PARTICIPATION OF THE POOR

Comparative Community Case Studies in the War on Poverty

PARTICIPATION OF THE POOR

Comparative Community Case Studies in the War on Poverty

RALPH M. KRAMER, D. S. W.
School of Social Welfare
University of California, Berkeley

Sponsored by
The Institute of Governmental Studies
University of California, Berkeley

Prentice-Hall, Inc., Englewood Cliffs, New Jersey

Library of Congress Catalog Card Number: 69-16753

Current printing (last digit):
10 9 8 7 6 5 4 3 2 1

Printed in the United States of America

Prentice-Hall International, Inc., *London*
Prentice-Hall of Australia, Pty. Ltd., *Sydney*
Prentice-Hall of Canada, Ltd., *Toronto*
Prentice-Hall of India Private Ltd., *New Delhi*
Prentice-Hall of Japan, Inc., *Tokyo*

PREFACE

"War," "mobilization," and "crusade" have been some of the typical titles given to American efforts at social reform as well as mass fund-raising appeals. Whether the appeals are aimed at wiping out cancer, destroying blight, opening opportunities, or eliminating mental illness, these metaphors give the impression of an innovative, massive, and once-and-for-all effort. The launching of the war on poverty in 1964 was no exception to this community tradition, with its broadly stated intent to do no less than help the poor raise themselves out of poverty. A slogan that often became a battle cry was "maximum feasible participation" or, as it was sometimes called, participation of the poor. It was this controversial element of the antipoverty program that caught the imagination of the politicans, the professionals, the poor, and the public. Initially, little attention was paid to this "sleeper" clause in Title II-A, Section 202(a)(3) of the Economic Opportunity Act of 1964, but it quickly became the aspect of the Community Action Program that was regarded as either its most distinctive accomplishment or its worst feature.

Shortly after the Economic Opportunity Act was passed in August of 1964, I decided to study the inception of the Community Action Programs in the San Francisco Bay Area to see how various communities would implement the legislative mandate to secure the maximum feasible participation of the groups and areas to be served. As a teacher of community organization in the School of Social Welfare at the University of California, I had a professional interest in citizen participation. I therefore saw an unusual opportunity to observe at first hand in cities where I have lived and worked for many years, the creation of a new form of social planning, linking the federal government, the local community, and the poor. For the next three years I was essentially concerned with these questions: How did the Community Action Program get organized? How did the Community Action Program respond to the demands for greater representation of the poor? How did the poor participate?

Originally, I selected nine communities in four counties and with the help of some students reconstructed the decision-making process whereby a Community Action Program was established in each of them. Drawing largely on interviews with the members of the initiating groups, a summary of these findings was published in *Social Work,* Vol. 12, No. 4 (October 1967), pp. 68-80, under the title "Organization of a Community Action Program: A Comparative Case Study." This initial investigation also served as an exploratory study in which some of the critical variables were identified and a theoretical framework designed for continuing monitoring of a Community Action Program. The results of the subsequent developments are contained in the case studies and comparative analyses that comprise this book. Because of practical considerations, I decided to reduce the number of communities for subsequent analysis to five: Berkeley, Contra Costa County, Oakland, San Francisco, and Santa Clara County, with a more intensive and consistent focus on the last three. Oakland, San Francisco, and Santa Clara County were selected because of their decentralization into 18 different target areas that permitted fairly systematic comparisons on both the community and neighborhood levels, and because their Community Action Programs had different auspices, structures, and orientations.

Although I observed as many of the meetings of these Community Action Programs as I could and interviewed most of the leading participants, I could not have completed this study without the work of an able and conscientious group of graduate students at the University of California from the departments of City and Regional Planning, History, Political Science, and Social Welfare. These research assistants were indefatigable in carrying out their assignments, but I alone take full responsibility for the detailed account of the case studies and the interpretation of the data. Among those students whose help is gratefully acknowledged are: Natalie Becker, Marjorie Myhill, Polly Bart, Clare Denton, Morton Elkins, Robert Feinbaum, Ruth Goodman, Adja Gorbach, and Paul Terrell. Jack Bloom, Joan Heifeitz, and Sally Wilt assisted in the editing of the case studies.

The attempt to order and analyze social processes as complex and as fluid as those described in this field study is obviously fraught with many hazards and difficulties for a researcher. Most of the data was derived from direct observation and interviewing, with newspaper accounts and official documents used primarily for supporting and illustrative purposes. I have tried to be as objective and careful as I could in verifying information and in interviewing the various partisans in the key conflict situations reported here. The comments, corrections, and suggestions of some of the principal protagonists in Oakland, San Francisco, and Santa Clara County who read the case studies of their communities are especially appreciated. The study also relied on the interest and cooperation of those participants in the Community Action Programs and delegate agencies who gave us the benefit of their opinions. The help of hundreds of staff and board members as well as government officials is hereby acknowledged. Constructive suggestions on various chapters were also made by my colleagues Davis McEntire, Harry Specht, Robert Pruger, and Anatole Shaffer.

Portions of Chapter 6 were presented at the 1966 annual meeting of the Pacific Sociological Association in Long Beach, California. Thanks are also due to Mrs. Leatha Peterson, secretary in the School of Social Welfare, who cheerfully typed many sections of this work. To Stanley Scott, Assistant Director of the Institute of Governmental Studies, my appreciation for its support during 1965-67, which enabled me to devote a portion of my time to this study.

Finally, I want to express my thanks to my wife, Hadassah, and my daughters, Miriam, Alisa, and Debby, to whom this book is dedicated, for their patience and encouragement during these last three years.

RALPH M. KRAMER

ABBREVIATIONS

ASC	Area Service Center in Santa Clara County
APB	Area Planning Board in San Francisco
CAP	Community Action Program
EOA	Economic Opportunity Act of 1964
EOC	Economic Opportunity Council/Commission, the Community Action Agency in San Francisco/Santa Clara County
OEDC	Oakland Economic Development Council, the Community Action Agency in Oakland
OEO	Office of Economic Opportunity
TAAC	Target Area Advisory Committee in Oakland
TAO	Target Area Organization, generic name for the neighborhood group officially related to the Community Action Program

CONTENTS

PARTICIPATION OF THE POOR

Comparative Community Case Studies in the War on Poverty

1

PRELUDE: FOUR MODES OF RESIDENT PARTICIPATION

Happy is he that wisely considereth the lot of the poor
—PSALMS

This is an account of how "maximum feasible participation" of the poor in the war on poverty was interpreted in five San Francisco Bay area communities during 1965-67. As a comparative case study of an unprecedented governmental effort to induce social change in the local community, it is an analysis of some of the consequences of an innovative but ambiguous social policy and, on another level, of an attempt by various groups to translate social and political ideologies into action.

The Economic Opportunity Act of 1964 consisted of seven Titles loosely tying together a wide range of old and new programs to combat poverty. Its most controversial features were contained in Title II-A, Section 202 (a) (3), authorizing the creation of Community Action Programs (CAPs), which were to be "developed, conducted and administered with the maximum feasible participation of residents of the areas and members of the groups served."[1] The ostensible purpose of Title II was to stimulate local communities to take the initiative in developing programs and mobilizing their resources in a concerted and coordinated manner for a broadly based, long-range attack on poverty. As a major incentive to organize a representative structure for planning and administration that would reflect the collaboration of the major governmental and voluntary interests con-

[1] Note that the poor as such are not referred to in this key phrase. The other Titles of PL 88-452 (as amended in 1965, 1966, and 1967) deal with work-training programs for youth and relief recipients; loan programs for marginal farmers and small businessmen; VISTA (Volunteers in Service To America), literacy training, etc. Although a new federal agency, the Office of Economic Opportunity, was created to administer and coordinate these programs, some were under the jurisdiction of other federal agencies such as the Departments of Labor and Health, Education and Welfare. One of the purposes of the local CAP was to draw on the entire range of federal antipoverty programs and presumably bring together what Washington had put asunder, since it has been estimated that there are now over 400 federal grant programs for local communities.

cerned with poverty, communities were offered up to 90 per cent federal financing of approved projects. It was, however, the inclusion of the concept of "maximum feasible participation" of the poor that lifted the CAP out of the traditional category of a grant-in-aid or technical assistance program and introduced a new set of political and social issues that may have an impact on local communities for many years.

Originally, the decision to organize CAPs in the San Francisco Bay area involved the development of consensus among two sets of influential people, elected officials and public and private agency executives, with virtually no direct involvement of the residents of those pockets of poverty designated as "target areas."[2] In order to move the Community Action Program into the next stage, it became necessary to secure the "maximum feasible participation" of the poor. What did this mean? Did it imply an advisory relationship in which the poor were to be consulted as consumers whose opinions should be taken into account along with those of other interest groups? Or should the poor have a more substantial part in planning programs and in policy making? Did maximum feasible participation imply administrative control of the program by target area residents? Furthermore, who could speak for or represent "the poor"? Did the poor refer to *all* residents of the target area, or only those with an income below some stated maximum?

These questions reflected a general confusion over the basic meaning and intent of the whole CAP that was never satisfactorily resolved. As one somewhat disillusioned original supporter put it,

> What are they [CAPs] supposed to do? Are they to make trouble—or prevent trouble? Create small controversies in order to avoid large conflicts—or engender as much conflict as they can? Hire the poor, involve the poor, or be dominated by the poor? Improve race relations or enhance racial pride? What is it Washington wanted? The simple answer to these complicated questions is that Wash-

[2] The use of military terminology in the war on poverty was as pervasive as it was inappropriate. References to social services as "weapons" in an "arsenal," to staff members as "poverty warriors," and programs as an "assault" or "attack" conjure up false images of a concerted, planned, and massive program. The "mobilized" resources committed to this engagement were less than 1 per cent of the federal budget and a negligible fraction of GNP. Clearly, this was a token reconnaissance or skirmish at best. On the deeper significance of this military approach, see Edgar S. Cahn and Jean C. Cahn, "The War Against Poverty: A Civilian Perspective," *Yale Law Journal,* Vol. 73, No. 8 (July, 1964), 1317-52. Among the more general critiques of the poverty program, see Martin Rein and S. M. Miller, "Poverty, Policy, and Purpose: The Dilemmas of Choice," in Leonard H. Goodman (ed.), *Economic Progress and Social Welfare* (New York: Columbia University Press, 1966), pp. 20-64 and Nathan Glazer, "The Grand Design of the Poverty Programs," *New York Times Magazine* (February 27, 1966), p. 21.

> ington wanted a great many things that could not be simultaneously had.[3]

Because of the ambiguity inherent in the legislation, the shifting policies of the Office of Economic Opportunity and its reluctance to specify the meaning of "maximum feasible participation," as well as the delegation to each community of the power to organize its own program, each CAP faced the same dilemmas: how to make policy decisions in the face of uncertainty regarding the meaning of what came to be called "resident participation"; how to identify and select those who could speak for or represent the poor, and how to involve the poor in a relatively brief period of time in a manner that would not unduly hamper the process of program development. As a result, it is not surprising that the concept of the participation of the poor was perceived in multiple and divergent ways by various groups with high stakes in the war on poverty in Berkeley, Oakland, San Francisco, and Contra Costa and Santa Clara counties.

The nature of these community decisions and their consequences can be understood by analyzing four interrelated and yet somewhat conflicting modes of resident participation that operated with OEO sanction on both the community and neighborhood levels. Each of these modes also contained contrasting interpretations of purpose, out of which controversial issues arose. Summarized in Table 1 are the views of the role of the poor as participants in four aspects of the war on poverty (policy making, program development, social action, and employment); the ostensible goal and substantive content of these activities, and the key, problematic issue found in each one.

Underlying these issues and reflecting the diverse economic, political, and social service goals of the CAP are two opposing orientations toward the causes of poverty and the appropriate organizational strategies, both of which were sanctioned by OEO. In the first, poverty is defined in terms of individual deficiencies and the emphasis is on *changing people so they*

[3] Daniel P. Moynihan, "What is 'Community Action'?" *The Public Interest,* No. 5 (Fall, 1966), 4. Cf. Barbara Carter, "Sargent Shriver and the Role of the Poor," *The Reporter,* Vol. 34, No. 9 (May 5, 1966), 17-20; Earl Raab, "Which War, Which Poverty?" *The Public Interest,* No. 3 (Spring, 1966), 44-56; *Examination of the War on Poverty: Hearings Before the Subcommittee on Education and Labor, House of Representatives,* 89th Congress, First Session (Washington, D.C., Government Printing Office, 1965), pp. 346-61; 415-23; 600-606. While the ambiguities caused by the multiple goals of the Economic Opportunity Act produced conflict and organizational strain, they also made for political viability, since disparate groups could each pursue their own interests within the CAP. A brilliant discussion of the conflict in statutory goals is found in "Participation of the Poor: Section 202(a) (3) Organization under the Economic Opportunity Act of 1964," *The Yale Law Journal,* Vol. 75, No. 4 (March, 1966), 599-629. Also, see Charles E. Silverman, "The Mixed-up War on Poverty," *Fortune,* Vol. LXXII, No. 2 (August, 1965), 156-61, 218-26.

TABLE 1
Four Modes of Resident Participation

Goal	*Content of Activity*	*Role of the Poor*	*Issues*		
1. Participation in policy making by the representatives of the poor	CAP policy making	Governing board members	*Participation* by the poor in a tripartite coalition	*or*	*Control* of the CAP Board by the representatives of the poor who constitute a majority of the members
2. Target area feedback and utilization of service	Program development	Social service consumers	*Centralization* of power in the CAP with advisory functions delegated to the target area organization	*or*	*Decentralization* of power, with planning, policy making, and administrative authority vested in the target area organization
3. Redistribution of power to affect changes in community policies	Social action	Political constituency	*Social service programs;* community organization used mainly for information and referral purposes	*or*	*Political* power; community organization used to foster social action and community development
4. Job experience	Employment in CAP	Staff members	*Merit* system qualifications for employment of indigenous people	*or*	"Need," reward for loyalty (*patronage*), or both as criteria for employment

can function more effectively. The poor are considered to be in need of improved social services such as better education, job training, health, welfare, and legal programs that will help them move out of their impoverished condition and compete more successfully. Accordingly, the CAP was to be primarily concerned with redesigning, coordinating, and redistributing community resources in the most efficient way to an underserved portion of the low-income population. This perspective was associated with a belief in the importance of centralizing power in the CAP and the delegation of rather limited advisory functions to neighborhood organizations largely dependent on the CAP. The target area residents and their representatives were seen as one among other groups of participants in the decision-making process, but definitely not as the controlling element. Along with this view was a commitment to the traditional values of administrative efficiency, including merit system qualifications for employment and program development criteria for success.

The other orientation regards poverty as inhering in the social and economic systems and persisting because of the "powerlessness" of the poor. Consequently, this view holds that *only as the poor acquire political influence* can they change the community policies and conditions that prevent them from acquiring their fair share of society's goods and services. While those holding the former point of view may also be concerned with changing institutions by means of the judicious leverage of financial incentives, in this second view, significant alterations in policy can be better achieved by social action utilizing the solidary strength of poor people. Accordingly, this orientation saw target area residents in control of the CAP, with planning, policy making, and administrative authority decentralized and invested in neighborhood organizations that should be given the greatest autonomy. In this view the CAP was regarded more as a social movement whose success was to be measured by increased power accruing to the poor and by changes in institutions so they function more equitably for the poor.[4]

Each of these four different modes of resident participation will next be identified briefly. Its rationale will be noted, as well as the issues generated by the tension between competing values and assumptions regarding the purpose of Title II-A and the meanings imputed to maximum feasible participation. This guiding framework will be used to analyze the five community case studies, which are focused on the ways in which each CAP interpreted its mandate to involve the poor. Based on this ex-

[4] A typical expression of this orientation can be found in Warren C. Haggstrom, "The Power of the Poor," in Frank Riessman, Jerome Cohen, and Arthur Pearl (eds.), *Mental Health of the Poor: New Treatment Approaches for Low-Income People* (New York: Free Press, 1964), pp. 205-23.

perience, some implications will be suggested for future efforts to promote the participation of low-income citizen groups in community decision making.

1. CAP Policy Making

The first mode of resident participation involved the process of CAP decision making in which the poor were cast in the role of policy makers as voting members of the governing board of directors. In this capacity, the representatives of the poor were regarded by OEO as essential members of a tripartite coalition, along with the major governmental and voluntary welfare agencies, and the leadership of important elements in the community such as labor, business, religious, and minority groups.[5]

Much of the official rhetoric of the OEO was devoted to this mode of resident participation and it is the one that was promoted with considerable determination by the federal agency.[6] Drawing largely on a pluralist view of the political system and the ideology of citizen participation, the rationale for involving representatives of the poor in policy-making roles was based largely on the democratic conviction that people should have a voice in the decisions affecting them. Consequently, the CAP was expected to plan *with* and not *for* the residents of the target areas.

A commitment to the involvement of the affected population groups is usually hortatory on the part of most governmental and voluntary agencies seeking to advance their organizational goals. However, in the war on poverty there was a stronger than usual determination to close the gap

[5] During the initial months of the program in 1964, OEO had few specific requirements pertaining to resident participation other than that the proposed CAP had to submit a plan for eventually securing the participation of the poor. In February, 1965, six months after the Act had passed, most communities had received copies of the *CAP Guide,* which outlined the various purposes and means of securing resident participation, as well as the minimum standard of one representative, preferably a potential recipient, from each of the areas singled out for priority attention. In Region VII, which included most of the western states, all CAPs were informed on April 7, 1965 that no later than June 1, they were expected to comply with this policy. On October 29, 1965 a regional guideline of one third—the "three legged stool"—as a minimum for the proportion of representation of the groups and areas to be served was formally announced in anticipation of an OEO regulation. Regional CAA Bulletin SSR-16.

[6] After 18 months, OEO claimed that over 5,000 persons from target areas were on community action boards and another 21,000 were employed as nonprofessionals. Assistant OEO Director Hyman H. Bookbinder declared: "I think that issue (representation) is now basically solved . . . by and large it can be said that the communities of America have accepted in principle and in action the involvement of the poor in the general management of community action programs." A speech delivered at the first annual meeting of the National Association of Community Development, cited in *Community Development,* Vol. 1, No. 4 (May, 1966), p. 6.

between ideology and practice. The lack of success of previous efforts to help the poor was ascribed by many to the failure of social agencies to take their clientele into account and to involve them in the program planning process. In order to avoid "welfare colonialism" or the "paternalism" of the traditional social services, OEO strongly encouraged communities to bring into the mainstream representatives of the low-income population previously excluded or at least not usually involved in the making of decisions regarding allocation of social service resources.[7] The CAP board of directors was seen as a new community forum and social service planning center wherein the broadest spectrum of community interests were to be represented, including those of the clientele. For some, this objective was regarded as the primary one.

> I think the most important thing is that we have created a vehicle for providing a dialogue between the so-called power structure and the members of the community, which never existed before. We're sensitizing a great number of the white majority to the problem and at the same time allowing some of the civil rights types to see that these people are concerned. I think that's a big step.[8]

Ideally, this type of participation would require that delegates to the CAP board of directors be elected by means of a democratic process that would insure some accountability to a low-income constituency whose views could be authoritatively represented. It also assumed that the information brought by the low-income delegates regarding neighborhood needs, problems, and attitudes was closer to reality because "the poor know best what they need." Apart from its emblematic function, then, this policy-making role of the poor relied on the development of a communication channel between the target areas and the CAP board of directors. The establishment of this channel was not left to chance, because the presence of representatives from the target areas on the board of directors of the CAP was a functional necessity if the program was to be sanctioned

[7] On the alienation of the poor from the institutions supposedly designed to help them, see Richard A. Cloward and Richard M. Elman, "Poverty, Injustice and the Welfare State," *The Nation*, Vol. 202, No. 9 (February 28, 1966), 230-35. This idea is also expressed in an official OEO publication: "For years, poor people have been isolated from the processes through which policy is made. They are offered services, and they can take or leave them. If they take them, they are in danger of becoming dependent on an institution over which they have little or no control. If they leave them, they remain poor and pass their poverty on to their children. Poverty is not just a lack of money; it is also a feeling of helplessness, of being controlled by outside forces." *Community Action: The Neighborhood Center* (Washington, D.C.: Office of Economic Opportunity, July, 1966, p. 8.

[8] Norvel Smith, executive director, Oakland Department of Human Resources, in an interview quoted in the Oakland, California *Tribune* July 31, 1966, p. 1.

and funded by OEO.[9] Although neither the EOA nor the *CAP Guide* stated that the representatives of the poor had to be poor themselves, the CAP was required to comply with the changing criteria of OEO if it was to be regarded as a legitimate community body officially recognized to wage the war on poverty.

In view of the insistence by OEO on the novel requirement that representatives of the poor must participate on the community policy making level, the evolution of this concept is significant. There is a long history of voluntary efforts to encourage the social participation of low-income persons in their neighborhoods, beginning with the settlement movement in the last quarter of the nineteenth century. Shortly before World War I, the Cincinnati Social Unit experiment flourished, embodying many of the "innovations" introduced in the war on poverty.[10] In 1934, a self-help approach to the organization of slum neighborhoods was undertaken in the name of juvenile delinquency control by Clifford Shaw and his associates in the Chicago Area Project, a concept that was revived in the 1960's by the President's Committee on Juvenile Delinquency and Youth Crime.

Inclusion of the requirement for maximum feasible participation, however, seems to be more immediately related to the experiences with citizen participation in urban renewal, the community development ideology of self-help, and the projects funded by the "gray areas" program of the Ford Foundation and the President's Committee on Juvenile Delinquency. Perhaps the most notable predecessor is Mobilization for Youth in New York City, although the agency coordination goals of the CAP were not in character with Mobilization's somewhat adversary stance toward local agencies.[11]

[9] This process is similar to "formal co-optation" as described by Selznick, whereby the representatives of the poor on the CAP board of directors "fulfill both the political function of defending legitimacy and the administrative function of establishing reliable channels for communication and direction." His next comment is somewhat prophetic: "In general, the use of formal co-optation by a leadership does not envision the transfer of actual power. The forms of participation are emphasized but action is channeled so as to fulfill the administrative functions while preserving the locus of significant decision in the hands of the initiating group." Philip Selznick, *TVA and The Grass Roots: A Study in the Sociology of Formal Organization* (New York: Harper Torch Books, 1966), p. 14.

[10] A useful account of the history of neighborhood organization in the United States can be found in Sidney Dillick, *Community Organization for Neighborhood Development: Past and Present* (New York: William Morrow & Company, Inc., Publishers, 1953).

[11] Descriptions of some of these predecessor programs can be found in: Solomon Kobrin, "The Chicago Area Project—A Twenty-Five Year Assessment," *The Annals*, Vol. 322 (March, 1959), 19-29; William C. Loring, Jr., Frank L. Sweetser, and Charles F. Ernest, *Community Organization for Citizen Participation in Urban Renewal* (Boston: Massachusetts Department of Commerce, 1957); Melvin B. Mogulof,

As far as is known, there was no pressure from the poor or any other organized political group for inclusion of the requirement for maximum feasible participation. There is no reference to the concept in the Congressional hearings on the original bill, and there was no evidence that Congress was strongly committed to participation of the poor. Although some of the interested congressmen and the task force from the executive office of the President, who between them wrote the Community Action Title of the Economic Opportunity Act, were receptive to the idea that originated in the President's Committee on Juvenile Delinquency that the poor would benefit from involvement, their major concern was to provide incentives for social service planning and coordination.[12] Thus arose the concept of the "umbrella" organization—the CAP—which would represent an alliance among all the agencies and interests in the community concerned with poverty.

Although involvement of the poor seemed to be compatible with the ideal of social service cooperation as found in the juvenile delinquency program, in the war on poverty attempts to secure participation of the poor often resulted in prolonged controversies. One reason was that it was possible for the CAP to be established outside the existing governmental framework, thus leading inevitably to a power struggle. Another factor was that the diffuseness of the legislation encouraged conflicting interpretations of maximum feasible participation. For example, opposing the official view of the poor as participants in a community coalition

---

"Involving Low-Income Neighborhoods in Anti-Delinquency Programs," *Social Work,* Vol. 10, No. 4 (October, 1965), pp. 51-59. A concise summary of the origins of resident participation is found in Lillian Rubin, "Maximum Feasible Participation: The Origins, Implications, and Present Status," *Poverty and Human Resources Abstracts,* Vol. II, No. 6 (November-December, 1967), pp. 5-18. A thoughtful analysis of the gray areas projects, delinquency prevention programs, and the CAP appears in Peter Marris and Martin Rein, *Dilemmas of Social Reform* (New York: Atherton Press, 1967).

[12] Useful accounts of the legislative history of the Economic Opportunity Act can be found in: Elinor Graham, "Poverty and The Legislative Process," in Ben Seligman (ed.), *Poverty as a Public Issue* (New York: Free Press, 1965), pp. 251-71; Sar A. Levitan, "Planning the Anti-Poverty Strategy," *Poverty and Human Resources Abstracts,* Vol. II, No. 1 (January-February, 1967), 5-15; Daniel P. Moynihan, "What is 'Community Action'?" *The Public Interest,* No. 5 (Fall, 1966), 4, and "The Professionalization of Reform," *The Public Interest,* No. 1 (Fall, 1965), 6-16; "Participation of the Poor . . ." *Yale Law Journal,* Vol. 75, No. 4 (March, 1966), 602-605; Richard W. Boone, "What is Meaningful Participation?" *Community Development,* Vol. 1, No. 5 (June, 1966), 27-32; Roger H. Davidson, "Poverty and the New Federalism" in Sar A. Levitan and Irving H. Siegel (eds.), *Dimensions of Manpower Policy: Research and Programs* (Baltimore: The Johns Hopkins Press, 1966), pp. 61-80). In all these discussions, there is general agreement on the strong influence of the civil rights struggle in precipitating the legislation; and, although the concept of maximum feasible participation was inserted by professional reformers, the subsequent controversies were evidently unanticipated.

formulating CAP policy was the belief of minority spokesmen that the representatives from the target areas should *control* the program by constituting the majority of the members of the governing board and the executive committee. While perhaps at variance with the concept of the CAP as a coalition, this view was a logical extension of the basic rationale for this mode of resident participation. If the war on poverty was going to be a novel and substantial departure from the conventional approach to the planning and administration of social service programs, then, it could be argued, the poor or their representatives should constitute the majority of the policy-making board. Taking the slogans of "resident participation" and "self-help" seriously, proponents of CAP control by the poor asserted that not only was there a legitimate claim on administration of this program by the poor themselves, but only in this way could the intended purposes of the legislation best be achieved. That is, as low-income persons learned how to take responsibility and acquire citizenship skills, they would become more capable and less dependent. Or, as expressed in the *CAP Guide:*

> The long range objective of every community action program is to effect a permanent increase in the capacity of individuals, groups, and communities afflicted by poverty to deal effectively with their own problems so that they need no further assistance.[13]

A community coalition in which the poor are the minority, it was said, would insure a continuation of the *status quo* because of the inevitable compromises required. If change was sincerely desired the poor must be given an opportunity to express their wants and manage their own affairs and be permitted to make their own mistakes.

This view emerged with particular force early in the experience of San Francisco and with somewhat less intensity later in Contra Costa County, Oakland, and Santa Clara County. In each of these communities the struggle for control took a characteristic turn that we will describe. In comparing the case histories of the CAPs, we shall note the conditions under which these two views—participation versus control—emerged; with what groups they were identified; what strategies were employed; and the dynamics of the power struggle as the CAPs responded to the pressures on them to maximize the influence of the target areas.

[13] *CAP Guide,* page 7. Toward the end of the second year, Sargent Shriver reaffirmed OEO policy that: "We have no intention, of course, of letting any one group, even the poor themselves, 'run the jobs' or 'run the programs.' That's not *community* action . . . [which is] maximum feasible participation by *all* segments of the community . . . and that *must* include the intended beneficiary of that program." Memo from the Director, Subject: Involvement of the Poor in All OEO Programs, September 9, 1966, pp. 1-2.

2. Program Development

A second mode of resident participation took place on the neighborhood level and was linked to the first through the elected representatives to the CAP's board of directors from the target area. The core process was one of program development; here the poor were initially viewed primarily as consumers who could give useful advice and suggestions to those responsible for the planning and delivery of social services. According to this view, a concern with resident participation was akin to market research and the quest for a high-quality service or product. The requirement for maximum feasible participation was justified by Sargent Shriver on the following grounds:

> . . . it is desirable for the same reason that a business concern tries to find what the consumer thinks of his product. You would not be in business 20 minutes if you did not run consumer surveys . . . We are trying to find out what the poor people really think about what all the rest of us are doing theoretically for their benefit.[14]

Resident participation was thus seen as a means of securing reliable feedback from clientele. As members of a vast consumer panel, the poor as citizen-clients had an advisory role: They were to be consulted by the institutions supposed to be serving them, and it was expected that their opinions regarding program preferences and priorities would be helpful in generating new and more effective social services.[15]

But information regarding the wants or "perceived needs" of the poor was not the only reason for seeking to involve them in advisory relationships to the CAP. It was also assumed that a neighborhood-based organ-

[14] Interview with Sargent Shriver reported in the *San Francisco Sunday Examiner and Chronicle,* December 12, 1965, section IV, page 1. Another analogy that was used by Mr. Shriver was that of the client's relationship to an architect whereby the former participates in the planning without doing the actual designing. See also Jules Witcover and Erwin Knoll, "Politics and The Poor: Shriver's Second Thought," *The Reporter,* Vol. XXXIII (December 30, 1965), 23-25. Later, greater stress was laid on actual conduct of programs by indigenous groups although the coalition concept persisted; ". . . the poor across this nation—want no structure or service built and manned and controlled entirely by outsiders." Shriver, Memo of September 9, 1966 (see footnote 13).

[15] There is a growing literature on what has been called "public consultation" in the field of physical planning, in which similar advisory roles are proposed along with somewhat the same ambivalence and ambiguity regarding the decision-making power of the client. See David R. Godschalk and William E. Mills, "A Collaborative Approach to Planning Through Urban Activities," *Journal of The American Institute of Planners,* Vol. 32, No. 2 (March, 1966), 86-95; Harvey S. Perloff, "New Directions in Social Planning," *op. cit.,* Vol. 31, No. 4 (November, 1965), 297-304.

ization affiliated with the CAP would encourage the use of the decentralized social services available in a multiservice center. This belief was based on some of the socio-therapeutic benefits ascribed to participation, e.g., if people were involved in the planning of a program they were more likely to regard it as theirs to support and promote. Without some organized effort to engage the poor it could be expected that they would exercise their traditional power to refuse to be clients. Since the success of the program required that, at the very least, potential clients be informed of the availability of compensatory educational, legal, health, welfare, and employment services, the organizational maintenance requirements of the CAP and its delegate agencies reinforced this need to reach clientele by means of some form of neighborhood organization.

In the larger urban centers, neighborhood councils and advisory committees were organized by the CAP. Rather limited powers and functions were delegated to a presumably representative assemblage of residents who were recognized as the official arm of the poverty program in the neighborhood. Among the major functions usually assigned to such target area organizations were the following: (1) the election of representatives to the board of directors of the CAP and to delegate agency advisory committees; (2) review and evaluation of, and sometimes including a veto power over, delegate agency programs and personnel assigned to the neighborhood; (3) direct sponsorship or subcontracting service programs such as information and referral, and community organization; (4) advisory or policy-making powers relating to a multiservice center in program planning priority setting, recruiting and selecting staff, and evaluation.[16]

There were, then, three distinct roles involved in these functions. The neighborhood organization had a *service* role whereby it operated as a planner, advisor, sponsor or administrator of social services and their interpreter. It had a *political* role when it served as spokesman, advocate, and negotiator of neighborhood interests in the wider community, and an *educational* role as a vehicle for citizen participation and leadership development.

The conflict between participation versus control of the CAP governing board found in the first mode of resident participation is reflected in this second form in the strain between the *advisory* and consultative roles usually ascribed to the poor initially and their desire to assume more *policy-making* functions in planning, sponsoring, and administering services, as well as in reviewing, screening, and vetoing programs for their area. This issue developed in varying degrees in all the CAPs studied, and none was able to restrict the neighborhood organizations solely to

[16] *Community Action: The Neighborhood Center,* pp. 7-8.

advisory functions. All of the communities soon faced the demand for enlarging the policy roles of target area residents not only by means of additional representation on the CAP governing board and executive committee, but also by decentralizing authority and granting more decision-making power to the neighborhood organization itself.

In analyzing the experiences of the neighborhood organizations, we shall note the ways in which the various groups struggled to attain a sense of identity and purpose and how they sought to increase their authority progressively from involvement in planning to policy making and to direct operation of programs. We shall be interested in what they did with the power given to them originally and how they acquired greater autonomy. In this process, we shall also note the extent to which target area residents were involved in program development and the character, role, and influence of the target area organization.

3. Social Action

The third type of resident participation was the most radical and controversial of all, and for many persons the possibility of increasing the power of the poor was either the most objectionable or the most encouraging feature of the CAP. According to this view, the poor were an underdeveloped political constituency that needed stimulation and nurturing. It was assumed that the "powerlessness" of the poor perpetuated poverty, and only as low-income persons were organized and mobilized as an effective pressure group could they begin to influence city hall, the schools, and the welfare and housing bureaucracies.[17] In addition, it was believed that the social service agencies upon whom the poor were dependent would be more likely to change if they were prodded by their clientele. Since the poor lacked the resources necessary for interest group bargaining in urban politics, OEO was expected to support the development of indigenous organizations in low-income areas through which the poor could overcome their traditional disengagement and begin to assert their influence in the community decision-making processes from which they had been excluded. Within OEO, a militant faction of the staff interpreted their congressional mandate so as to justify "organizing the poor" to become a more powerful force in changing the policies of community in-

[17] Warren C. Haggstrom, "The Power of the Poor," in Frank Riessman, Jerome Cohen, and Arthur Pearl (eds.), *Mental Health of the Poor: New Treatment Approaches for Low-Income People* (New York: Free Press, 1964), 205-23. Richard A. Cloward, "The War on Poverty: Are the Poor Left Out?" *The Nation*, Vol. 201, No. 3 (August 2, 1965), 55-60.

stitutions affecting their lives.[18] Legitimacy for governmental support of the emergence of the poor as a new special interest lobby with a constituency relationship to OEO could be found in the precedent of the county agricultural extension system for farmers and the Wagner Act for labor union members. Indeed, Sargent Shriver described the Economic Opportunity Act as constituting

> . . . for the poor what the National Labor Relations Act was for unions . . . It recognizes the principles of representation, full participation, of fair bargaining. It establishes a new relationship and new grievance procedure between the poor and the rest of society.[19]

Consequently, as a federally sanctioned and supported "intrusion" of a new structure and resources into the community's social service and political subsystems, the CAP appeared as a new decision-making center with the possibility of control not only over the allocation of compensatory and supplementary social service resources, but also over the policies of other community institutions. Among those also committed to the creation of new power centers in the urban slums were a host of civil rights, religious, ethnic, student, and "New Left" groups with various motivations, ideologies, and strategies. Particularly where there was an active civil rights movement, the war on poverty provided a natural opportunity for such groups to utilize the CAP structure to help ethnic minorities make the transition from "protest to politics." [20] In this way, the social action interpretation of maximum feasible participation led to struggles, evidently unanticipated, between mayors and their "insurgent poor" that

[18] "A promising method" of implementing maximum feasible participation was "to assist the poor in developing autonomous and self-managed organizations which are competent to exert political influence on behalf of their own self-interest." *Community Action Workbook, Office of Economic Opportunity* (Washington, D.C., 1965), III A.7. This workbook was subsequently withdrawn from circulation.

[19] Sargent Shriver in a speech to an audience at the Yale Law School as reported in *Community Development*, Vol. 1, No. 5 (June, 1966), p. 5.

[20] Bayard Rustin, "From Protest to Politics: The Future of The Civil Rights Movement," *Commentary* (February, 1965), pp. 25-31. See also Raab, "Which War, Which Poverty?" *The Public Interest*, No. 3 (Spring, 1966), 45-56. On the involvement of the "New Left" see the following: Paul Jacobs and Saul Landau, *The New Radicals: A Report With Documents* (New York: Vintage Books, 1966), pp. 70-73; Norman Fruchter and Robert Kramer, "Community Organizing," *Studies on the Left*, Vol. 6, No. 2 (March-April, 1966), 31-61; Tom Hayden, "Community Organizing and the Newark War on Poverty," *Liberation* (November, 1965), pp. 17-19; Paul Bullock, "On Organizing the Poor: Problems of Morality and Tactics," *Dissent*, Vol. XV, No. 1 (January-February, 1968), 1-7.

not only failed to change the balance of urban political power, but also affected congressional support for the CAP.[21]

There were, however, substantial differences in the strategies aimed at increasing the power of the poor, ranging from self-help and cooperative efforts in the neighborhood to the use of conflict tactics in attacking the public bureaucracies and slumlords. These approaches, in turn, reflected discrepant views regarding the why and how of community organization among low-income residents. For example, should such organization be undertaken within or outside the CAP structure? Should political power be sought directly or indirectly, now or in the long run? In this process, are the social services a diversion, a means to political involvement, or an end in themselves?

Among those who defined poverty as a function of powerlessness were those who looked to Saul D. Alinsky, a nationally known, conflict oriented, professional organizer of the poor, as their ideologue and hoped to organize the poor for tests of strength with the "power structure" by relying on rent strikes, demonstrations, picketing, and other overt forms of protest. As part of their community organization philosophy, they sought to induce conflict and to avoid becoming involved with health and welfare services to individuals and families on the grounds that these perpetuated "welfare colonialism" and diverted attention from the need for redistribution of power.[22] According to this perspective, the chief value of the CAP was less the social services that it might provide than the opportunity to utilize the structure for political purposes.

> The hope for the poverty program was not that it would wipe out poverty overnight, but that it would begin to revive the instruments of representative government which lie in wreck and ruin in the fast-growing Negro slums that are the core of the American city.[23]

Although some of these militants saw possibilities for social action within the CAP, most of the others were more realistic and concentrated their

[21] J. David Greenstone and Paul Peterson, "Reformers, Machine and the War on Poverty," a paper presented at the 1966 annual meeting of the American Political Science Association, New York City, September 6-10. Based on an examination of the war on poverty in New York, Chicago, Los Angeles, and Philadelphia, the authors concluded that cities with strong party organizations were less likely to involve the poor in decision-making roles.

[22] Saul D. Alinsky, "The War on Poverty: Political Pornography," *Journal of Social Issues*, Vol. 21, No. 1 (January, 1965), 41-47. For a sympathetic account of Alinsky's methods see Charles E. Silverman, *Crisis in Black and White* (New York: Random House, 1964), pp. 308-55.

[23] *Ramparts*, Vol. 4, No. 10 (February, 1966), p. 40.

efforts outside its "umbrella" on the assumption that government could not possibly support efforts for change which would lead to community conflict and a redistribution of power.

Another approach was represented in a series of variations on what was essentially a *community development* model whereby the poor were to be organized around social service issues directly affecting them with the objective of improving their daily living conditions and at the same time gaining skills in decision-making and in exerting influence. These efforts, which were to be undertaken *within* the CAP, were not always distinguishable from the second type of resident or consumer participation, although they were usually aimed at those not involved in the official target area organization. Riessman, for example, delineated a "third force" stance for indigenous groups organized under CAP auspices, in which *service-based* social action was clearly distinguished from those forms of angry protest based on agitation because of grievances. It was argued that such CAP-sponsored organizations could appeal to less militant and unaffiliated elements among the poor and could mediate between the latter and the established agencies in pressing for better development and delivery of more effective social services.[24] Others, such as Cloward, stressed the political power potential of ethnically based social welfare structures with control over the antipoverty programs and funds for their slum neighborhoods.[25]

Within this latter conception of community organization among low-income persons, there were at least five types of organizations that could be promoted by a CAP:

(1) "social brokerage" groups concerned with the needs of a special clientele such as slum or public housing tenants, relief recipients, working mothers;

[24] Frank Riessman, "Anti-Poverty Programs and the Role of the Poor" in Margaret S. Gordon (ed.), *Poverty in America* (San Francisco: Chandler Publishing Co., 1965), pp. 403-12. A more recent statement of Riessman's concepts of the consumer participant and citizen-client can be found in "The New Anti-Poverty Ideology" prepared for the Planning Session, White House Conference on Civil Rights, November 17-18, 1965, in *Poverty and Human Resources Abstracts,* Vol. I, No. 4 (July-August, 1966), 5-16. These views are challenged in "Debate Between Bookbinder and Alinsky" in *Communities in Action,* Vol. 1, No. 2 (July, 1966), 22-27.

[25] Cloward calls for a "new social welfare voluntarism" whereby institutions under expressly ethnic control such as HARYOU-Act, could be used by the poor to develop vehicles to influence important spheres of public policy and eventually overcome class inequality. While he declares that "the growth of ethnic separatism is a pre-condition for eventual penetration of ruling circles and full economic integration," this is not regarded as revolutionary; rather, "the controversy over the involvement of the poor has its roots in relatively moderate ideologies—self-help, local autonomy, democratic collective action, and the importance of ethnic separatism. The struggle, in short, is in the tradition of urban politics and nothing more." See fn. 17.

(2) self-help or neighborhood improvement associations;
(3) functional or non-profit community corporations that operated a social service program (day care or a credit union) or performed some economic function on a cooperative basis (housing repair or food sales);
(4) *ad hoc* groups focused on a specific social or political issue;
(5) coalitions of existing low-income organizations brought together as a council or federation.[26]

Each of these groups could be organized along residential, ethnic, or functional lines, and the extent of the commitment to social action could vary on the part of the members as well as on the part of the sponsoring CAP.

Thus, the major issues posed by this third interpretation of maximum feasible participation arose out of the means-ends choice between organizing a social service clientele or fostering a political constituency. It is here that one can see most clearly the conflict between and confusion in the statutory goals for a CAP. If increasing the power of the poor is the objective, then three problems must be faced: First, organizing around social services could become an end in itself, displacing broader political concerns. Secondly, it is still an open question whether social service and political functions can be performed equally well by the same type of organization. While the former may represent a practical way of bringing people together around a common interest and acquiring some resources and experience for them, there is some impressionistic evidence that Gresham's Law may operate—one function may drive the other out. It is not clear whether this is due to the "corrupting" or co-opting influence of funds or to realistic limitation on available time and interest.[27]

[26] Most of these are discussed in George Brager and Harry Specht, "Mobilizing The Poor For Social Action," *The Social Welfare Forum* (New York: Columbia University Press, 1965), pp. 197-210, and Frances Piven, "Participation of Residents in Neighborhood Community Action Programs," *Social Work,* Vol. 11, No. 1 (January, 1966), 73-80.

[27] The long history of neighborhood organizations under a variety of auspices reveals the difficulty of combining service functions with even coordination or milder forms of citizen action. See Dillick, *Community Organization for Neighborhood Development: Past and Present* (New York: William Morrow Co. Inc., Publishers, 1953), pp. 95-166, It may be that these two functions require somewhat different structures and strategies and that they appeal to different types of people and interests. A similar analysis is found in Martin Rein and Robert Morris, "Goals, Structures and Strategies for Community Change," *Social Work Practice 1962* (New York: Columbia University Press, 1962), pp. 127-45. An excellent analysis of the relationships between services and organization is found in Robert Perlman and David Jones, *Neighborhood Service Centers* (Washington, D.C.: Department of Health, Education, and Welfare, The Welfare Administration, 1967), pp. 70-74.

Finally, organizing the poor for political action raises the question of the extent to which government can or should subsidize protest and opposition from its citizens even if the latter are seriously disadvantaged in the bargaining process because of their poverty. The experience with public funding of citizen groups with a social service or social action function indicates that it is a high-risk, unstable, and precarious operation, as the experience of the Syracuse Community Development Association and Mobilization for Youth testifies.[28] Organizations of low-income residents are confronted with the paradox of being dependent for their sanction and financial support on community institutions whose policies they will inevitably seek to change. Under these conditions, how militant or effective can they be? In analyzing this mode of resident participation we shall observe the purposes, patterns, and trends in community organization efforts in the target area both in and outside the CAP. We shall note the conditions under which social protest and action occurred as well as the ways in which the tension between social service and social action was dealt with.

4. Employment

The fourth and perhaps least controversial way in which the poor could participate was through employment as aides or in other nonprofessional roles, some of which were defined as "new careers" in educational, health, welfare, legal, and correctional agencies.[29] Employment was originally regarded as the primary, perhaps sole form of resident participation. The rationale for employing the poor, apart from its obvious economic benefit, was based in large part on an indictment of the professionalism and "credentialism" of the educational and welfare systems and their failure to come to grips with the causes of poverty. Two attributes of the guild system of the helping professions were attacked: its restriction of the right of entry and practice to those with formal education and training, and its professional ideology, which seeks to adjust the individual to

[28] A brief history of the demonstration project in Syracuse is found in Erwin Knoll and Jules Witcover, "Fighting Poverty and City Hall," *The Reporter*, Vol. 33 (June 3, 1965), 19-22, and Lawrence Davis, "Syracuse: What Happens When the Poor Take Over," *ibid.*, Vol. 38, No. 6 (March 21, 1968), 19-21. See also Herbert Krosney, "Mobilization For Youth: Feuding Over Poverty," *The Nation*, Vol. 199, No. 19 (December 14, 1964), pp. 455-61.

[29] For an imaginative if somewhat overly optimistic analysis of the possibilities of expanding this mode of participation as part of a national solution to problems of automation, unemployment, and poverty, see Arthur Pearl and Frank Riessman (eds.) *New Careers For The Poor* (New York: Free Press, 1965). By 1967, almost 94,000 nonprofessional jobs had been filled, including over 50,000 in summer Head Start programs.

society rather than to try to change the community. These beliefs were behind the conviction of some of the major architects of the Economic Opportunity Act that not only should the poor have more to say about their needs and ways of meeting them, they should also not be kept from working on their own programs because they lacked formal degrees and credentials.[30]

A double benefit was supposed to flow from the employment of poverty area personnel by delegate agencies and by the CAP itself: It could help change the individual *and* the agency that employed him. The indigenous staff member would learn better work habits, become motivated to improve his skills, and become an effective interpreter of the agency's policies and programs to the neighborhood. At the same time, he would bring into the agency his distinctive perspective and first-hand experiences with life in the poverty area. Presumably, this might have some influence in making the professional staff and agency policy more sensitive to the real needs of their clientele. Thus, employment of the poor was seen as a means of stimulating both individual and organizational change, as well as inducing more flexibility in the helping professions.

The possibility of obtaining a job served as one of the strongest incentives for participation, since many persons mistakenly assumed that an antipoverty program would naturally be a source of a large number of new jobs. Indeed, it was said by many that the poor did not want power; they wanted jobs. The CAPs, in their concern with "manpower problems," were, however, oriented toward job training and preparation rather than job development. The relatively small number of nonprofessional jobs, in contrast to the seeming proliferation of professional positions that required formal education and training, naturally produced much frustration. The failure to meet expectations regarding employment resulted in a continual pressure from the target areas to develop more jobs for poor people and to minimize the usual requirements of formal education and experience.

Out of these tensions emerged the first issue pertaining to employment: the extent to which eligibility for employment in an antipoverty program should be based on some actual or potential capability to perform the required tasks, or on "need," or as a reward for ethnic or political loyalty.[31]

A second set of issues arose from some of the possible consequences of this form of resident participation. One pertained to the need for upward

[30] See references in fn. 12.

[31] For a related discussion of some of the concepts underlying this issue, see James Q. Wilson and Edward C. Banfield, "Public-regardingness as a Value Premise in Voting Behavior," *American Political Science Review*, Vol. LVIII, No. 4 (December, 1964), 876-87.

career mobility and the institutionalized reluctance of the professions to permit this. This reluctance threatened to produce a new form of "peonage" in which nonprofessionals, unable to qualify for other than the lowest order of positions, would constitute a large pool of persons, disproportionally drawn from ethnic minorities, who were frozen in their job classifications.

The other set of issues concerned the hazards of co-optation, whereby those employed in the poverty program could lose their identity with the low-income population from which they came and develop a vested interest in the agency employing them. This might be reflected in a leadership drain, with the most able persons making the transition from citizen to staff, thus eliminating their participation in the policy-making, program development and social action aspects of the war on poverty.[32] In this way, employment of the poor could conceivably militate against achievement of the goals of the other types of resident participation.

In examining the CAPs, we shall see to what extent these tensions appeared, what their effects were, and how tensions were resolved.

In summary, then, there were four different modes of participation by the poor in the war on poverty. They represent the principal and divergent interpretations of Title II-A of the Economic Opportunity Act that were rooted in contrasting conceptions of poverty and how one might deal with it. At different stages of their organizational careers, CAPs emphasized one or another of these types of involvement in policy making, program development, social action, or employment.[33] Vying with each other as the foremost requirement of the poor were: participation, social services, power, and jobs.

Whether the conflict engendered by this ambiguous social policy was functional or whether the attempt to reconcile social control and social change objectives was successful cannot be answered simply, since this judgment depends on one's conception of the purposes of the war on poverty and on the particular community under discussion. In selecting for study a group of communities in a major metropolitan region, I hoped that an analysis of their experience would suggest some future policy guidelines for involvement of the poor in large-scale efforts for social change. This analysis may suggest some answers to the question of whether the poor can really be organized into a massive effort to lift themselves out of poverty and powerlessness.

[32] The nonpolitical character of a civil service is expressed in OEO Community Action Memo No. 23, which prohibited any person employed in an OEO-financed program from membership on a CAP policy-making body.

[33] A somewhat different analysis of the characteristic phases of a CAP is found in Melvin B. Mogulof, "A Developmental Approach to the Community Action Program Idea," *Social Work*, Vol. 12, No. 2 (April, 1967) 12-20.

The purview of the case studies is *not* the total scope of CAP policy and program; rather, it is this one, most distinctive aspect of the CAP: *the choices made regarding involvement of the poor and some of their consequences.* In three of these communities, issues of decentralization and the power to be given to the neighborhoods were critical decision areas, and the CAPs in San Francisco, Oakland, and Santa Clara will also be compared more intensively on the other three modes of participation in chapters 7-10.

A note on methodology: The case studies were based on data collected by the author and seven students, who between them monitored hundreds of meetings during the two-year period of 1965 and 1966 on both the community and the neighborhood levels. In addition, a selective sample of leaders and members was interviewed and a wide range of CAP documents such as minutes, reports, memoranda, and newspaper clippings were analyzed. The comparative analysis of the findings in chapters 6-10 dealing with the pattern of conflict resolution between the CAPs and the neighborhood organizations, and the character, role, and influence of the four types of participation in the target area must, because of the case study methodology, be regarded as sources rather than as tests of hypotheses. Since the five CAPs were scarcely three years old at the completion of the study, conclusions regarding impact and outcome must also be viewed as a preliminary and tentative assessment of consequences.

The account of how these five communities went about involving the poor and the analysis of the findings in the light of basic political and social policy issues should, in addition to their intrinsic historical interest, contribute to a better understanding of the relationship between citizen participation and social planning with implications for the social service and political systems in the community. If we can learn from this experience, we may be able to consider the lot of the poor with greater wisdom and be more effective in changing it for the better.

I

COMMUNITY CASE STUDIES

. . . What is involved in the war against poverty is a political struggle—not a federalized community chest in which men of good will from all sectors of society will get down to work with good hearts and pull together, but a struggle over how to make certain economic and social decisions in which there are few pros and cons.[1]

[1] Michael Harrington, "Poverty and Politics," in George H. Dunne (ed.) *Poverty in Plenty* (Washington, D.C.: P. J. Kenedy, 1965), p. 51.

2

COMMUNITY CASE STUDY OF THE SAN FRANCISCO ECONOMIC OPPORTUNITY COUNCIL

Maximum feasible participation . . . are words that expanded the social revolution in San Francisco into a chain reaction of unrest and distrust that has left its mark on every major civic improvement project attempted here in recent years.[1]

The development of the antipoverty program in San Francisco and the subsequent struggle for control between the Mayor and a coalition of target area leaders from Negro, civil rights, and neighborhood groups is one of the few instances of a dramatic shift in the balance of power. The program was initiated by the Mayor with a limited conception of resident participation and the role of the target areas. Within a year, however, elected representatives from the target areas comprised 51 per cent of the membership of the Economic Opportunity Council (EOC) and its executive committee, and the four Area Planning Boards (APBs) had full authority over funds, program, and personnel in their neighborhoods.

Although ostensibly the issue was maximum feasible participation, the battle over representation of the poor was in reality a power struggle between the Mayor of San Francisco and a group of young minority-group spokesmen, most of whom had leadership roles in prior civil rights protest activities and in opposing redevelopment in the Western Addition neighborhood of San Francisco. Through this power struggle the war on poverty became the successor to the civil rights movement by providing a sanction for middle-class ethnic activists to speak for the poor and to organize them as a constituency that might be used as pressure on community institutions. In the process of its development, however, the EOC was transformed into an arena of conflict between various minority factions, and between the central administration and the areas, that pre-empted the participation of the poor.

[1] John F. Shelley, former mayor of San Francisco, EOC *Journal,* Vol. 1, No. 5 (July, 1967).

Passage of the Economic Opportunity Act in August, 1964 came after San Francisco had experienced three major sit-ins: one at the Sheraton-Palace Hotel in February, one at the Cadillac agency on Auto Row, and one at the Bank of America the following month. A key role in these demonstrations was played by a confederation of civil rights groups organized in August, 1963 called the United San Francisco Freedom Movement (UFM). This confederation consisted of the NAACP, CORE, and the Ad Hoc Committee to End Discrimination, the latter a loose collection of twelve student groups. Among the most active leaders in the UFM were those who later played a major part in the fight with the Mayor over the composition of the EOC. These included Wilfred Ussery, a national chairman of CORE, Bill Bradley, chairman of San Francisco CORE, Kenneth Simmons and Edward Rice of Freedom House, and Kermit Scott of the Urban League. In the subsequent breakup of the UFM coalition, several of the most prominent civil rights advocates who had differed among themselves were pushed aside by some of these younger militants from the Western Addition. Most of the latter had also been involved in Freedom House, which was established in March, 1964 in the Fillmore district (a Negro ghetto) to oppose the redevelopment of the A-2 section of the Western Addition. With the aid of college students, 15 block clubs were formed and hundreds of residents were involved that summer in protesting the city's plans to redevelop the remaining portion of the Western Addition, which contained one-third of the Negro population of San Francisco. Although their efforts failed when the San Francisco Board of Supervisors voted unanimously to proceed with the plan, these experiences in politics and community organization served as a training ground for many of the active Negro residents and for the cadre of civil rights leaders identified with CORE and Freedom House. Thus, when the Economic Opportunity Act was passed, there were numerous groups in San Francisco particularly sensitive to the political possibilities of the maximum feasible participation clause. When Mayor John F. Shelley began meeting with various community representatives to discuss the organization of the EOC, there was no disagreement between the "official" Negro leaders who were invited and the "young Turks" that this program could be a means of enhancing Negro power in San Francisco. Apart from the possibility of controlling a new resource, the anti-poverty program appeared to provide a unique opportunity to organize the Negro grassroots community more effectively for political purposes since neither Freedom House nor the UFM and its constituent organizations had ever reached into the community sufficiently to develop an authentic constituency for whom it could speak.

The EOC Appointed

The original Economic Opportunity Council of 39 was appointed by Mayor Shelley on September 2, 1964 and held its first meeting nine days later. Incorporation as a nonprofit organization, which took place on October 23, was a matter of expediency, since it represented a way of avoiding the slow legislative process involving the establishment of a new city commission.[2]

The EOC was to have a membership of 50, all appointed by the Mayor and consisting of representatives from five sectors of the community: business, labor, social agencies, racial and ethnic groups, and public members. The Mayor particularly wanted strong representation from business, industry, and labor since he believed that only in this way could the CAP be used to develop new job opportunities. Although the Mayor had requested certain agencies and groups to submit names of possible nominees, the actual appointments were made by him, and it was made clear from the beginning that he intended to control the Council and the program. An executive committee of 11 was appointed; it had policy-making powers until July 30, 1965.[3]

From the beginning there seems to have been a tacit understanding that the war on poverty was going to be a "Negro program." Everett Brandon, a young Negro stockbroker with relatively little administrative experience, was appointed as the executive director of the EOC at the insistence of some of the Negro leaders who had originally urged the Mayor to move quickly and establish a CAP. These included Carleton Goodlett, M.D., editor of the *Sun-Reporter,* Terry François, a member of the Board of Supervisors, and Dr. Arthur Coleman, who was appointed by the Mayor as the chairman of the EOC.

Four target areas of widely varying size, demographic characteristics,

[2] Because several months of hearings were required to establish the San Francisco Human Relations Commission, the Mayor was determined to bypass this procedure in order to start the Community Action Program as quickly as possible. The rationale for establishing a nonprofit organization instead of an official city agency was mentioned by the Mayor in the August 9, 1965 minutes of the EOC.

[3] The executive committee was composed of the following: Reginald Biggs (department store executive); George Choppelas (attorney); John Crowley (AFL-CIO Labor Council); Herman Galegos (Director, Youth Opportunities Center and Mexican-American leader); Reverend J. Austell Hall (Minister, Bethel A.M.E. Church); Earl Raab (Jewish Community Relations Council); Reverend Taam (Chinese Community); Mrs. Claire Gold (Head Start Program representative); Dorothy von Beroldingen (attorney); and Roger Hernandez (Spanish Speaking Citizens).

and extent of poverty were designated in the Mission, Hunters Point, Western Addition and Chinatown sections of the city. Although these areas contained over 100,000 low-income persons and 80 per cent of the Negro population of the city, almost half the poverty-stricken people in San Francisco lived outside the boundaries of the target areas and the one with the highest concentration of low-income persons, the "Tenderloin," was not originally selected as a target area.[4]

Residents were expected to organize interim and then permanent planning boards which would then have veto power over programs and personnel assigned to their areas, although this provision was not widely understood. No guiding criteria were proposed for their size, composition, or methods of selection, as these matters were to be left to the discretion of each target area. In contrast to the practice in Berkeley and Oakland, direct election of target area delegates to the EOC or its executive committee did not get beyond the discussion stage, and it was only after an eight-month struggle that the executive committee agreed to the idea that each area could elect one representative to it.

The initial strategy in San Francisco, then, consisted of the establishment of a mayor's committee, organized as a nonprofit corporation, and a rather vague plan for the establishment of advisory bodies in the four neighborhoods. At the same time, because of the rather tense civil rights situation during the summer and fall of 1964, and the defeat of Proposition 14, a state-wide open housing law in November, city hall recognized that it would be unwise to move ahead in program development without some involvement from the groups and areas to be served. Accordingly, the EOC decided that some of the poor should be consulted regarding their notions of what they needed. Beginning in November and December of 1964, "contact teams," consisting mainly of social agency staff members on loan and volunteers, interviewed selected families and individuals to ascertain their preference for services and their conception of needs. The EOC claimed that over three thousand interviews were conducted in San Francisco for this purpose, involving 40 meetings and numerous "dialogues" between EOC members who visited poor families in their own homes.[5] There was, however, the fact that little or no control was exercised over the selection of respondents and the types of questions

[4] The four original target areas were estimated to include 61 per cent of the San Francisco families earning less than $4,000 in 1959; 50 per cent of the unemployed persons in the city; 85 per cent of the Aid to the Families of Dependent Children cases; 62 per cent of the Old Age Assistance cases and 43 per cent of the persons aged sixty-five or more. These and other details of the target areas can be found in *A Preliminary Report on the Activities of the Economic Opportunity Council of San Francisco, Inc.*, February, 1966, pp. 8-9.

[5] *Ibid.*, p. 4.

asked may have encouraged unreal expectations, as well as confusion regarding the scope and content of the war on poverty.

The service preferences ranked by the respondents were supposed to be fed back into an elaborate planning process in which governmental and voluntary agencies would design projects based upon the facts of poverty as gathered by a research firm and the expressed demand of the potential consumers. These proposals were then to be presented to the EOC for their review and eventual approval.

The Fight With the Mayor

It was not possible for this plan to be fully implemented, because shortly after the appointment of the EOC, two groups were formed that strongly protested to the Mayor about the composition of the Council.

Speaking on behalf of the poor in the target areas was a loose coalition of about twenty-five civil rights, ethnic minorities, neighborhood, and social clubs that called itself Citizens United Against Poverty (CUAP) and the Mission Community Action Committee, consisting of some spokesmen for the Spanish-speaking minority. CUAP grew out of a meeting in the Macedonia Missionary Baptist Church on February 26, 1965 when a resolution demanding that the poor have a greater voice in the poverty program was drafted and sent to the Mayor. It specifically asked for a delay in submitting program proposals to OEO until such issues as the following were "resolved in consultation with the poor": the right of target area residents to review and veto programs; employment policies that would not exclude those lacking formal education and professional training, and majority representation of the poor on the executive committee of the EOC.[6]

The Mayor's initial response to this request was simply to ignore it. He avoided meeting with the CUAP delegates, and the subject was not even discussed at subsequent EOC meetings.[7] Annoyed at the Mayor's lack of response, CUAP sent him a telegram on April 19 requesting a meeting to discuss their demands, to which the Mayor again did not reply. On April 30, 1965, Dr. Carleton Goodlett, a spokesman for CUAP and editor of the *Sun-Reporter,* strongly criticized the Mayor in the press, saying

[6] A copy of the resolution is found in the EOC minutes of May 21, 1965 and in Willie Thompson, *Enemy of the Poor* (San Francisco, 1966), pp. 21-24. The latter, a pamphlet, is an account of the fight with the Mayor written by one of the CUAP leaders.

[7] On March 5, 1965 the EOC did discuss representation with Dr. Melvin Mogulof, regional manager for Community Action Programs, who said that one representative from each area would satisfy OEO, and, if the EOC met infrequently, the poor should be included on its executive committee.

that ignoring the requests of CUAP for election of its representatives to the executive committee was an insult to the Negro community. Goodlett was quoted as saying that Mayor Shelley had forgotten that he received his majority vote from the "black belts." The chairman of the local chapter of CORE, Bill Bradley, also sent telegrams to Governor Brown, Sargent Shriver, and various congressmen urging the suspension of all antipoverty funds.

On that same day Dr. Arthur Coleman, chairman of the EOC, was quoted in the press as saying that the antipoverty program in San Francisco belonged to the poor people and they would run it. Mayor Shelley had exercised proper authority in setting up the Council in order to be able to receive federal funds, but the Mayor could not run the EOC. Coleman added:

> We have completed plans for turning the neighborhood antipoverty programs over to the people of the neighborhoods. They will run their own programs—not in name but in actuality.[8]

Brandon, executive director of the EOC, referred to the Council's hopes for obtaining $2 million from the federal government, which would enable them to start planning programs within a month. He also added that because the poor know more than anyone what they need, poor people in the four target areas would send delegates to the Council's executive committee. The next day, May 1, after two months of negotiations, the executive committee of the EOC, consisting entirely of mayoral appointees, unanimously approved the idea that one person be appointed from each of the area boards to the executive committee and that similar measures be taken when further poverty areas were declared.

This concession still did not meet CUAP's demand for majority control by the target areas, which were in the process of creating interim boards of directors. As a result, the next few months witnessed a series of confrontations, open skirmishes, charges, and countercharges by the Mayor and CUAP and its supporters. In answer to the claim that he was trying to control the program, the Mayor reasserted the necessity for governmental accountability if the city was going to serve as the fiscal agent and provide 10 per cent of the funds. He also accused the CUAP of being a "self-appointed and self-anointed group engaged in a power grab." Members of the executive committee were told on May 14 that CUAP had managed to control meetings in the Mission district, Hunters Point, and the Western Addition, and the Mayor, speaking angrily, declared:

[8] *San Francisco Examiner*, April 30, 1965.

> I think a power play and politics are being thrown into it and we are not going to get anywhere that way . . . the city has to take some hand in the thing. They (CUAP) want the city to pay, but they don't want the city to do anything about it. Well, by God, I won't go for that and I want the people to know that.[9]

CUAP answered these charges by describing itself as a democratically elected representative group, determined to express the needs of the poor. There was, indeed, no public challenge to CUAP's claim to speak on behalf of the groups to be served. It was the Mayor, not his appointees on the EOC, who strongly opposed majority representation of the target areas. Invoking its interpretation of maximum feasible participation, CUAP again demanded a delay in submitting program proposals for funding beginning in July until the issue of representation had been resolved and until the neighborhoods had elected 8 out of 13 members of the executive committee. The Mayor fought bitterly against this demand and insisted that he name the representatives from the neighborhoods. Eventually there was a dramatic confrontation between the Mayor, CUAP, and each of the area boards on May 20 at a meeting of the executive committee. The Mayor finally gave his verbal approval to a reorganization of the executive committee in which the target areas themselves might elect 8 out of the 13 members.[10] By this time, it was becoming clear that CUAP could prevent the EOC from meeting the OEO deadline of June 30 for program proposals, since some indication of area approval was required.

Although he had ostensibly yielded majority control of the executive committee, the Mayor did not give up his fight. Together with Mayor Samuel Yorty of Los Angeles, he appealed to the United States Conference of Mayors, convened over Memorial Day in St. Louis, and to the OEO, in an effort not to let the program leadership slip entirely out of his control. At the Conference of Mayors, Shelley joined Yorty in introducing a resolution accusing OEO of "fostering class struggle." OEO's insistence that "the poor must dominate this thing," Shelley warned, would have the effect of wrecking the program by removing it from the control of city officials. He was quoted as insisting, "the elected city officials must retain control." [11]

While the Mayor was out of town, CUAP, the target area representatives, and the Urban League were successful on May 28 in persuading the executive committee to rescind its action of the day before in approving the submission of $3.1 million in program proposals to OEO. Although

[9] *San Francisco Examiner,* May 15, 1965, p. 1.

[10] EOC executive committee minutes, May 20, 1965.

[11] As quoted in Charles Silberman, "The Mixed-up War on Poverty," *Fortune,* Vol. LXXII, No. 2 (August, 1965), 158.

this first package of 16 programs was forwarded, it was agreed that no further policy decisions would be made until a new executive committee could be appointed with a majority of its members elected from the target areas, nor would funds be allocated for programs until the target areas had an opportunity to review and revise the original proposals.[12]

Shelley returned to the city from the Conference of Mayors claiming the support of OEO and Vice-President Hubert Humphrey for his position that no single interest should dominate the program. On June 7, Vice-President Humphrey met with a delegation of mayors and was quoted as saying that he was shocked to learn that control of the program by the poor was an idea prevalent around the country. Shelley, reassured by this, did nothing to carry out his promise of May 20 to reconstitute the executive committee. He indicated a willingness to enlarge the executive committee (which would have had the effect of maintaining his control), but he made no move to fulfill his original commitment to give majority representation to the target areas.

Shelley's statements on June 8 clearly indicated that he had changed his mind:

> . . . there'll have to be further reorganization of the program here and more people pulled in, including representatives of business, labor and the Board of Supervisors and the general citizenry. Berry (OEO Director of Community Action Programs) said clearly that it was never intended that recipients of the program should control or run it. Such control is a little ridiculous when you consider the fiscal responsibility City officials assume when they take office.[13]

He further said that he was not prepared to detail what form of organization the executive committee would take: "there are some people who don't care whether there is a program or not—they simply want power. I want a program." [14]

The EOC was not convened during a seven-week period of doubt and uncertainty from May 20 to July 9, while the Mayor was under frequent attack for having reneged on his word. Goodlett said on June 5

> He made an agreement. The only currency in a politician's bank is his word. What is Mayor Shelley's word? The Negro community

[12] EOC executive committee minutes, May 28, 1965.

[13] *San Francisco Chronicle*, June 18, 1965, p. 10. For an account of the organization and administration of a CAP that largely conformed to these ideas of Mayor Shelley, see Seymour Z. Mann, *Chicago's War on Poverty* (Chicago: Center for Research in Urban Government, Loyola University, May, 1966).

[14] *Ibid.*

of San Francisco is awaiting with interest what action, if any, Shelley will take in the matter.[15]

Coleman said on July 8 that if Shelley would "honor his commitment to give the poor control of the program we can move right into action." [16]

This issue was then fought out at the EOC meetings during August of 1965 and was marked by a dramatic walkout on August 11 by all the Negro representatives for the Western Addition and Hunters Point when audience participation in the meeting was ruled out of order.[17] The EOC was boycotted by these two neighborhoods for three weeks, during which time OEO officials stated that they were satisfied with the present composition of the Council.[18]

The final battle took place at the EOC meeting of August 31, at which 39 organizations, with the sole exception of the Chamber of Commerce, spoke in favor of majority representation of the poor.[19] Mayor Shelley's name was hissed, jeered, and booed at every mention. In the face of this impressive opposition, and with the reverberations of the Watts riots still in the air, he capitulated: "There seems to be a very strong feeling that control of the program should be with those who are involved in it." [20]

Coleman concluded:

> I think it is great. I think the general public is in support of the idea of majority control by the poor—the concept of them having some control of their fate is profound. I am optimistic about the program. I think it is a big breakthrough.[21]

EOC Reorganized

Following this meeting, the EOC was reorganized with 23 mayoral appointees and 24 elected representatives, 6 each from the four target

[15] *San Francisco Chronicle,* June 5, 1965, page 10.

[16] *San Francisco Examiner,* July 8, 1965, page 7.

[17] EOC minutes, August 9, 1965 and August 11, 1965.

[18] EOC minutes, August 23, 1965. Earlier, Theodore M. Berry, OEO director of Community Action Programs, was quoted as stating that "The structure of the Executive Committee can be evaluated and perhaps expanded." *San Francisco Chronicle,* June 5, 1965, p. 3. Subsequently, there were rumors that Congressman Philip R. Burton was able to persuade Berry to disclaim his support of Shelley and to urge him to accept the demands of the target areas.

[19] EOC minutes, August 31, 1965. Although it was threatened innumerable times with falling apart because of internal feuding, CUAP was held together by the determination of the civic, professional, and intellectual Negro leaders who, despite personal and ideological differences, were all committed to no compromise on the principle of majority representation of the target areas on the EOC.

[20] *San Francisco Examiner,* September 2, 1965, p. 1.

[21] *Op. cit.,* p. 14.

areas, and an executive committee of 15, which included 8 representatives, 2 each from the target areas. The fight with the Mayor shifted the direction of the war on poverty in San Francisco, altering the distribution of power between the representatives of the neighborhoods who spoke for the poor, and the Mayor. The target areas gained a majority of both the 47-member city-wide Council and the 15-member executive committee, and the Mayor, who had initially appointed the whole Council, found himself in a subsidiary role. While he continued to exert influence on the EOC in various ways from the sidelines, he never attended their subsequent meetings. Broad powers over program and personnel were subsequently voted to each of the target areas, including the authority to: approve all programs operating in their neighborhoods; elect representatives to the EOC and executive committee; operate information and referral and community organization programs, and employ the necessary personnel for these tasks. Section 8 of the bylaws adopted in September of 1965 described the authority of the Target Area Action Boards as follows:

> (a) Powers:
> (i) to initiate programs. All programs that require any action by the Council . . . must originate in the Area Boards or receive prior written approval by the Area Boards . . . before such programs shall receive consideration by the Council. In the event a program proposes to serve more than one Area, written approval must be received from each Area to be affected.
> (ii) to set program priorities, institute program changes, changes in agencies or groups or originally designated to perform specific programs and delete and/or add needed programs within the limit of the funds designated for the respective target areas.
> (iii) Personnel. Persons to serve as Area Director must be approved by the Target Area Action Boards. In consultation with the Area Director all other Area staff shall be hired only with the approval of the Target Area Action Boards.[22]

In this way, the structure of the EOC was altered to give the area boards authority over all of the activities of the poverty program within their geographic jurisdiction, although there remained numerous ambiguities about the relationship between the staffs of the central administration and the areas.

The bylaws provided for an unprecedented degree of decentralized power in the neighborhoods. The first place in which the area boards

[22] This section of the bylaws is found in *A Preliminary Report* . . . p. 7.

were able to assert their newly won authority during September and October was in the realm of program planning. In order to meet the OEO funding deadlines of June 30, an initial package of 16 programs had been prepared by agency representatives and submitted to the executive committee on May 28. When, in accordance with the new bylaws, these were submitted to the area boards for their approval, Western Addition rejected all but five, Mission and Hunters Point rejected three each, and Chinatown approved them all. As a result, there was considerable variation in the programs found in each area, although virtually all of them were sponsored by established agencies such as the schools, the Urban League, the San Francisco Bar Association, the police department, Catholic Social Service, Cameron House, International Institute, public housing authority, and so forth.[23]

Among the programs adopted by all four boards, "Area Development" was the most significant. Using the rhetoric of community development, the Area Development Program embodied the ideology articulated by CUAP earlier, and it subsequently became the dominant rationale for the war on poverty in San Francisco; namely, organizing the poor to exert leverage on existing community institutions as the best use of the limited funds and time available. The original plan for neighborhood organization was submitted by Wilfred Ussery, former CUAP leader and Chairman of the Western Addition Interim Area Board Structure Committee, who later became its area director. The plan, designed by Ussery and two other architects, Kenneth Simmons and Henry Schubart, called for the division of the Western Addition into five districts of 50 to 60 blocks each and 32 neighborhoods of 8 to 10 city block units. Although policy and administration were to be coordinated on the area level, each neighborhood was to serve as a primary unit of involvement by electing a representative to the area board.

There were thus three distinct planes of operation: (1) the area, where policy was set by the board and administered by the director and his staff; (2) the district, conceived as a level where residents could gain easy access through service centers to various programs and which would also sponsor conferences, workshops and meetings; and (3) the neighborhood, approximately eight to ten square blocks, which would be the size

[23] EOC minutes, October 29, 1965. Citywide programs adopted included: Bay Area Urban League Job Development program ($65,308); San Francisco Bar Association project to release indigent prisoners on their own recognizance (OR) ($47,356). In addition, the following were approved: Health care beyond screening (all but Western Addition); social services in public housing (Mission only); social casework services (Chinatown and Mission); police-community relations (all but Western Addition); compensatory and remedial education programs (all but Western Addition).

of the unit for a field worker. There was to be one central office for the entire area and five district service offices, each of which would be staffed by an organizer and his assistants. The emphasis was clearly on organization to the exclusion of service programs.[24] As Ussery stated it:

> Organization was a prerequisite to actual service programs . . . there was an urgency to this in order to bring programs from 1965-66 up from the people instead of down from the agencies.[25]

This elaborate plan was presented to the EOC on September 29, 1965 and endorsed by a vote of 31 to 1. Members of the Council joined in hailing the proposal as courageous, innovative, and visionary, although representatives from the other areas made it clear that this approval would not necessarily obligate them to proceed in the same manner as the Western Addition.[26]

Each of the four target areas had its own special character and developed a board that reflected its distinctive orientation to the opportunities presented by the EOC. For example, the Western Addition, with its tradition of Negro political and civil rights activities, embarked upon a most extensive program of community organization but was virtually consumed by factional conflict. Chinatown, on the other hand, reflected the stable consensus of a conservative traditionalism fostered by a cultural enclave and sought to work as closely as possible with the established agencies. The ethnic heterogeneity of the Mission underlay its firm antiestablishment stance and an intense political process that practically exhausted the entire board. An isolated, impoverished Negro ghetto, Hunters Point also sought to organize itself and to seize the opportunities for staff employment in the program. Central City brought together Tenderloin denizens and a group of committed professionals concerned with modern-day rescue. Each target area was quite autonomous, and together they comprised a loosely knit collection of experiments in citizen participation.

[24] "Western Addition Area Development Plan 1965," pp. 1-3 (mimeo.). For a perceptive analysis of the significance of the priority given to area development, see *Examination of the War on Poverty*, Staff and Consultants Reports, Prepared for the Subcommittee on Employment, Manpower and Poverty of the Committee on Labor and Public Welfare, U.S. Senate, Vol. VII (Washington, D.C.: Government Printing Office, September, 1967), pp. 2179-2202.

[25] EOC minutes, October 29, 1965, pp. 4-6.

[26] *Ibid.* Each of the areas did establish an area development program that included the two major functions of information and referral and community organization. Although the latter was carried out in somewhat different ways in each target area, the information and referral (social service outreach) was essentially similar in attempting to relate individuals to various benefit systems in the community. Community organization was utilized to develop the area organizational structure as well as to assist groups in various forms of self-help.

Western Addition: Negro Politics

Containing the oldest Negro community in San Francisco, the Western Addition is the heart of the 18th Assembly and Fifth Congressional Districts, and the historic base of civil rights movements, social reform, and politics for Negroes. Consisting of approximately three hundred blocks in which over 62,000 people live, 43 per cent of whom are Negro, it contains one-third of the Negro population of San Francisco. In the ten years between 1950 and 1960, the Western Addition lost one-fourth of its population on account of redevelopment, but whereas half of its white population moved, the nonwhite population increased by one-third. Although there are substantial numbers of middle-class persons, two-thirds of the families have incomes of less than $6,000 per year. *De facto* segregation in schools and housing, high rates of unemployment twice as high as in the rest of the city—and extensive dependency on public assistance characterize the area, as well as an extremely high degree of social organization, in the form of churches, lodges, associations, social clubs, and so forth.[27]

Out of this community emerged a group of young, militant civil rights activists who had fought discrimination and redevelopment and taken the initiative in forming CUAP, and who were subsequently involved in the organization of the Western Addition interim board. At the request of the executive committee of the EOC, an organizing committee or interim board of directors of 21 was formed on May 14, 1965. Over half were civil rights workers from CORE or Freedom House, including a leadership nucleus of six men who were involved in a struggle for personal power that influenced the character of the fight with the Mayor and the subsequent history of the San Francisco program.[28]

The sole purpose of the interim board was to lay the ground work for the election of a permanent board, hopefully by the end of the year. During the summer of 1965, while the fight with the Mayor raged, the interim board established the priority of community organization for the

[27] This data was derived from the United Community Fund of San Francisco, *A Profile of the Western Addition 1960,* June, 1964, and EOC Research Department reports.

[28] These included the following: Wilfred Ussery, a national chairman of CORE, and chairman of the Western Addition Structure Committee; William Bradley, chairman of San Francisco CORE; Kenneth Simmons of Freedom House, who became program coordinator on the central staff of EOC; Ed Rice, chairman of Freedom House, vice-chairman of the board of Western Addition (later a member of the central administration staff); Willie Thompson, a self-appointed spokesman for the poor and former CUAP leader; and Kermit Scott, staff member, Urban League.

Western Addition, set out the ground rules for election procedures, and established an Area Development plan by which "the poor may build their own mode of self-government and thereby to promote self-help, cooperation and self-expression." [29] Ideologues such as Ussery, Simmons, and Schubart articulated a philosophy that was a mixture of neo-Populism and community development. They perceived the Area Development Program as a way of implementing maximum feasible participation and providing a means for the political socialization of the Western Addition. An elaborate plan for elections was formulated with high hopes that not only would the poor select their own representatives, but many of them would be participating in a democratic process for the first time in their lives.

For a variety of reasons the elections went very slowly, even though the entire seven-month budget of the Western Addition was allocated for neighborhood organizers. In the beginning, board member volunteers were able to secure some interest in the elections, since there were no income requirements (i.e., *any* resident, regardless of his economic status, could vote, or run for a position on the area board). Gradually, during October and November, fewer and fewer people turned out to vote, and it was agreed to stop the elections until 15 neighborhood organizers could be hired to take over this responsibility. By December only five board members had been elected, so the interim board actually persisted for almost eleven months until April, 1966, when the permanent board of 32 was finally elected. By then most of the interim members either were elected to the permanent board or had obtained positions on the area staff. Several thousand persons took part in the voting for the 32 board members.

Although many regarded themselves as "poor," the majority of the board were middle-class persons, including four or five property owners, and all of them were employed, including the seven women who were elected. Their ages ranged from thirty to fifty. Only four board members were acknowledged to be "real" poor people, and low-income persons in general were bypassed as the more ambitious, affiliated, and active members of the Negro community sought membership on the area board. The prospect of funds, a better job, or power seems to have been the main incentive for participation.

From the first moment of Ussery's selection as area director in September, when his colleague Schubart cast the only dissenting vote against him, he was under continual attack by several personal and political enemies who consistently challenged his administrative authority as executive.

[29] "Report from Western Addition Interim Area Board," in *A Preliminary Report* . . . p. 30. The election procedures and process are described on pp. 34-40 of the latter document.

A battle for control of the board took place, characterized by pervasive distrust, shifting alliances, and endless squabbling. The principal conflicts took place around the criteria for the employment of staff and the priority assigned to organization of the Western Addition over social service programs.

As an administrator, Ussery and his supporters favored hiring staff with some attention to qualifications, whereas one of his major antagonists argued for rewarding loyal and faithful workers: "Some day you'll need a job . . . how would you like it if your mother or girl friend needed a job?" Increasingly the meetings were plagued by petty and violent quarrels as various factions sought to influence the selection of staff. Ussery was accused of trying to find jobs for his friends and supporters and, indeed, at one time over half of the organizers were CORE members. Since the budget of the Western Addition was close to $400,000 and provided for over a hundred jobs, such as neighborhood organizers and coordinators for leaflet distribution and telephone contact, it was no wonder that there was such a bitter struggle between the executive and his board over the authority to allocate these funds and select personnel.

Eventually, a stalemate was reached when the chairman of the Personnel Committee, an opponent of Ussery, refused to convene his committee. As a result, for many months in 1966 there were 48 unfilled positions. The situation was aggravated by the fierce competition for the relatively few jobs by an extraordinarily large number of applicants. For example, at one time there were 220 applications for 14 neighborhood organizer jobs. Unsuccessful and disgruntled applicants produced a growing number of dissidents and one thwarted job seeker in particular was alleged to have led a major attack on Ussery.

The other source of discontent was in the priority assigned to the Area Development Program, which required that all the funds be used to employ staff to organize the neighborhood as the preliminary to the development of programs that were to be initiated by the poor themselves. Ussery and his allies had regarded the victory over the Mayor as primarily an opportunity to develop a structure for organizing the community, but organization of the poor took an enormous amount of time and staff. Personnel were not available in sufficient number owing to the internecine fighting or because of the budget cuts. Board members grew increasingly restive and impatient for some programs and began asking when they would see some other benefits from the war on poverty apart from a few jobs going to a favored few.[30]

[30] The Area Development Program with its intent to organize the unaffiliated poor was also perceived by some board members as a threat to the established Negro organizations.

The issue of priorities came to a head around a demonstration project, sponsored by the San Francisco Family Service Agency, which had considerable backing in the neighborhood and which was strongly opposed by Ussery and others on the grounds that it did not originate in the Area Planning Board. Over 250 residents attended a meeting on January 11, 1966; it was evident that there was popular support for endorsing a proposal to provide a small number of jobs to mothers who would be developing some programs for children. Ussery and his supporters argued for maintenance of the principle that the program must come from the people themselves, but the board voted to endorse the agency's proposal.[31]

Ussery also antagonized other segments of his board, who resented what they regarded as his attempts to control the board through the influencing of elections, the hiring of staff, and the constant invoking of deadlines, thus "reducing the board to a rubber stamp." Many board members assumed that they would be paid for participation or could use their position as a means of obtaining a job or approval for a special project in which they were interested. When these hopes did not materialize, board members grew increasingly frustrated and directed much of their hostility toward the staff. Disruptive, factional fighting also prevailed around the decisions relating to approval of programs, and there seemed to be more interest in their political aspects than in the goals and methods of the services.

With the bulk of the staff assigned to the promotion of elections and replacements (six permanent members had to be replaced; two joined the staff and four got jobs elsewhere), there was little time for other community or program development efforts. The redevelopment plan for A-2 was not strongly opposed, and only one abortive attempt at social action occurred at a Rally for Justice called on behalf of 19 Negro maids allegedly fired by the Hilton Hotel on a discriminatory basis.

Eventually, toward the end of the summer of 1966, 28 neighborhoods were organized, each with a 15-member council whose chairman represented the neighborhood on the board. However, no more than half of the board members reported back to these councils and only 6 of the 28

[31] Other programs operating in the Western Addition were: The Performing Arts Workshop, Legal Services, Head Start, Summer Youth Employment, Urban League Job Development, and Own Recognizance Bail. All but the first were citywide. As a demonstration, the Western Addition Parents Project was funded under Section 207 of the Economic Opportunity Act and was not in the same category as other Community Action Projects. Participation of low-income residents in the Family Service Agency as nonprofessionals and as members of the board and advisory committees was credited by the executive as having a major impact on the agency's policies and practices in the community. Although this involvement in the antipoverty program may have been resented by other agencies, the executive believed that it led to much better public relations in the low-income community.

councils were believed to be functioning actively. Many of the board members were reluctant to convene their neighborhood councils because, according to the bylaws, they could be voted out at a single meeting, although this only occurred twice.

These personal vendettas and endless squabbling were accompanied by widespread newspaper publicity. At one point the area director was engaged in battling various board members and staff members who had complained to OEO and the FBI that the neighborhood organization plan was a "communist thing," and he was also deeply embroiled in the attempt to oust the executive director of the EOC.

Eventually a secret rump meeting of the board was called in September, 1966 and the area director was dismissed. He refused to resign, claiming the meeting was illegal, although admitting that the permanent board had never acted on his original appointment by the interim board. He accused Brandon of interfering, but when a second meeting took place, although no charges were leveled, Ussery was fired for the second time in two months. Another group of board members claimed that *they* were the authorized representatives of the Western Addition, and the matter went to the EOC for adjudication. There was considerable reluctance to act on this claim because it represented an admission that the area boards could not function on their own. The outcome of the dissension-ridden situation was that the entire board had to resign. With 20 of its members serving as an interim board, a new set of elections was held in January and February of 1967. Ussery was eventually permitted to resign, having grown weary and discouraged about the possibility of using the war on poverty as a vehicle for the political and social regeneration of the Negro community.

The Western Addition represented a noble political experiment, but the original goal of maximum feasible participation of the poor was subordinated in an internal struggle for power between the board and staff. The unity of the Western Addition against the Mayor was quickly shattered as factions emerged and alliances shifted in the fight over control of staff and policy making. Negro politics prevailed, and although a shaky organizational structure emerged after a year, its composition, representative quality, and capabilities fell far short of the intent of the architects of the Area Development plan.

The Mission District: Ethnic Politics

The Mission district was the largest target area, encompassing about one-fifth of the land area of San Francisco and a population of approximately 140,000, of whom one-fourth were considered impoverished. Characterized by an extraordinary ethnic and cultural diversity, the Mission area contained over twenty different Spanish-speaking nationality groups, of which the Mexican-Americans were the largest bloc. It also included substantial numbers of Negroes, Orientals, Filipinos, American Indians, and "Anglo" residents.[32]

Following the work of volunteer contact teams, a broadly based Mission Area Organizing Committee was convened by the EOC staff members in March, 1965, consisting mainly of organizational and ethnic representatives. It functioned until December, when the bylaws were completed that provided for the elections of 38 board members consisting solely of low-income residents over sixteen years of age. Provision was originally made for five delegates each from six neighborhoods plus eight members-at-large, but large sections of the Mission area were subsequently transferred to the fifth target area, Central City.[33] The stipulation that only low-income persons could be elected to the permanent board disqualified most of the members of the organizing committee, but the majority of the members-at-large elected at a street fiesta, who turned out to be among the most influential persons on the board, were also formerly active on the organizing committee.

Although elected by fewer than six hundred residents, the Mission area board had the distinction of being the only one all of whose members had to meet low-income criteria. In this sense, it constituted one of the very few instances of maximum feasible participation of the poor. While Mexican-Americans, some of whom did not speak English, comprised the largest group on the board, no one ethnic bloc had a majority. As a result, there was constant jockeying for power and office between individual board members. There were few stable alignments except that of the Negroes, most of whom were women, and the younger members of the board—several were in their late teens—who were usually opposed by most of the Mexican- and Latin-Americans and the American Indian representative. Only half of the active board members were presumably concerned with the interests of a particular neighborhood since they had been elected on a geographic basis, although they tended to communicate more often with their own ethnic group than with the sub-area that elected them. Furthermore, every one of the more influential members was affiliated with some ethnic or political organization whose interests he sought to advance, and these identifications tended to be much more significant than low-income status. For several indigenous board members, this was

[32] Mission Area Community Action Board, "Poverty Progress Report," submitted to Social Service Committee of the San Francisco Board of Supervisors, August 18, 1966, pp. 1-2.

[33] *A Preliminary Report* . . . pp. 11-12.

their first organizational experience and the beginning of a leadership role.

The weekly meetings of the board were usually marked by considerable tension and personal wrangling. The first chairman, a young, politically liberal, sophisticated Mexican-American attorney was succeeded by a Negro college student who, aided by the presence of a growing number of visitors attending the meetings, was able to maintain more orderly proceedings.

Major struggles ensued, centered around employment of staff and the selection of programs, as the board members sought to protect or advance their personal or ethnic interests. As a result, the Mission lagged somewhat behind the Western Addition and Chinatown in getting organized and did not employ its area director, a bilingual former parole officer named Alex Zermeno until February 14, 1966. By the end of the year, it had hired only three other professionals and 25-35 community aides out of a total of 72 authorized positions.[34] An enormous amount of meeting time was devoted to discussion of staff qualifications, since the board was unwilling to delegate this responsibility to the area director, and they were equally zealous in their determination to get members of their ethnic group appointed. Race was pitted against race; as described by one board member "it was like throwing a bone to a bunch of dogs who immediately began to fight over it."

There was also conflict between those who wanted to use staff positions as a reward and form of patronage and those who wanted to hire on basis of qualifications, although both sides were in agreement that jobs should go to the indigenous poor, preferably those who were also Spanish-speaking.

By the summer of 1966, five district offices were established and ten aides assigned to information and referral duties. Fifteen organizers were deployed on the grounds that "community organization" was given top priority on the basis of 900 replies to a needs survey in January, 1966. A major controversy ensued when the director insisted upon and won the exclusive claim of his staff to Area Development funds in opposition to several board members who had hoped to secure financial support for the organizational efforts of their own association. Approximately half of the funds of the Area Development Program were devoted to the organization of 11 grassroots and public housing tenant groups. These organizations, which required substantial amounts of staff time, sought a variety of improvements in neighborhood conditions, such as better garbage collection, rodent extermination, clean-up campaigns, school lunches and a well-baby clinic. Although some of the members of these neighborhood groups were elected to the Mission area board, it proved difficult to

[34] Mission Area Community Action Program, "Rationale for Budget Application for February 1967 to January 1968," p. 1. Prepared for EOC submission to OEO.

sustain these organizations and all but a few eventually disintegrated. Perhaps more successful was the investment of staff time in providing information and referral services that were used by over two thousand persons in the first seven months of 1966.

Mission area board and staff members also helped organize and promote the Mission Council on Redevelopment (MCOR) outside the framework of the Area Development Program. A very loose coalition of over sixty organizations, MCOR pressed the San Francisco Redevelopment Agency and the Board of Supervisors to include funds for a planning grant to the neighborhood so they could hire their own independent planner and advise the agency, and it also demanded veto power over any final plans for the Mission district that were proposed by the redevelopment agency. Ultimately, MCOR was successful in influencing the Board of Supervisors to halt future redevelopment planning for the Mission. The way in which the principle of resident participation was invoked by MCOR was criticized by a newspaper editorial writer:

> There is an underlying power struggle here, led by ideologists for the view that where the poor are affected, the poor should make the decisions. This theory will not work in designing and building a $20 million redevelopment project. Whatever pressure for it the Mission Council may bring, the Supervisors should hold out against the power play.[35]

The other major issue concerning the board was program development; here again, the Mission was distinctive in rejecting virtually all of the 23 agency proposals and accepting on March 29, 1966 mainly those submitted by indigenous groups, some of whom were organized by its own Area Development staff. In the spring of 1966 there was much log-rolling as the various programs were considered each week, with approval going to those that could muster the most support regardless of the substance of the program. These indigenous programs, developed largely by Spanish-speaking groups, were in addition to city-wide programs operating in the Mission such as the OR bail project, police community relations, legal assistance, health screening, job development and some compensatory and after-school tutorial programs.

The board insisted on having representatives on the policy-making body of the sponsors whose programs were approved for funding. In addition, staff members were assigned to monitor these new programs, with the understanding that funds could be cut off if there was improper administration. Performance of these monitoring duties was evidently not fol-

[35] *San Francisco Chronicle,* October 14, 1966, p. 46.

lowed through consistently, as both board and staff members became uninterested in this function.

When the time came for new elections in November, 1966, only three of the 25 board members were willing to run again. Instead of an all-indigenous board, the new election rules permitted one of the five persons from each district to be over the maximum poverty income. A virtually completely new board of directors was elected by a turnout of fewer than four hundred voters, and in some places it was claimed that only area staff members cast ballots. The new board included 10 members of one Spanish-speaking organization that had made a concerted effort to nominate them. Sixteen of the 25 were laborers, recent immigrants, and were participating in a community group for the first time. The morale of this second board was considerably lower than the morale of the first, and a quorum was frequently unavailable. In part this may have been a reaction to the retrenchment in funds toward the end of 1966, although the Mission area did not lose any staff positions because of this cutback. In January, 1967, the area director resigned, followed by several other professionals. Subsequently, the board and the staff seemed to drift with little sense of purpose, as a succession of directors departed. The various indigenous organizations, however, continued to be funded and constituted new, structured enclaves offering tutorials, English classes, and job finding and training programs to small groups.

During its short, vigorous life as the only indigenous low-income board, the Mission area illustrated over a period of 10 months some of the possibilities and limitations of an ethnically mixed policy-making body responsible for allocating close to half a million dollars and employing a staff of almost fifty persons. With relatively few possibilities for tangible rewards for themselves and subject to conflicting pressures by various interest groups, it is no surprise that most of the participants fought hard for power for themselves, their ethnic groups, or both, on the assumption that in this way the poor, with whom they were closely identified, would benefit.

Chinatown: Traditional Stewardship

Although there is a public image of Chinatown as a colorful, prosperous community that is an integral part of the tourist attraction to San Francisco, this exotic facade hides a community of 40,000, of whom 40 per cent live in poverty in some of the worst and most expensive substandard housing in the city. There are high rates of unemployment, rising delinquency, and serious public health problems. Because of cultural patterns that stress the social responsibility of the extended family, "saving face," and a reticent, nonmilitant approach to problems, the existence of serious deprivations in Chinatown has usually not been officially recognized,[36] and it was included as a target area by EOC staff only after the insistence of some of the more assertive younger spokesmen for the Chinese community.

Although over six hundred persons were sought out by EOC contact teams early in November, 1964 to determine the "needs of the poor," the involvement of low-income persons was not regarded as a high priority by the area board. On May 4, 1965, two representatives each from seven organizations were invited by two EOC staff members who later became the area director and community organization director, to form an interim board that would carry out the mandate to form a permanent board with the maximum feasible participation of the poor. The organizations included the Chinese Six Companies, Chinese American Citizen Alliance, Chinatown-North Beach District Council, Greater Chinese Community Service Organization, Chinese Chamber of Commerce, Chinese Christian Union and the North Beach Place Improvement Association. Several months later it was decided to request representation from the Catholic Archdiocese, two Chinese veterans organizations, International Ladies Garment Workers Union and the Italian and Filipino communities, together with some representatives from the fields of education, social work, and medicine. In addition, efforts were launched through the Area Development Program to find up to six low-income persons from the Ping Yuen public housing project in Chinatown who could be elected to the board, but over a year elapsed before the first representative was seated.[37] Imperceptibly, the interim board became the permanent board, since no elections were held nor were bylaws adopted. Criticized by some because of its overwhelmingly middle-class, professional character, the board's composition and character were defended by its leadership on the grounds that there were no organizations of the Chinese poor, who have always been a voiceless class.[38] Many of the Chinese poor, it was pointed out, were recent immigrants, understood no English, and worked long hours, frequently at night, and were thus unavailable for meetings. In addition, to admit being poor would be to lose face in the community. As one board member put it, "the poor have enough troubles without having to

[36] Chinatown-North Beach Area Board, "Poverty Progress Report," submitted to Social Service Committee of the San Francisco Board of Supervisors, April 21, 1966, pp. 1-8.

[37] A rather detailed history of the board is found in "Progress and Development of the Area Board," May, 1965–June, 1966, EOC Chinatown-North Beach Area office, 10 pp. (mimeo).

[38] One of the few public challenges to the representative character of the Chinatown board was made by J. J. Choy and is described in *The Bay Guardian,* Vol. 1, No. 1, October 27, 1966.

go to endless meetings, too." For example, when the board decided to include North Beach in its target area, the Chinese members of the board seemed quite embarrassed at the prospect of the North Beach Tenants Improvement Association voting for a "recipient" to be elected to the board, believing that it was not proper since no one would want to be put in such a position. Also, despite a long history of discrimination against the Chinese in California, there were no organized groups comparable to those in the Negro community fighting for civil rights. As a result, there was no serious challenge to the elitist philosophy of representation and of the traditional stewardship whereby the more concerned and sophisticated delegates from key civic groups would administer the program until the disadvantaged overcame language and other cultural handicaps, including reluctance to be labeled as poor.

Meanwhile, the board made every effort to take full advantage of the opportunities to bring badly needed educational and health programs into Chinatown. In sharp contrast to the board in Western Addition, the Chinatown board was not at all interested in fighting the Mayor, obtaining power, or waiting for plans to emerge out of a yet-to-be-organized low-income constituency. Instead, the attitude of the board was that programs should be activated without delay. At its second meeting on May 12, 1965, while the other areas were still debating resident participation and supporting CUAP, the Chinatown interim board passed a resolution endorsing the EOC's program proposal. Hence, it was no surprise that on August 30, 1965, the Chinatown Board, in contrast to the other area boards, voted full approval of all the agency-developed proposals. As the chairman, Father Wong, stated, "organization had to commence through traditional agencies which are necessary instruments by which people can be reached."[39]

In addition to bringing into Chinatown additional English language classes, social services for the elderly, case work services, health screening, medical care, family planning, education, summer youth employment, and tutorial and study centers, an area development program was launched with 18 community aides. Low-income residents were sought out in the public housing projects, in sewing factories, and in selected census tracts to determine their needs and inform them about the antipoverty program and the availability of information and referral services. The referral services succeeded in generating hundreds of inquiries in the area office each week regarding citizenship, employment, and welfare matters.[40]

An intensive organizational effort culminated in the formation in

[39] EOC minutes, October 29, 1965.

[40] "Poverty Progress Report," pp. 9-31. The other areas assigned almost three times as many jobs in area development as Chinatown, 65-70 as opposed to approximately 23 in the latter.

April, 1966 of the Ping Yuen Improvement Association, the first grassroots association to be formed in Chinatown. The association subsequently elected four representatives to the board late in 1966. Their participation and role were, however, exceedingly limited since only one, an eighteen-year-old college freshman, could speak English. Although the Ping Yuen Association, with considerable staff help, elicited and considered a variety of tenant complaints and developed an elaborate organizational structure, it accepted without protest the failure of the Public Housing Authority to grant it permission to use a meeting room after months of deliberation. Not able to effect any significant changes in housing policies, it functioned as a rather weak organization sponsoring essay contests and informational programs.

The board as a whole had more cohesiveness, continuity, and stability than the boards in any of the other areas, though perhaps at the price of considerable apathy, relative lack of controversy, and a reputation for being a "rubber stamp." It viewed with considerable distaste the power struggle between central and area staff members and restrained its own area director after he became involved. Many board members, being mainly Chinese middle-class professionals with a sprinkling of Italian and Filipino representatives, were unhappy with the over-representation of Negroes on the central staff and felt that the EOC, because of its internal conflicts, had made little impact on improving the lot of the poor.

Major conflicts in the Chinatown-North Beach Board occurred around the priority of the Area Development and language center programs, with the North Beach contingent favoring the former and the Chinese representatives favoring the latter. Characteristically, controversies around the resignation and replacement of the executive director, Larry Jack Wong, were resolved outside meetings in order to maintain the appearance of a dignified consensus. Considerable favoritism and patronage were involved in the selection of staff but did not have the disruptive consequences these practices produced in the Mission or Western Addition.

Thus, the Chinatown-North Beach Area Planning Board represented a mingling of the old and the new, the traditional community interests and some of the younger, more liberal elements joined by representatives of the poor, who performed a largely symbolic role. Consisting largely of the responsible, community-minded leaders, and concerned mainly with efficient program implementation, the Chinatown board succeeded in bringing some compensatory social service programs into the area and informing a small number of persons about the existence of poverty and the uses of current community resources. Although some new leadership emerged, it had little following and was not necessarily identified with some of the more popular programs sponsored by the Chinatown board, such as the language center. Because of the lack of consistent reporting to and from its organizational sponsors, the board tended to become another enclave with no strong roots in the community.

Hunters Point–Bay View: A Hilltop Ghetto

The distinguishing feature of this target area was its bleak isolation—physical, racial, and economic—from the rest of San Francisco. Almost a third of its 51,000 persons lived in the largest single concentrated block of public housing units in the city, and 5,000 of them lived in dilapidated "temporary" units built during World War II. Hunters Point had the largest proportion of children of all the target areas; 45 per cent of its population was under twenty-one, and two-thirds of the youngsters had some sort of juvenile crime record. Its unemployment rate was at least double that of San Francisco, reflecting, in part, the low educational attainment of its residents: Three out of four had less than a high school education and one-third had less than a grade school education. More than one-half of the families in the target area were headed by single parents, and although only 51 per cent of the total population was nonwhite, in three of the five districts comprising the target area 91 per cent of the families were Negro. Other dreary statistics describe the familiar attributes of a dark ghetto in which racial discrimination created a colony of impoverished people deprived of opportunities for decent education, housing, and jobs.[41] A social island where hopelessness prevailed, Hunters Point contrasted sharply with the Western Addition in its lack of civil rights organizations, churches, voluntary associations, and middle-class residents.

Organization of the Hunters Point target area began in May, 1965, when hundreds of leaflets were distributed by EOC staff announcing a mass meeting to establish an organizing committee that would determine the composition, number, and method of selecting a permanent board. Over three hundred persons attended and nominated a 15-member organizing committee that provided for geographic, ethnic, and occupational representation.[42] Because of pressures to meet the June 30, 1965 deadline of OEO for program submissions, the Hunters Point organizing committee decided "not to use time-consuming democratic elections throughout the community."[43] Instead, it believed that it was sufficiently representative for each member to submit a list of candidates to vie for the

[41] Additional data regarding Hunters Point can be found in the "Area Development Proposal 1967," submitted by EOC to OEO, pp. 1-6.

[42] *A Preliminary Report* . . . pp. 14-16.

[43] *Ibid.*, p. 16.

remaining seats on the board, and in this manner a board was selected that served until community elections took place almost a year later in the summer of 1966.

Although there was no income limitation, most of the board members had low incomes, and were evenly divided between men and women. The latter, all of whom lived in public housing and had considerable organizational experience, dominated the board. Most of the board members were active participants in one of the nine block organizations started by George Napper in the two public housing areas. Napper was a student at the University of California School of Criminology, who later became the area's first executive director. Membership in these block organizations was cited as evidence of the means through which resident participation could take place. In general, the board members were those who had traditionally assumed community leadership roles in Hunters Point, and in contrast to those in the Mission and Western Addition, the area meetings here were much less marked by controversy. They were dominated by a clique of four or five women, members of a matriarchy, who were known as energetic community workers. At the same time, relationships between the executive and the board were more harmonious than they were in the Western Addition and in the Mission.

From the very beginning, staff employment was a critical issue. Hunters Point also embarked upon an extensive Area Development Program in which, ultimately, 78 persons were employed with a monthly payroll of $40,000. Competition for these nonprofessional jobs as community aides was keen, and there were usually two or three times as many applicants as jobs, with the result that the board was frequently accused of favoritism. There was a good deal of envy in the housing projects when jobs were being passed out. Hundreds expected cash payments, and instead they saw their neighbors benefiting.[44]

While it was agreed that only indigenous low-income residents should be hired—only two of the top positions were filled by college graduates—there were still frequent conflicts over need or qualification as a criterion for employment. Also, while the three top jobs were held by men, the next six were won by women who had been involved in community work for over 10 years. Many of the board members also applied for staff positions, as well as jobs in the programs of delegate agencies, and they had to be replaced by new board members. Since no procedure had been established for this, the matter of structure and the representativeness of the board went unresolved for many months.

A pattern of supporting indigenous organizations similar to the pattern

[44] *San Francisco Chronicle,* October 26, 1966, p. 1; *Washington Post,* August 28, 1966, p. E-1.

established in the Mission was also developed at Hunters Point, and funds were approved for a new, nonprofit Housing and Community Development Corporation, as well as the Hunters Point–Bay View Community Center. In part, this was a result of overlapping membership among the board and other organizations in Hunters Point and members' previous experience with the Youth Opportunities Center, which had sensitized them to the possibilities of federally financed projects as a source of jobs and funds.

The composition of the board was substantially altered by elections in the summer of 1966, for which aides went door to door with ballots to be completed. Prior to this, candidates campaigned actively. Many of them saw election to the board as a way of getting known and possibly obtaining a job in the antipoverty program, whereas others thought they would get paid for being on the board. In the election, 85 per cent of the public housing units voted; in one district of 792 units, 516 persons voted.[45] This first election, coming over a year after the board was appointed, increased the proportion of women, although several younger men were also elected to the board and only three of the original board members were left. Gradually this board, too, experienced disenchantment and a falling off of interest in response to the power struggle between the EOC and area staff members, the cutback in OEO funds, and the subsequent plans for reorganizing the antipoverty program. Also influential, of course, was the impact of the tragic shooting of a sixteen-year old boy by a policeman on September 27, 1966 that touched off a three-day riot, the worst in San Francisco's history.

The heart of the effort to secure maximum feasible participation at Hunters Point was mainly in the Area Development Program. The community was divided into four districts and a main office, to which teams of information and referral aides, together with community organizers, were assigned. Over three hundred persons a month were assisted by these information and referral aides in dealing with a wide range of economic, health, legal, and social problems. The community organizers helped establish 13 block clubs in three districts and assisted some of the existing ones, which had been established by the Youth Opportunity Center. Most of the block leaders, who had been paid $50 per month, were hired as aides and their clubs later incorporated into the Area Development Program. Several needs surveys were conducted, which discovered that child care, education, job training, and employment were regarded as the most urgent necessities.

Under the leadership of John Dukes, a former board member who

45 San Francisco EOC, "Hunters Point-Bayview Area Development Proposal 1967," p. 7.

succeeded George Napper as area director in October, 1966, there was considerable agreement between the board and staff on the importance of short-term, visible, and tangible program goals. In contrast to workers in the Western Addition, the community workers (whose title was changed from "community organizers"), attempted both informally and officially to help develop small projects and services desired by residents, rather than to promote organization *per se*. For example, mothers' clubs were formed in each of the five districts. Community workers helped them plan and organize a cooperative nursery in which over a hundred parents were involved and helped several church groups to prepare a proposal for Neighborhood Home Health Care, which was also funded. Five youth groups were established and classes organized to teach various clerical skills. The block clubs focused primarily on improving the physical aspects of the neighborhood, their efforts included refurbishing rest room facilities in a local elementary school and guarding another school on weekends to prevent vandalism.

The number and scope of these projects was not, however, commensurate with the expectations aroused by the various needs surveys and the publicity about the antipoverty program, with the result that confidence and interest in the program gradually declined. Much of the disappointment and resentment was projected onto the EOC staff members, who were accused of not really reaching the poor and of only being interested in holding onto their jobs. The board became increasingly divided and dominated by a new matriarchy when Dukes left to become the acting director of the EOC in June of 1967. Dissension increased among the board members, two area directors were fired, and by the end of the year, the organizational structure had almost disintegrated.

Because of its pervasive role in the Hunters Point area, the Public Housing Authority was the object of most of the attempts to change agency practices. On an individual case-by-case approach, the Area Development staff were able to help bring about some modifications in staff attitudes and in policies on evictions, charge schedules, and earnings of minors.

Largely as a result of the pressures generated by an eight-month rent strike begun in November, 1966 by a tenants' union organized outside the EOC framework, the Housing Authority agreed to a year-long moratorium on evicting unemployed families and consented to an investment of $150,000 in rehabilitating some temporary housing units. For years the Housing Authority had insisted that nothing could be done about their condition, and shortly afterwards, the city agreed to invest another $350,000 in aiding the rehabilitation program.

Other gains were made in the housing field through the agreement of the redevelopment agency to consult with the Joint Housing Committee, consisting of another group of Hunters Point residents who were ultimately involved in planning for the future of 150 acres on which 300 temporary housing units were located. Through their overlapping membership in both the Joint Housing Committee of the redevelopment agency and the independent Community Development Corporation, these Hunters Point residents were able to extract an unusual concession in getting the redevelopment agency to agree to erect new low-cost housing under the nonprofit corporation's sponsorship before any demolition would take place. Still another expression of resident involvement in housing policy was the support given by the Area Planning Board to the city's selection of their area as a site for a Model Cities Planning application, but this action was strongly opposed by the white residents of adjacent neighborhoods, who, led by MCOR, forced the Mayor to abandon this plan.

Despite the development of new organizational structures in response to the opportunities and challenges presented by various governmental agencies, the basic conditions and decisions affecting the future of Hunters Point were unchanged. At Hunters Point, maximum feasible participation of the poor meant that upwards of a hundred persons were able to secure some full- or part-time staff positions and several hundred more were involved in block meetings concerned with improving some of the worst abuses in public housing. Hopes were raised, but the extent of changes brought about in this ghetto were negligible. As the editor of the antipoverty newspaper put it: "The most outstanding thing is that everything is the same. This is the problem."

Central City: Target Tenderloin

Although eight pockets of poverty were identified in the initial EOC surveys, because of limited funds only four were designated as target areas when the program was launched in September of 1964. Pressures to designate the downtown Tenderloin district as a fifth target area were exerted toward the end of 1965 by a group of ministers, physicians, lawyers, psychologists, and social workers who had a professional interest particularly in the unattached youth and young adults who drifted into the central downtown portion of San Francisco, where serious problems of prostitution, drug addiction, alcoholism, and venereal disease and a host of other health and social problems were manifest. These efforts were largely spearheaded by the former interim director of the Mission area, Calvin Colt, who later became area director for Central City. Colt had been influential in identifying the special character of the Central City area and in pressing for its separation from the Mission.

Understandably, there was considerable resistance by the other target areas to divide the San Francisco allocation from OEO into five parts instead of four. In addition, they feared a possible disturbance in the balance of power held by the ethnic minorities in the EOC, since the representatives of the Tenderloin would probably be white. A strong case was made by this group of energetic professionals, who received considerable support from the Glide Foundation, a downtown church organization, in undertaking surveys and calling attention to the "young reject in our society."[46] The Central City Citizens Committee was then formed in the spring of 1966 to secure recognition for the Central City as a fifth target area, which would make it eligible for OEO funds.

Although its research committee had recommended admission of Central City in February, the EOC rejected staff recommendations despite a strong presentation by Colt, who was supported by Assemblyman John Burton and labor leader Harry Bridges. Major opposition to Central City came from Coleman and Brandon, who sought to delay the decision. To dramatize their demands, Colt and his committee picketed the EOC offices and requested the Board of Supervisors to withhold its matching funds until Central City was a target area. The Central City Citizens Committee obtained the support of OEO, which also threatened the EOC that it would condition future grants on the inclusion of program funds for this area.

As a result of these combined pressures, the EOC reconsidered its actions and on May 25 approved an area budget of $124,500 for the next six months and set aside $100,000 for programs to be determined by the interim board.

Despite the reluctance of the EOC, a staff contact team of 15 persons was sent into the area early in April to interview residents and ascertain needs. These efforts paved the way for an election, completed by June 22, in which several hundred persons voted for an interim board of 24, which selected a woman minister, Deaconess Phyllis Edwards, as chairman. In July their two representatives to the executive committee were invited to sit in ex officio. Subsequently the EOC bylaws were changed to permit full representation from the Central City.

Two-thirds of the board were low-income residents, and the rest represented organizations and churches in the area. The board, in contrast to some of the others, was quite cohesive, much less factional, and not dominated by any one ethnic group, and was even singled out for praise by Mayor Shelley for its effectiveness! Later, it also diverged from the pattern

[46] The Rev. Edward Hansen, Mark Forrester, the Rev. Fred Bird, *The Young Reject in Our Society,* 33 pp. (process) available from Glide Urban Center, 330 Ellis Street, San Francisco; also the Tenderloin Committee, "A Funding Proposal for the Tenderloin Project," 322 Ellis Street, 8 pp. undated. See also, EOC minutes, February 23, 1966, p. 4.

followed by the other areas by abandoning the practice of conducting elections on a geographic basis for representatives of the poor. Instead, it relied more on representatives of organizations with a predominately low-income constituency in order to achieve more authentic and reliable participation in a less costly manner.

The EOC and the Target Areas

These, then, were the target areas, and this is how resident participation in the war on poverty functioned in the neighborhoods. What attracted more public attention, however, was the war between the EOC and the target areas, and it is to this theme that we now return.

With the conclusion of the fight against the Mayor, the issue of *representation* of the poor—or at least the target areas—was more or less settled in San Francisco by September, 1965 when the new bylaws were adopted. In contrast, in the other CAPs this issue was not finally resolved for a year. This did not mean that the *control* of the CAP was no longer in dispute. On the contrary, the San Francisco program was marked by a pattern of continual strife between central administration and the area staffs over who had power over what. This rancorous conflict was engendered in part by the ambiguity of the bylaws, which did not stipulate the nature of the relationship between central and the area staff. Because the areas could initiate program and employ personnel, the central administration lacked sufficient authority to coordinate, set priorities, or review the plans of the areas. This anomalous relationship between central administration and the areas was also exacerbated by the clash of individual ambitions, personal rivalries, and opposing ideologies regarding the war on poverty. As in Santa Clara, the key actors who were arrayed against each other came from the professional staff, in addition to the chairman of the EOC, Dr. Coleman. In the struggle against the Mayor for majority control in the neighborhoods, the executive leadership of the EOC, both Coleman and Brandon, had more or less maintained the united front with the area staff and their boards. Once this objective had been obtained, however, a persistent struggle for personal power ensued that was marked by recurrent battles in which each faction sought openly or covertly to oust the other. Arrayed against Coleman and Brandon was a coalition of area directors headed principally by Ussery, along with Kenneth Simmons, EOC program coordinator, and Joseph Arrington, assistant director, who were the most prominent members of the central staff allied with the anti-Brandon forces. Supporting Coleman and Brandon in time of need were such

Negro political leaders as Supervisor Terry Francois, Assemblyman Willie Brown, and Dr. Goodlett, who were originally consulted by the Mayor in the formation of the EOC.

The antagonisms between central administration and the target areas were expressed in the preference of the former for social service program and the preference of the latter for Area Development, as well as in their jockeying for power. Brandon, as the executive, was naturally most concerned with meeting OEO deadlines for program submissions so San Francisco could take advantage of the nearly $2 million in funds that had originally been set aside as its "guideline" beginning on July 1, 1965. Brandon felt that the success of the EOC would depend on the extent to which the resources of various federal programs could be brought into the target areas to provide support on a wide scale for the economic betterment of the area residents.

The first batch of programs to survive the review by the four target areas in September, 1965 were all sponsored by established agencies with little involvement of local residents. It was expected that the next group of proposals would emanate more from the expressed wishes of the target areas through their involvement in need and priority determination, together with the actual development of program proposals. At the same time, a deadline date of March 30, 1966 required that this process could not be a leisurely one. In view of the investment of over one-third of all EOC funds in Area Development, much depended on the capability of this program to stimulate a high degree of resident participation in the formulation of program. As noted earlier, the task of organizing the poor in all the areas proved to be exceedingly difficult, and there were many doubts regarding the effectiveness of this program. In the Western Addition, where it was envisioned that the programs would come from the people—"we can't assume what people want us to do for them . . . they must tell us"—an April all-day "grits and gripes session," for which over two thousand people turned out, produced few if any concrete proposals for program.[47] Later, OEO rejected all but two of the six programs submitted by the Western Addition, and for the next year Area Development funds were cut below the requested levels.[48] Other program proposals developed by indigenous groups assisted by the staff of

[47] *San Francisco Examiner,* April 3, 1966.

[48] However, this still provided more money for Area Development for the six-month period from July, 1966 to January, 1967 than for the previous 11 months. Whereas Chinatown and the Mission had 100 per cent of their budget for Area Development approved, Hunters Point received only 50 per cent and Western Addition only 33 per cent of their original requests. The disproportionate amount of funds being placed into Area Development as opposed to service programs was decried by OEO.

the Mission also required considerable working over before they could be acceptable.

Although programs approved by an area board could be overturned only by a two-thirds vote of the EOC, there was considerable resistance to the EOC review process by area board members, who considered their action as final and, on the other hand, by the mayoral appointees on the EOC, who objected to the lack of adequate time to study the proposals.

Thus, the EOC, like all of the other CAPs, faced tensions produced by the conflict between the need to develop fundable proposals within a deadline period and the concern for maximum feasible participation; between the goal of a competent program and the goal of a competent community. In this case, Brandon was identified with the former, Ussery and his supporters with the latter.

Apart from this ideological difference between moderates and militants within the Negro community,[49] the conflict was highly personalized. Brandon, like Ussery, was under fire almost from the day the EOC got started. Inexperienced in politics and administration, he was nevertheless the "favorite son" candidate of the Negro leaders with whom Mayor Shelley consulted. His chief supporters were Coleman and several members of his central staff who were indebted to him for their jobs and who were allied with the personal enemies of Ussery and Simmons who hoped to see them ousted. Because of some poor judgments in making a few staff appointments, Brandon also succeeded in antagonizing some of the Mexican-Americans and mayoral appointees, one of whom brought up a formal resolution that requested Brandon's resignation following his employment of a public information officer in January, 1966 after this applicant had been turned down by the executive committee. It was because of this error that Simmons was able to get a group of Negro leaders together to meet with the Mayor on January 10 to seek Brandon's dismissal on the grounds of incompetence. Coleman walked out of this meeting and subsequently called for Simmons' resignation, which was refused.[50] Despite strong pressures applied by the area directors and Arrington, all of whom threatened to resign, the target area representa-

[49] Whereas the "moderate" leader in the Negro community seeks welfare ends such as the tangible improvement of the community or the provision of better services and living conditions, the "militant" leader looks for improvement of the status of the community. James Q. Wilson, *Negro Politics, The Search for Leadership* (New York: The Free Press, 1965), pp. 185 and 218. In San Francisco, the moderate Brandon saw the EOC's success as being contingent upon increasing the variety of services available to the poor, while Ussery, a militant, saw the participation of the poor as the primary goal to be achieved.

[50] *San Francisco Chronicle*, January 12, 1966, p. 2; January 13, 1966, p. 4.

tives on the EOC were unwilling to fire Brandon on these charges and the matter was left alone for over two months.

The next attack on Brandon occurred several months later as a result of Ussery's challenge to the $600,000 budget for present and future central staff, which currently provided for 30 persons. The 1966 budget for central administration was approximately equal to the total budget for at least three of the target areas, and the latter also included Area Development. Ussery argued, with the support of all the other area directors, that such a large budget would confuse further the ambiguous relationship between area directors and central staff, to whom the area directors were responsible, and the authority of the executive director. Instead, he proposed that a coordinator be appointed, responsible only to the target area boards. Brandon reacted to this proposal by sending a letter to the area boards telling them that their directors had acted without their consent; later, he and Coleman spoke at a Western Addition meeting where they further assailed Ussery for seeking to amass power for himself. Coleman insisted that OEO and the Board of Supervisors would not approve such a position and that he personally would not sign any financial warrants if the ultimate powers for expenditures lay in the target areas.[51] Ussery replied that there were sufficient checks on any expenditures to prevent misuse of funds and that they had fought the Mayor for precisely this principle of all power to the target areas.

Brandon's next move, on May 10, was to fire Kenneth Simmons—for the third time. Simmons refused to leave, claiming that the executive committee had to approve the dismissal and that the firing was not done in writing.[52] Ussery denounced the dismissal of his ally, Simmons, and declared: "The issue at hand is a simple case of the central office moving to acquire through intimidation what CUAP won from the Mayor." He charged that this was done by "employing on the central staff only people with unswerving loyalty to the Executive Director, who buy the idea of recentralizing the power as it now exists in the target areas in favor of the central office." [53] Indeed, the reason behind the firing was widely thought to be the EOC's desire to reassert its authority over the Western Addition's antipoverty campaign. A marathon, eight-hour, all-night closed session of the executive committee heard the charges against Simmons (that he was "incompetent, abused professional trust and undermined staff morale") but he was reinstated by a vote of 10 to 2.

The Mayor was also obliquely involved in this affair, since all of his appointees voted for Simmons' reinstatement. Coleman interpreted this

[51] *San Francisco Examiner,* April 28, 1966.
[52] *San Francisco Chronicle,* May 10, 1966.
[53] *Sun-Reporter,* May 14, 1966.

as a lack of confidence in his leadership and stated that he would resign as of June 1. This resignation did not take place, because members of the Negro community privately put pressure on Coleman to remain, out of their fear that one of the mayoral appointees would be named chairman.[54]

Two weeks after the closed meeting that reinstated Simmons, conflict between Coleman and the mayoral appointees who were on the executive committee broke into the open when Coleman cancelled an executive committee meeting scheduled for June 1. Seven members of the executive committee insisted on meeting anyway and passed a resolution censuring their chairman for not recognizing the legitimacy of their request.[55] Responding to this action, a group of 50 Negro leaders met on June 7 and passed a resolution that was sent to the Mayor expressing full support of Coleman and asking the Mayor to remove his five appointees, who consistently attempted to "disrupt, discredit, and destroy" the antipoverty program.[56] The outcome was again a stalemate for both sides, as Coleman's opponents did not get any support for their position, nor was there any attempt to remove them from the EOC, which went on to express "complete confidence in all members of the Council."[57]

At this same meeting of the executive committee on June 22, Mayor Shelley attended for the first time, warning them against "internal family feuding" and urging them to clear the divisive atmosphere that someone has "planted" because it was destroying the EOC's ability to get money from the federal government and the Board of Supervisors.[58]

The Mayor failed to acknowledge his own role in planting the seeds of dissension. At a meeting a month earlier of the Board of Supervisor's Finance Committee, which was debating the 10 per cent local share of the EOC's funds, about $210,000, the Mayor was quoted as saying

> I have a very definite feeling that this program is headed in a direction we don't want . . . it has the potential for setting up a

[54] *Ibid.*, May 28, 1966.

[55] *San Francisco Examiner,* June 23, 1966.

[56] EOC executive committee minutes, June 8, 1966. Most of the mayoral appointees were regarded by the target area representatives as having a very limited knowledge of the EOC and its program because of their lack of involvement in other than monthly meetings.

[57] EOC executive committee minutes, June 22, 1966.

[58] *Ibid.*, p. 3. The image of the EOC in constant conflict was widely promoted in all the mass media and seems to have contributed to some of the distrust in the target areas and on the part of the established agencies. This aspect of the EOC was perhaps best expressed by one of the activists, who is reputed to have said: "As long as Sam pays and we know we cannot do much about poverty with a few million dollars, we might as well keep things moving. It is much better that way."

great political organization. Not mine. Because I have had nothing to say about it.[59]

The Mayor and Coleman traded charges that the former wanted to set up a city commission to run the poverty program and wrest control away from the poor, but the Mayor insisted that was not his intent.[60] Nevertheless, the Mayor was highly critical of the way in which the program was being run. "It may be well-organized," he said, "but I have not seen enough of the benefits seeping down to the public in the way of programs." Mayor Shelley felt that the EOC had lost control over the target areas and reasserted his original position that only with broad-based business, labor, and neighborhood and community support would the program be able to succeed.

During this period, the Mayor's relationship to the EOC was described as "very remote"; communication with Coleman broke down, a number of his appointees resigned from the Council, and he was unable to find people willing to accept appointments. At one point he told the executive committee that he had spoken to over thirty-five people and that all refused positions on the Council.[61] Furthermore, his appointees had a very spotty attendance record. Over an 11-month period, four of his appointees were absent seven or more times, whereas only one of the target area representatives was absent more than three times.

Further evidence of the deep division within the EOC was the close vote—15 to 12—on the proposal to organize a fifth target area in the Central City. This proposal was opposed by the original target areas largely because it would upset the balance of ethnic representation in the EOC. Pressures from OEO and from the Central City Citizens Committee were responsible for a reversal of this vote, and on May 25, 1966, Central City was eventually included. This resulted in enlargement of the EOC to 30 target area representatives and 17 mayoral appointees and the same distribution of 10 and 5, respectively, on the executive committee.

On one issue, however, there was a high degree of consensus, although the pattern of its resolution was characteristic of the gap between ideology and practice. In March, 1966, OEO issued two guidelines, Memos 23 and 24, tightening regulations regarding employment in the poverty program. Among the controversial provisions were those prohibiting partisan political activity and membership in subversive organizations, limitations on beginning salaries (not to exceed 20 per cent more than previously earned) and future increases, and in addition, those requiring all partici-

[59] *San Francisco Examiner,* May 5, 1966.
[60] *San Francisco Chronicle,* May 23, 1966.
[61] EOC executive committee minutes, June 22, 1966.

pants to be "persons of good character." At the executive committee meeting of March 16, 1966, a resolution was unanimously adopted denouncing Memos 23 and 24 "as unconstitutional and not a part of the contract between the EOC and OEO." Dr. Coleman challenged Sargent Shriver to come to San Francisco and "meet us head on." Two officials, John Dukes, chairman of the Hunters Point area board (later to become its director) and Ussery, threatened to resign, and a third suggested a march on Washington if the rules were allowed to stand.[62] At the following week's meeting the full Council endorsed the action of the executive committee.

The matter rested until July, when OEO announced it would hold up $2.3 million in unpaid antipoverty funds for San Francisco until the EOC agreed to comply with the national policy. By this time the San Francisco budget included 14 programs amounting to $5.7 million, $2.2 million over the guidelines of 1965-66. On July 26, Dr. Coleman signed a statement of grant, in order to obtain release of funds for San Francisco, which affected 250 full-time jobs. One condition of the grant was the EOC's acceptance of Memos 23 and 24. Dr. Coleman presented the action to the Council at its meeting on July 27 as a *fait accompli,* arguing that since the directives were in process of being revised, the Council should confirm his signature on the grant. His position was strongly opposed by Central City, Western Addition and Hunters Point. Spokesmen for the latter said they would prefer to see the program closed down rather than take funds if these policies were allowed to stand. Nevertheless, the Council supported Dr. Coleman's position and at the same time, unanimously reaffirmed its opposition to the two memos. The minutes later stated that what was being voted was a "moratorium" on further attacks on the OEO rather than a concession.[63] Few members seemed to want to face the contradiction involved in their actions.

Subsequently, some minor changes were made in the rulings relaxing the good moral character requirement and making some modifications in salary requirements, but at the same time a rule governing conflict of interest was added, stating that "no person shall hold a job while he or a member of his immediate family serves on a Board or a committee of a grantee or a delegate agency." [64] This was an exceedingly significant change in that many nonprofessionals had continued to serve on the boards of neighborhood and other target area organizations. These restrictions on the employment and participation of the poor reinforced the earlier disillusionment with OEO policy on participation funds for

[62] *San Francisco Examiner,* March 17, 1966.

[63] EOC minutes, July 27, 1966, and *San Francisco Chronicle,* July 28, 1966.

[64] OEO, Community Action Memo No. 23-A, August 26, 1966.

meeting attendance and the expenses of low-income members had been deleted by OEO early in March.[65]

The persistence of the conflict between central and area staffs resulted in a conference on July 9, when these differences were aired, but with little change in policy. OEO had begun to crack down, however, and in addition to expressing its disapproval with the size of the Western Addition Area Development Program and the program's neglect of social services, it stated that it would not again authorize funds for the present level of central administration, with its 30-member staff, unless a management study recommended this.[66]

Central staff was subsequently reassigned from individual target areas to fields of service such as education, social welfare, aid to the aged, housing, employment, and legal services. In addition, each staff member was assigned to an EOC committee, only one of which, education, had been active. This latter committee came into being toward the end of 1965 as part of the requirement of the Elementary and Secondary Education Act that schools receiving funds must "cooperate" with the local CAP, but the EOC was never really able to implement its authority over poverty-related educational programs and controversies with the schools periodically arose.[67]

[65] In Community Action Memo No. 29, April 20, 1966, OEO had authorized payments to low-income members of boards who earned less than $4,000 a year and had to travel 25 miles or more on a round trip between their home and meeting place. This was superseded by the 1966 Amendments to the Economic Opportunity Act and embodied in Memo No. 29-A, February 21, 1967 providing for payment of $5 for each meeting attended, not to exceed two in one month, travel expenses, baby sitting, etc. Such payments were available only to those members of boards whose income was below a poverty guideline of $3,000 for a family of four. Since very few board members could meet such low-income criteria, both regulations had relatively little effect on participation.

[66] Bids for this contract ranged from $8,000 to $40,000, and the EOC, over the objection of Coleman and Brandon, awarded the contract to the Brenner Associates, a relatively unknown team consisting of a faculty member from San Francisco State College and two graduate students from the University of California, Berkeley, Department of City and Regional Planning. Their report, which recommended a major reorganization and further decentralization, was not acted upon by the executive committee, and for several months payment was delayed because of the questionable status and competence of the firm and its study. The qualifications of Brenner and Associates was also questioned by the federal auditor, and subsequently a new management study was authorized involving federal officials and business executives. The federal audit criticism of this contract is found in *San Francisco Examiner*, December 13, 1966, p. 1.

[67] At the instigation of the area directors in December, 1965, the executive committee had tried to halt funds for a proposed compensatory education program sponsored by the San Francisco Unified School District on the grounds that the EOC had not been consulted sufficiently and that the program as it was designed fostered racial discrimination. While some slight modifications were made and further attempts at coordination initiated, the relationship between the schools and the EOC was a generally abrasive one.

Beginning in September, 1966, the EOC was shaken by a series of events—from relatively minor to catastrophic—that led to a major shakeup and its embarking upon a new phase after the beginning of 1967.

The balance of power on the central staff changed as a result of the resignations of Arrington in September and Kenneth Simmons in November. Thus, two of Brandon's antagonists had departed, although Arrington became the Mayor's deputy for social programs and remained in city hall for six months.

Although the OEO appropriations bill for 1967 had not yet passed, it appeared as if a tremendous retrenchment in CAP funds were imminent. This would hit San Francisco particularly hard because it had received several million dollars over what its guidelines specified. In addition, it was learned that Manpower Development and Training funds were going to be removed from San Francisco and allocated to cities where it was believed the need was greater. This proved to be a tragic irony, because toward the end of September, the whole city watched in horror the violence that ensued at Hunters Point for three days following the fatal shooting of a sixteen-year-old boy by a policeman. This was the first racial disturbance in San Francisco in many years, and it indicated how little had been done by the antipoverty program to deal with the basic economic causes of unrest in this ghetto. Although a job center was set up by the Mayor, and seemingly hundreds of jobs were found, the actual record of placements was a dismal one.[68]

Considering the size of the likely reduction in OEO funds, there was relatively little effort made to mobilize the target areas to protest. Resolutions were adopted, some telegrams were sent, a few officials went to Washington, but except for a few local project sponsors who later picketed EOC and OEO offices, there was no channeling of organized opposition to the action of Congress.

In October the Western Addition board was again in the news, this time because a rump meeting of the board voted to fire its controversial director.[69] This time the conflict involved both board and staff and brought the perennially unresolved issue of the authority of the target area boards once more to the EOC. It looked as if only the intervention of the EOC could determine which was the legitimate representative board of the Western Addition, since there were several sets of claimants. However, in the name of preserving area autonomy and "not running

68 The aftermath of the Hunters Point riot is described in the *San Francisco Chronicle*, October 5, 1966, p. 1, and *San Francisco Examiner*, July 11, 1967, p. 16. One of its consequences was the ascendancy of younger men to spokesmen roles for Hunters Point and their use of the threat of a riot to obtain jobs and support for various programs.

69 *San Francisco Chronicle*, October 31, 1966, p. 1; November 1, 1966, p. 6.

downtown when we have problems," Coleman urged the EOC not to accept jurisdiction of the dispute and Ussery's appeal of his firing by an illegal meeting of the Western Addition board. Instead, Coleman urged the Council to send this issue back to the Western Addition board, although he did not say which board, to resolve the personnel situation with the aid of an arbitrator. This recommendation was confusing, since there were no rules for appeals by Area Planning Boards and there was complete chaos in the Western Addition following an attempted takeover by one board member and a group from one of the districts who went to the press and "fired" Ussery at a special meeting convened by telegram and with a questionable quorum. Coleman was rumored to have supported this new chairman as a way of eventually getting rid of Ussery. The situation dragged on. New elections were ordered in the Western Addition, and eventually Ussery, tired of fighting, was allowed to resign at the end of the year.

Finally, on December 11, a federal audit was released that charged that the EOC had misused thousands of dollars in unapproved expenditures and implied very loose and inefficient administration.[70] Two days before, Coleman submitted a surprise resignation to the Mayor, effective December 31, stating, "I don't have the support of my committee and I think some new blood is needed."[71] Brandon's resignation was also rumored, and he implied that the auditor's report was leaked to the press to force his departure. He defended each one of his expenditures and claimed that it was "punitive" and unethical for OEO to make an audit public without first giving the EOC a chance to study and explain it.[72] Basically, most of the items questioned involved authorization for travel allowance, misapplication of funds for personal use, illegal pay raises, unauthorized salary payments such as those funds paid to Western Addition community aides while they were picketing the Hilton, inadequately explained long distance phone calls, and purchase of office equipment at prices totaling $10,000 more than the cost if the items had been bought from the General Services Administration. Eventually, these items were "explained," but the suspicions about the caliber of central administration remained.

Mayor Shelley had considerable difficulty recruiting a successor to Coleman. On January 14, 1967 he eventually succeeded in persuading Municipal Judge Joseph G. Kennedy, a highly respected Negro jurist, to take the position after Kennedy had accepted and then changed his mind. The next day, the resignations of the area directors of Mission,

[70] *San Francisco Sunday Examiner and Chronicle,* December 11, 1966, p. 1.
[71] *San Francisco Chronicle,* December 12, 1966, p. 18.
[72] *Ibid.,* and *San Francisco Sunday Examiner and Chronicle,* January 15, 1967, p. 3.

Alex Zermeno, and Chinatown, Larry Jack Wong, who had been among Ussery's staunchest supporters, were announced, thus bringing about a complete new change in personnel, with only the area director of Hunters Point, John Dukes, the former chairman, and Calvin Colt in Central City remaining. By the end of the month most of the principal antagonists had departed. Only Brandon remained, and he was permitted to resign in June after some private disclosure of additional administrative abuses. One of the costs of the year-long battle was the loss in prestige of many of the middle-class spokesmen for the Negro community. Popularization of the concept of Black Power, rising militancy among the younger men in the ghetto, and disillusionment with the EOC had also weakened their position, with the result that there was even more fragmentation of power and doubt as to who could be legitimately identified as a "Negro leader."

Judge Kennedy had a different philosophy regarding the EOC and proposed "maximum community involvement." He recommended an open-end committee system on the EOC on every level, by which outside participation by professionals could be invited so that they could contribute expertise in the fields of employment, social welfare, education, recreation, and housing and development.[73] This attempt to bring back the established agencies that might have been repelled by the continual controversies was in keeping with Mayor Shelley's belief that maximum feasible participation

> . . . had been twisted to mean maximum participation by minority segments of the community but also opposition to participation by the community as a whole.[74]

The program outlook for the year was encouraging. The cutback in funds for 1967-68 proved to be less drastic than anticipated, and about $5.2 million was received for 35 programs, in addition to $10 million for special projects.[75] Nevertheless, the uncertainty and the organizational turmoil resulted in considerable turnover among the 250 persons em-

[73] *San Francisco Chronicle,* February 16, 1967.

[74] Statement by Mayor John F. Shelley submitted before the United States Senate, Labor and Public Welfare Sub-Committee on Employment, Manpower and Poverty, May 10, 1967 in San Francisco. Part of this statement appears in the *Journal,* official publication of the San Francisco EOC, Vol. 1, No. 5 (July, 1967), 14, 16.

[75] These included: Mission Neighborhood Health Center ($4 million); Narcotics Treatment Center in Central City ($987,000); year-around Head Start ($875,000); Summer Youth Employment ($600,000) and concentrated employment program ($4.3 million). About one-fifth of the total budget for city-wide and area service projects was allocated to Neighborhood Legal Assistance ($1,013,074). The EOC claimed that total employment (full-time and part-time, professional and nonprofessional) in all programs was approximately 2500. The *Journal, ibid.,* pp. 1-2.

ployed in the Area Development Program; apart from staff reductions in the Western Addition and Chinatown, this program seemed to have even less direction than before.

Gradually during 1967 the EOC moved toward an administrative reorganization recommended by a management study, which proposed consolidation and standardization of many functions that would strengthen the coordinating role of the central staff. John Dukes, formerly of Hunters Point, was named executive director in June, 1967 to replace Brandon, and by the end of the year, two other area directors joined the central staff. The EOC entered a new phase as a $15 million, large-scale social service planning center, increasingly concerned with the administration of programs and a closer working relationship with the established agencies.

Summary

In San Francisco the fight for maximum feasible participation evolved from a contest between the Mayor and minority spokesman for control of the program into a succession of power struggles within the target areas and between them and central administration. These struggles tended to preempt any substantial involvement of the poor themselves. From the beginning a prevailing pattern of rancorous conflict was established, which remained the dominant mode of confronting most program and administrative issues. The initial victory over the Mayor was achieved over an eight-month period by a coalition of ethnic minority groups led by former civil rights activists, and resulted in a reorganization in which the four target areas gained majority control of the EOC and administrative authority over their own funds, programs, and personnel. This made the San Francisco structure unique in the ostensible management of the EOC by the poor themselves. Each area, however, determined its own procedures for electing its board and developed a distinctive structure that reflected its history and the relative influence of different ethnic factions.

While the degree to which low-income persons themselves participated varied widely from an over-all indigenous board in the Mission to virtually none in Chinatown, most of the representatives of the poor were not impoverished themselves, but instead were working or middle-class persons. The conditions under which area elections were conducted and the small number of voters resulted in a process of self-selection favoring the more ambitious, upwardly striving, affiliated members of ethnic groups, who perceived themselves as spokesmen for the poor although most had little or no accountability to any low-income constituency.

All areas, heavily influenced by the leaders in the Western Addition, who saw an opportunity to organize the poor as an ethnic power base in the ghetto, gave priority to an Area Development Program. Each board became deeply involved in the administration of such a program and in the process of awarding close to three hundred jobs, mainly to neighborhood residents. Considerable jealousy and antagonism occurred between board and staff and various minority groups as they fought to control these new resources. Despite the fears and the hopes of opposing groups, the Area Development Program did not become a significant source of political power. It proved exceedingly difficult to organize the poor and to sustain any new infrastructure. Community organization sponsored by the areas resulted in some relatively minor improvements in neighborhood conditions, but there were no significant policy changes in any of the major community agencies except in public housing and in the effort to block redevelopment in the Mission, both of which were only indirectly related to the target area organization.

Because each board had sole jurisdiction over any programs, there was considerable diversity, with Mission favoring indigenous sponsors and Chinatown approving the programs of established agencies. The concern with social service programs was in general subordinate to the political struggles involving the OEO, the Mayor, the EOC and its executive leadership, central administration staff, and various ethnic factions on the boards. Two of the boards were sharply torn by such cleavages, whereas the remaining three were much more cohesive, but all were united in their opposition to the role and authority of the central administration staff.

Rooted in structural ambiguities, ideological differences, and personal rivalries, a continuous struggle for power ensued among Negro leadership factions around attempts to oust staff and a series of personnel and program issues. This struggle eventually resulted in the resignation of the principal antagonists and the reorganization of an area board. The addition of a fifth target area and the changing composition of other boards as most of the original members dropped out also altered the structural character of the EOC. Somewhat spent by its stormy career, and although still dominated by those representing the poor in the target areas, the EOC became less committed to an organizing strategy and increasingly concerned with the more efficient administration of social service programs involving broader community participation.

3

COMMUNITY CASE STUDY OF THE SANTA CLARA COUNTY ECONOMIC OPPORTUNITY COMMISSION

People within this community must realize that a program as poorly conceived and as poorly guidelined as the Poverty Act of 1964 would inevitably lead to mass confusion and a concerted attempt at take-over.[1]

The quiet agreement that surrounded the origin of the antipoverty program in Santa Clara County gave few clues to the turbulent nature of the controversy that would soon engulf it. Shortly after the Economic Opportunity Commission (EOC) was constituted, some Mexican-American leaders saw the possibilities of this new organization as a source of jobs, power, and status for their minority group, which had long been relegated to second-class citizenship. The success of the civil rights movement had awakened Mexican-Americans in California to the necessity of a more aggressive strategy to secure their rights and to improve their greatly disadvantaged position in the community. Aided by the confusion surrounding "maximum feasible participation" and the disproportionate number of impoverished Mexican-Americans in Santa Clara County it was not difficult to identify their cause with representation of the poor.

The political drive for ethnic control of the EOC was soon reinforced by demands for greater autonomy from the nine areas comprising the new organizational structure, and the "Anglo" executive director then became the target for both campaigns.

Although much of the early conflict centered around the person of the executive director, the basic issues at stake pertaining to the role and authority of the EOC persisted long after he was eventually ousted. These were the same questions that faced all the Community Action Programs as new resources and decision-making centers: How should

[1] William Fernandez, in a speech before the Inter-City Council, July 7, 1966.

power be distributed? That is, who should control the EOC, and how should the poor participate? In Santa Clara, the initial answers were short lived.

Planning for the antipoverty program in Santa Clara County began in March, 1964 with the formation of an *ad hoc* committee of nine agencies and organizations: four community councils, two chapters of the Community Service Organization, the Central Labor Council, the County Council of Churches, and the Catholic Social Service. In October, this committee, originally convened by the Community Council of Central Santa Clara County, presented a resolution to the Santa Clara County Board of Supervisors asking for the creation of an EOC to implement the Economic Opportunity Act of 1964, and to serve as the Community Action Agency for the entire county. The board adopted the resolution, which provided for a 15-member Commission with four representatives from local government, two each from business and labor, three from minority groups, and one each from groups representing agriculture, veterans' groups, schools, and the community councils. No attempt was made at this time to include members of the Commission who were themselves poor or who were selected by potential beneficiaries of the antipoverty program. The bylaws of the Commission did, however, call for an advisory board with spokesmen from 134 county agencies and organizations that had prior experience with the problems of low-income groups.[2]

The Santa Clara EOC first met on October 29, 1964, and was incorporated as a nonprofit agency in December, 1964. By February, 1965, it had received a $21,000 planning grant for program development from the OEO. At the first meeting, the EOC elected as its chairman Dr. Stanley Skillicorn, a neurologist with a long-standing interest in welfare services, and the representative of the community councils to the EOC. No one opposed the choice of Skillicorn as chairman.

Selection of an executive director proved a more arduous task. Of the more than one hundred applicants for the job of executive director, two local residents were the strongest contenders. One, Philip Buskirk, a labor representative on the United Fund staff, had been influential in the creation of the EOC and was highly regarded by the Mexican-American community as well as by organized labor. The other, Dr. Ernesto Galarza, a farm labor expert, had the endorsement of many Mexican-American associations. In the final selection these two were edged

[2] Original bylaws, Economic Opportunity Commission of Santa Clara County, Inc., February 1, 1966. An account of the process whereby the EOC came into being is found in Ralph M. Kramer and Clare Denton, "The Organization of a Community Action Program," *Social Work*, Vol. 12, No. 4 (October, 1967), pp. 68-80.

out by Arthur Potts, whose candidacy was promoted mainly by the representatives of government, business, and the social agencies. Though a newcomer to Santa Clara County, Potts had considerable experience in welfare administration, having served as a welfare officer in the Army and in the United Nations relief program in Asia, and as head of California's Aid-to-Needy-Children program. His most recent job as director of area planning for the Los Angeles Welfare Council was cited as evidence of his familiarity with the problems endemic to the poor in Santa Clara; like Santa Clara, Los Angeles has a sizeable and impoverished Mexican-American population.

Buskirk's and Galarza's supporters were skeptical about hiring an executive director who had not already secured the confidence of the county's representatives of minority groups, but they acquiesced to Potts' appointment.[3]

Planning Begins

After Potts began work on February 2, 1965 his reputation as a skillful administrator and program developer seemed borne out. Working with only the limited $21,000 planning grant, he hired a skeleton staff, including several Mexican-Americans, began soliciting program ideas from all over the county, and devised procedures for hiring additional staff and for informing the community of EOC's plans. The Commission, as the official policy-making body for the county's antipoverty program, showed little hesitation in approving its executive's program and policy recommendations.

Because of informal requests from the regional office of OEO, followed in April, 1965 by a specific directive that all CAP boards include at least one resident from each major target area to be served,[4] the Commission was advised to enlarge its original membership to 18 to include 3 representatives of the poor. Prior to this, during the early months of operation, only the NAACP representative urged broader representation of those to be served, and he cast the lone vote against adoption of the bylaws in November because of the inclusion of the Taxpayers Association and other organizations not noted for their prior concern with poverty. Representatives of labor, religion, and the Mexican-American community made no public criticism of the original Commission or its rules.

[3] Unless otherwise indicated, interviews with the participants constitute the primary source of data.

[4] Office of Economic Opportunity Regional Memo, *Resident-Recipient Participation on Policy Boards,* April 7, 1965. OEO Regional CAP Bulletin, *Board Representatives to Include Low Income Groups or Their Representatives,* May 3, 1965.

In February, the EOC appointed a task force headed by William Ellison, the representative from the NAACP, to work out procedures for selecting three representatives of the poor. The task force divided the county into six areas, and, after consultation with some local groups of residents, designated two people from each area, who decided that these new representatives of the poor to the EOC should have an income of less than $6,000, or be recipients of some service under the Economic Opportunity Act, and/or be able to read and have direct knowledge of the problems of the poor.

On June 7, Dr. Melvin Mogulof, CAP manager in the OEO regional office, was informed that three people who met these criteria were seated on the EOC by the end of May, and that the local residents who had assisted Ellison's task force in selecting these three were invited to join the EOC advisory board. Two of the three women who were the first representatives of the poor gradually became quite active on the EOC and impressed some of the commissioners with their participation. Also set forth in the letter to Mogulof was the commitment of the EOC to the "progressive involvement" of poor people, not merely in an advisory capacity on the area boards coming into existence, but also as policy-makers, administrators, and employees. By creating new organizations to supplement or replace traditional service agencies, by locating services close to where recipients lived, and by hiring semiprofessionals, the EOC hoped to expand greatly the numbers of poor people involved in a continuous relationship with the antipoverty program. Mogulof's warm reply to this letter praised the method used by the Santa Clara EOC to add representatives of the poor as "an extremely sound approach" and as a potential model for other communities.

Program Development

The major task facing the EOC during its first few months was the preparation of program proposals for submission to OEO by April 30, 1965 before its limited planning grant was exhausted, in order to secure funds for implementing approved programs during the remainder of the year. At Potts' suggestion the EOC agreed, in the interest of reserving sufficient time to work out detailed proposals, to forego any elaborate or extensive survey of the expressed needs and desires of the county's low-income population. In addition to consuming large amounts of time and money, such surveys seemed to produce a similar definition of needs, Potts argued, citing the experience of other communities.[5] By working

[5] Potts' report to EOC on progress in submission of program proposals to OEO, undated memo in EOC file, p. 7. Unless otherwise indicated, references are to documents in EOC files.

through existing agencies and organizations, and especially with those experienced in working with low-income persons, he believed that programs could be developed that would be geared to serving the best interests of the poor. From February on, therefore, the emphasis was less on the process of developing program ideas than on preparing a final, fundable proposal with as little expenditure of time and money as possible. Some grumblings of dissatisfaction were heard at this stage from Mexican-American spokesmen about the importance of organizing the poor before discussing any programs, or, in effect, of making community organization the major program of the EOC.

Though Potts stressed cooperation with existing agencies, he did not overlook either his own commitment to gradually involving the program's recipients in planning and administrative capacities, or the Economic Opportunity Act's "maximum feasibility" clause. In the application forms that he and his staff prepared for agencies wishing to submit proposals, Potts followed the OEO guidelines by insisting that in order to be eligible for program grants, an agency had to demonstrate

> the capacity to enlist the participation of residents of the areas and members of the groups to be served in the development, conduct, and administration of the proposed program.[6]

All EOC materials pertaining to program development were printed in English and Spanish, released to the press, announced at public meetings, and given wide distribution. Potts himself spoke before a number of community groups, urging them to submit proposals and promising them assistance in filling out applications. To review proposals, an elaborate procedure was set up that involved a number of task forces composed of agency delegates and wherever possible, of spokesmen from low-income groups. The EOC had its own Administrative and Program Development Review Committee. After a series of preliminary discussions and reviews, all proposals had to receive the endorsement of the full Commission before being passed on to OEO. Initially, then, it seemed that a concerted effort was made to solicit and give a fair hearing to program ideas from virtually anyone in the county. If some individual or group was not itself eligible to receive funds to administer a program, it could nevertheless urge an eligible agency to sponsor its program suggestion. Whether all groups and interests were actually given an equal chance to submit proposals, however, was increasingly questioned by both existing agencies and some Mexican-American spokesmen

[6] *Guide Instructions for Submitting Community Action Program Proposals to EOC*, February 2, 1967.

for the poor, who claimed that Potts was less interested in receiving different or new ideas through his program review machinery than in having his already set ideas approved.

Among those proposals rejected on the grounds that they would duplicate what was going to be offered by the EOC was one submitted by Community Service Organization leaders Albert Pinon and José Martinez for assistance in immigration and citizenship matters, a CSO project which was eventually approved a year later. An abortive attempt was made in April by Pinon to get support from other Mexican-American leaders for a letter requesting OEO to withhold funds from Santa Clara County because of Potts' inability to work with indigenous organizations. None of the other Mexican-American organizations represented knew enough about the EOC program to support this request, and because of this refusal to cooperate, CSO abandoned this initial effort.

About sixty proposals did go through the review procedure, and by late spring, OEO was requested to fund a number of separate programs such as Head Start, Neighborhood Youth Corps, and programs for literacy and small business assistance. These programs were directly administered by the EOC or operated through the Area Service Centers, and relatively little controversy was created around them.

Organization of the Area Service Centers

The heart of the EOC program, however, was the comprehensive request for the funding of Area Service Centers (ASCs). The plan was entitled "Enlisting Santa Clara County Community Action and Planning for Economic Opportunity" (ESCAPE), which envisioned a number of multiservice centers throughout the county with the objective of "improving the chances of the poor through education, work experience, social treatment services, citizen organization, economic incentives and effective co-ordinated administration."[7] It was around the board formation, program definition, and hiring policies of these centers that most of the controversies arose.

The county was divided into nine administrative areas roughly comparable in their incidence of poverty, and the EOC proposed to set up a service center in each area.

The areas designated were

1. Gilroy

[7] *A Proposal for Area Service Centers, under Title IIA of the Economic Opportunity Act sponsored by the Economic Opportunity Commission of Santa Clara County, Inc.*, pp. 2-4.

2. Morgan Hill, San Martin, and Coyote
3. Alum Rock, Evergreen, Berryessa, and Milpitas
4. San Jose East, Edenvale
5. San Jose West
6. Campbell, Cupertino, Saratoga, and Los Gatos
7. Sunnyvale and Santa Clara
8. Alviso and Agnew
9. Palo Alto, Mountain View, and Los Altos

Each center was to have a board of directors to be chosen by local agencies and residents, four staff members, and a director. In addition, the proposal called for at least ten semiprofessional positions, which presumably would be filled by low-income residents of the area. The budget for each center was estimated at $65,000, and the selection of *nine* areas was evidently decided upon by dividing the anticipated total allocation for Area Service Centers by an amount deemed sufficient to operate the centers for a year. Three centers were to be opened within 90 days, three more within six months, and the final three by the end of the year. The approval for the ASC proposals and other programs such as Head Start came through on July 10, 1965, and in spite of the organizational difficulties that subsequently ensued, all of the nine area boards or committees were established by April, 1966.

The initial proposal for the ASCs stated:

> The first phase in the establishment of Area Service Centers will be identifying and contracting with local area groups and organizations for the operation of the Center program. The recruitment of EOC co-ordination staff and Center administrative and program staff will be a part of the initial phase . . . *The next phase* will include the development and expansion of citizen participation in the operation and administration of the Center programs.[8]

While justified on the basis of administrative expediency—meeting the April 30 deadline—the EOC's commitment to the speedy development of structure and program *before* seeking the participation of the poor triggered many of the subsequent conflicts. Despite the wishes of several local groups to attempt to organize the poor first, EOC staff members were assigned to organize indigenous groups of low-income residents only in the Alviso area. Only by the end of the year, when it became clear that it would not be possible to comply with the OEO deadline for low-income representation, were organizing teams assigned to three other areas. Reflecting the feelings of those opposed to this initial policy of

[8] *Ibid.*, p. 4. Italics mine.

the EOC was the following statement issued jointly by the Gardner District Neighborhood Council (Area 5) CSO, Mexican-American Political Association (MAPA), the Interfaith Migrant Committee, the Mountain View Community Council (Area 9) and the San Jose Health Department that declared:

> In order to carry out the spirit of the Economic Opportunity Act of 1964 and to best meet the expressed needs of residents in poverty areas in Santa Clara County, we are convinced that it is mandatory to directly involve residents in early planning and program development. We urge that financing initially be restricted to neighborhood councils or their counterpart groups where such exists and to the development of neighborhood councils in poverty areas where such are . . . nonexistent.[9]

In five of the nine areas (1, 3, 5, 7 and 9), however, recently hired EOC staff members sought to establish a new interim area board of directors with which the EOC could contract by working with existing community councils, governmental and voluntary agencies, and ethnic associations that had already taken the initiative to begin planning for the antipoverty program. Controversies quickly arose in two areas (3 and 5) over the extent to which existing organizations would yield control to the EOC, the new area boards, or both on fiscal, personnel, and program matters, as well as the delineation of their geographic boundaries.

The negotiations about area autonomy dragged on from September to November, 1965. In a few cases, they became quite bitter as the local boards refused to sign the contracts, claiming that they had been promised much more control over their centers and that they had no voice in the writing of the standard agreement forms. Earlier, in a series of private meetings with Skillicorn, strong protests had been made by various spokesmen for the neighborhoods, who demanded complete budgeting and administrative autonomy. Because this was unacceptable to OEO, which had been sounded out informally, the final version of the ASC program was a compromise. Later, somewhat different representatives for several of the areas, in negotiating with the EOC, disavowed the right of the previous "leaders" to commit their neighborhood to the ASC proposal.

In four areas (2, 4, 6, and 8), new organizations were created by the five EOC staff members, and in two of them clashes between those who were politically right-wing and those who can be called left-wingers for control of the new board led to jurisdictional disputes, in one case between three separate community action committees. Right-wing ac-

[9] Gardner District Neighborhood Council, "Statement of Philosophy Regarding Community Action Projects in Local Areas," 1965.

tivity was also disruptive in Area 5, which subsequently elected a member of the John Birch Society to represent them on the EOC. Other controversies arose later over the required use of an eligible personnel roster, which was distributed by the EOC, for the hiring of staff. The area boards wanted to have complete control over the hiring of their employees and did not want to be limited by job specifications that seemed too restrictive, particularly with respect to the educational requirements. Favored candidates for the position of director or community development specialist often lacked the educational prerequisites, and the EOC agreed to substitute experience for education in defining the job qualifications for all ASC positions except that of social worker.[10]

In spite of these difficulties, all nine of the areas signed contracts for programs with the EOC by mid-November, 1965 and developed some kind of interim organizational structure. These organizations then began to plan for permanent boards, although few had any representation from the poor in their areas.

Mexican-American Enmity

These early efforts of the EOC to organize the areas and create boards of directors provided one major source of opposition to Potts' administration of the antipoverty program in Santa Clara. Many of the established agencies felt that their program proposals and concern for professional standards were not seriously considered even though there was an elaborate processing machinery. Various leaders of religious and ethnic associations concluded that the target population and programs developed by organizations close to them were being ignored. Mistrust in the areas was further engendered by the failure to offer firm encouragement to local groups that they would be the ones selected as the official arm of the EOC in their area. Finally, hostility was aroused by the struggle over the autonomy of the service centers, in which there were mutual accusations of "bad faith" and a "power grab."

These tensions were reinforced by the antagonism in several spokesmen for Mexican-American organizations aroused by Potts during his first few months in office. In Santa Clara County, people with Spanish surnames form by far the largest minority group, comprising 16 per cent

[10] Although Potts became identified with various objectionable parts of the job specifications and the Statement on "Authority and Responsibility of the EOC and the Area Service Centers," these documents were drawn up by a consultant, discussed with staff, committee members from the Advisory Board, and representatives of the poor as well as the administrative committee of the EOC, which finally adopted them after considerable modification.

of the county's population, slightly over one-fourth of the poor, but almost 50 per cent of the AFDC recipients. The largest part of this population, which has doubled in the last ten years, is Mexican-American and is found in certain neighborhoods in San Jose and in rural pockets both north and south of the city. In recent years there has been a surge of increased political activity, militancy, and feuding among Mexican-American organizations.

Some of the Mexican-American leaders were initially aggrieved when Potts was selected over Galarza, and in particular, they were anxious to see more Mexican-Americans in top staff jobs within the EOC. Shortly afterwards, stories began to circulate that Potts treated the poor arrogantly and paternalistically. In early March, Lino Lopez, head of the Mexican-American Community Service Project, took Potts on a tour of the Mexican sections of San Jose. Lopez claims that Potts listened disdainfully while Lopez described the problems of the residents, then laughed and said, "I don't believe your garbage." Although it was denied by Potts, this story was widely circulated among Mexican-American groups. In the six months following this encounter Lopez also claimed that Potts made no effort to contact his agency. On the other hand, it was not generally known that Potts had supported the award of a special contract for the consultation services of Lopez when the Community Service Project was in serious financial difficulties. In return for $5,000, Lopez conducted several "seminars" on Mexican-American culture for ASC staff members.

Still other sources of opposition were Potts' disparagement of a program proposal submitted by the CSO, which would have expanded their immigration and citizenship services, as well as his conflict with an east San Jose group much influenced by CSO. The latter organization believed that the EOC's proper role was to function solely as a fiscal agent and technical advisor to local organizations, with indigenous constituencies, which would actually operate the programs. In this view, they were joined by spokesmen for labor and religious organizations. As they watched the EOC take on the role of central planner and developer of new programs, CSO leaders concluded that Mexican-Americans were again being excluded and that "establishment" agencies would gain complete control of the antipoverty program.

Still another organization was antagonized when in August, Isaias Aguilera, head of the San Jose chapter of the MAPA, withdrew an invitation to Potts to speak before the MAPA. In a letter that he sent to the press and to the regional office of OEO as well as to Potts, Aguilera deplored the lack of understanding between the EOC staff and the poor. He charged that the Mexican-Americans were "purposely ignored," while "the benefits of the War on Poverty are going to others . . . than the disadvantaged," and said "We stress again the need to appoint to positions at policy-making levels Mexican-Americans who are best qualified by virtue of their knowledge and sensitivity for the problems you purport to counter." [11]

Mexican-American leadership came together in July when Nash Galindo, EOC consultant, with Potts' consent, called an informational meeting of various influential Mexican-Americans to inform them of the staff positions that soon would be available, and to encourage their participation in the program. The group decided to meet informally once a month, and was soon known as the "Roundtable." Although the Roundtable clearly did not originate as a response to Mexican-American dissatisfaction with Potts, ironically it soon became such a forum. At the EOC meeting of August 19, 1965, a spokesman for the Roundtable presented a statement accusing the executive director of discriminating against Mexican-Americans in his hiring procedures and of reneging on a specific promise to hire a Mexican-American as deputy director. Potts denied the charges and noted that nine members of EOC's 25-man staff were of Mexican descent, and that this number would have been larger if several others had not declined job offers made to them. In addition, many Mexican-Americans had been hired by the Head Start Program mainly as semiprofessional aides. As for the complaint about the deputy director's job, Potts said he had made no commitment to hire anyone for the job, especially since a management consulting firm hired to study the EOC staff might find the job unnecessary. Potts also reminded the Commission that in June, 1965, it had defeated by a 10-3 vote a motion to appoint a Spanish-speaking person as deputy director. This vote was the result of a forceful protest by one of the original three representatives of the poor, a Negro woman who strongly opposed including or excluding ethnic qualifications or designation in any job specification. The Commission was satisfied with Potts' answers; the Roundtable was not. Skillicorn agreed, therefore, to appoint a three-man committee, headed by Dale Scott, Executive of the County Taxpayers Association, to confer with MAPA and other Mexican-American organizations about their grievances.

Criticism of Potts' handling of the antipoverty program was also the subject of informal discussions between Potts and members of the OEO regional office. These complaints, mostly about the "maximum feasible participation" clause, organizing and administering the ASCs, the hiring of staff, and the composition of the EOC, were filtering in through OEO field representatives, Tom Cutler and John Martin. Potts' answer to these complaints was that discussions at every level delayed moving rapidly

[11] EOC, *Mexican-American Dispute Chronology,* p. 1.

enough to actually get the programs in operation. He often went on to question the motives of his critics and to suggest that the regional OEO was interfering with his independence. At the same time, OEO staff began to question the educational requirements for the job roster, suggesting that experience could replace education, and recommending better publicizing of job openings, as well as more encouragement for the training of nonprofessional aides for higher staff positions. Potts continued to insist on job applicants' meeting fixed and relatively high standards. In a letter to Mogulof, dated August 13, 1965, Potts said that Mexican-American and Negro leaders agreed with the principles underlying his hiring procedures, and that, despite reports to the contrary, people hired as nonprofessionals could expect to be upgraded.

Potts also replied to complaints to the OEO that he had ignored certain program proposals by saying that all proposals received equal attention, but that he was annoyed with hastily prepared, limited proposals submitted by organizations with no previous experience in alleviating poverty. In this category he placed most of the prominent Mexican-American organizations, which he claimed were not, with one exception, welfare or educational agencies, but rather social and political associations. Potts also pointed out that only 16 per cent of the county's poor families had Spanish surnames, and added that the EOC had a responsibility to serve *all* low-income groups.[12]

Several days later on August 17, 1965, OEO field representative Martin reminded Potts that in spite of numerous prods during the summer, the EOC had made no further efforts to increase the number of low-income board members since the three representatives were first added in May. Since then, nine areas had been designated but none of their representatives had been admitted to the board of directors. The EOC was warned that future grants from OEO might be conditioned upon the addition of area representatives. Potts made no official reply to this letter nor was it shared with staff. Perhaps Potts included the three representatives of organizations with low-income constituencies as comprising the necessary one-third (6 out of 18) of the board who represented the poor, but in addition it seems clear he had planned to add representatives from each area as soon as they were properly organized.

The three-man grievance committee appointed by Skillicorn at the August 19 EOC meeting met for the first time on September 2, with Potts and five spokesmen from Mexican-American organizations. Everyone agreed to postpone discussion of the deputy director's position until the report of the management consultant firm was released. The Mexican-American delegation seemed pleased to hear that many jobs were

[12] Potts' letter to Mogulof, August 13, 1965.

still open and assured Potts they would recruit applicants if he sent them appropriate forms. A second meeting on September 23, which was to discuss programs, did not materialize because several of the Mexican-Americans did not appear. Plans for a third meeting were cancelled when in early October, one of the members informed Potts that the Mexican-Americans preferred not to discuss any of their other complaints until a decision had been made to hire a deputy director.[13] Skillicorn made a number of informal requests to the Mexican-Americans to set up a dialogue on any basis and although they agreed individually to look into the possibility, a meeting never took place.

Potts later charged that the Mexican-Americans deliberately undermined the proceedings of the grievance committee. It is true that a general pattern of obstructive Mexican-American behavior emerged during the next few months; in public, they expressed a desire to cooperate, but at the same time they resorted to public protests and publicity for their grievances and went directly to the OEO in lieu of participating in discussions with Potts or Skillicorn. Also, they called out large numbers of mostly Spanish-speaking persons, who picketed EOC offices and meeting places whenever some conflict erupted. Demonstrations were organized at EOC meetings by Mexican-American leaders in collaboration with Anglo supporters from labor and Democratic Party groups. These meetings were packed to capacity and were characterized by widespread heckling, booing, stamping, and cheering, all directed by what appeared to be a claque.

By mid-October, the collapse of the grievance committee left matters at an impasse. Aguilera appeared before the San Jose City Council to ask that it withdraw from the EOC and apply for its own Community Action Program. He also persuaded the county's Republican and Democratic general committees to ask the EOC to appoint a Mexican-American as deputy director.[14]

Of greater significance was that at least eight Mexican-American organizations, notorious for their inability to agree on most matters of policy, began meeting together for the first time to discuss ways to secure redress for their grievances.[15] Aguilera, already an outspoken critic of the EOC and of Potts, was also part of the Roundtable, but its prime movers were Pinon of the CSO and Lino Lopez, of the Community Service Project.

[13] EOC, *Mexican-American Dispute Chronology*, p. 2.

[14] *Ibid.*, p. 13.

[15] The eight signatory organizations were: American Legion, Post 809; San Jose Renters and Home Owners Council; Community Service Organization; American G.I. Forum, Santa Clara; Mexican-American Political Association; International Longshoremans and Warehousemans Union Local #6; American G.I. Forum, San Jose; and the Mexican-American Unity Council Task Force.

Lopez had never gotten along with Potts, and Pinon had failed to pass the oral examination for the job of director of the EOC's small business assistance program. He had furthermore clashed with Potts over the development of a service center in the Alum Rock area of San Jose. Both Lopez and Pinon were regarded by Potts as the architects of the "conspiracy" directed against him.

In October, the spokesmen for the eight organizations released to the EOC and simultaneously to the regional and Washington OEO offices and to the press a list of 10 complaints and demands, requesting that EOC funds be frozen until a thorough investigation of the program was made.[16] The 10 "grievances and demands" concerned the hiring of members of minority groups for policy-making and supervisory staff positions; the relaxation of certain job requirements; the granting of genuine autonomy to the ASCs on all matters except funding; and the publicizing of all program proposals 30 days prior to their submission to the Commission. Heading the list, and by far the most controversial of all, was a demand that "sixty percent of the EOC . . . be comprised of target area people and/or their representatives from the community organizations," with these people to be selected by area residents and organizations.[17] Until this time, the major effort of the Mexican-Americans had been aimed at increasing the EOC representation of organized Mexican-American groups. The demand for majority control of the EOC by the poor had evidently been included upon the advice of a respected Mexican-American leader in San Francisco, who had been one of the strategists of Citizens United Against Poverty in its fight with Mayor Shelley.

"Well, that's a dinger," was Potts' initial reaction to the document. He told the press he would welcome an investigation since he had nothing to hide. He urged that the Mexican-American signatory groups be included in such an inquiry in order to assess the validity of their claims to represent the best interests of the poor. "Are they asking for special privileges for the Mexican-Americans?" he asked rhetorically.[18] Some of the Commissioners of the EOC joined with Potts in believing that men like Pinon and Lopez were more interested in advancing their own political ambitions than in genuinely combatting poverty by involving more poor people in the various aspects of the EOC. They felt that the regional OEO office did not understand the difficulties involved in getting "real" spokesmen for the poor and also questioned whether their Mexican-American spokesmen had actually secured the endorsement of most of the signatory groups. Skillicorn said that it was "a crime and disaster for the Mexican-

[16] EOC, *Mexican-American Grievances and Demands* and Cover Resolution.
[17] *Ibid.*
[18] San Jose *Mercury News*, October 15, 1965. Potts' news release, October 14, 1965.

American groups to threaten the county's anti-poverty program." He cited their withdrawal from the special grievance committee as evidence of their unwillingness to negotiate their complaints peaceably. When questioned by the press over OEO's role in the dispute, Mogulof said they would immediately investigate, and "nothing takes precedence over this kind of concern, even if it is based on allegations." He further said that it would be "not only desirable but mandatory that a Spanish-speaking person be employed in a top staff position." [19]

Toward EOC Reorganization

On October 25, 1965, OEO sent to the EOC a letter that had critical significance. OEO requested that within 30 days, interim delegates from each of the nine target areas be seated on the EOC and that within 90 days, ways be worked out to select permanent representatives from these areas. Also within 30 days the EOC was to report in detail on how the service centers were to influence program and staffing policies, and on how the "top staff group reflects knowledge of and capacity to work with those of Mexican-American ancestry." OEO also asked that the EOC refrain from making any major policy decisions on either the autonomy of the service centers or on hiring policies "until adequate interim representation is placed upon the board." As if to take the edge off this ultimatum, the letter concluded that

> . . . it is critical for all of us to constantly re-examine the way in which we fulfill our Congressional mandate for maximum feasible involvement. The most exciting part of these times is the constant change in what constitutes 'feasibility.' I know that you and the Santa Clara Commission will remain alert to changing conditions and be aggressive in fashioning a program which leads, rather than follows.

Simultaneously (on October 26), Mogulof released a directive to all CAP groups in the area directing that a minimum of one representative from each area to be served be included on CAP boards, and he suggested that at least one-third of the people on the boards be drawn from the "groups and areas to be served," so as to make them an "equal partner of the public agency and general community sectors in decision-making." [20] The coincidence of the new OEO directive to all CAP boards lent particular support, although perhaps unintentionally, to the demands of the Mexican-American organizations against the Santa Clara EOC. These

[19] *Ibid.*
[20] OEO Regional CAP Bulletin, *CAP Board Structure*, October 29, 1965.

organizations mimeographed copies of Mogulof's October 25 letter and the October 26 directive and sent them, along with their protest, to public and private groups throughout the county. Skillicorn and other EOC commissioners were particularly angered at the practice of OEO in sending copies of all their correspondence with the EOC to members of the Mexican-American community so that the latter actually received such letters before the commissioners could get their copies from the EOC office.

The Fall Assembly of the Santa Clara Council of Churches, meeting in early October, had previously passed two resolutions in support of the Mexican-American demands. One called for a Spanish-speaking person to be hired as deputy director or some other high-level position; the other urged majority representation of the poor on the EOC, with low-income families from each of the nine areas to elect these representatives. The NAACP branches in San Jose and Palo Alto similarly endorsed Mexican-American demands on hiring, but not on majority representation.[21]

Potts reacted as if the request to alter the composition of the Commission was a complete surprise to him and as if the seating of interim representatives represented only a "crash solution" to problems requiring much more time to work out. In a formal reply to Potts, Mogulof denied, as politely as he could, that there was any truth in Potts' complaint about being caught unawares by the requests to alter the Commission's structure. He added a quote from a letter to the regional OEO office from Mrs. Gertrude Stevens, director of the Department of Migrant Ministry, Santa Clara Council of Churches, in which she claimed not to have been aware of any of the 30 committee and agency meetings Potts referred to as being an intrinsic part of working out programs for the service centers. Mogulof said to Potts that in view of such comments as Mrs. Stevens' as well as others, "the efforts you are making, while acceptable on paper, have either not been communicated to those being worked with, or, in fact, are not being satisfactorily carried out." Apparently satisfied with Potts' reply that the directors of the Neighborhood Youth Corps and of program development would both be of Mexican-American ancestry, Mogulof softened his requests on hiring a deputy director, and on personnel policies or program decisions. He warned the Commission, however, to move cautiously in making decisions during the interim period so as not to preempt the decision-making effectiveness of the permanent Commission. Furthermore, the OEO would not insist on a 30-day deadline for interim representatives, but would expect progress to be made within that period.[22]

[21] Santa Clara Council of Churches, *Fall Assembly Resolutions*. San Jose NAACP, *Resolutions*. Palo Alto NAACP letter to EOC, November 18, 1965.

[22] Mogulof's letter to Potts, November 1, 1965.

All this controversy renewed the fears of some of the commissioners that their efforts would be obstructed by higher levels of government. Although many commissioners believed that the poor should not dominate the EOC, the Commission began at once to bring itself into accord with the latest OEO guidelines. Mexican-American leaders, the Council of Churches, and the NAACP did not press a demand that more than one-third of EOC members be from target areas.

On November 1, Skillicorn appointed an *ad hoc* committee to formulate the new bylaws and other procedural changes for reorganizing the EOC in accord with the regional OEO's October 29 guidelines. The committee was composed of 20 members drawn from each of the ASCs, the EOC advisory board and included one of the signatories of the October protest letter. In a letter to Skillicorn, Robert Rodriguez, a spokesman for the Roundtable, advised Potts that all eight organizations expected to be seated on the committee. Skillicorn replied the committee would become too unwieldy and offered instead to seat one more representative of the eight. The Mexican-Americans then appealed to OEO and appeared at the first meeting of the *ad hoc* committee demanding that 10 of their delegates be seated, in addition to members to fill the two vacancies already mentioned. Finally, the 10 were allowed to participate as non-voting members. The chairman of the *ad hoc* committee, Leonard McConnell, a Family Service Agency executive, preferred to avoid another confrontation with the Mexican-Americans. As a result, about 12 nonmembers of the committee participated in its deliberation and even voted for the final reorganization plan.

Meanwhile, Potts prepared a reply to the Mexican-American "grievances and demands." He pointed out the current proceedings of the *ad hoc* committee to add more target area representatives, and he again deferred discussion of the deputy director's post until the management consultant's report was made. On the alleged failure "to move with reasonable speed" on programs and staffing, his reply reviewed the impressive program accomplishments of the EOC in the first few months of its existence, and pointed out that programs would have been delayed even further if more time had been spent in discussions with recipients.[23]

About this time the management consultant's report on staff structure was released and discussed at the Commission's November 18 meeting. The report recommended that the deputy director's position be eliminated in the interests of better communication between Potts and his department heads. It was stated that the executive director was so accessible "that

[23] Potts' letter to Mogulof, November 10, 1965, p. 4.

his time for a major management task—reflective thinking—may be insufficient."[24]

The report was accepted without approval after the November 18 meeting engendered a heated debate with charges that the consulting firm had "sold out" and countercharges. Despite the recommendation of the management report, Potts began to realize the political effectiveness of appointing a Mexican-American as deputy director even though two more months would go by before an appointment would be made. Nash Galindo was the Mexican-Americans' choice for the post, but after the controversy began he resigned under pressure from his EOC staff position. Potts subsequently seemed to ignore Mexican-American preferences on candidates for the post.

In addition to the conflicting pressures regarding the employment of a Mexican-American deputy director, the EOC found itself in the midst of a major reorganization. In order to comply with the OEO deadline for representation from each of the areas, on November 18 the EOC approved three alternate methods for the selection of interim representatives. By the end of December, six delegates had been selected. Some manipulation of the selection or election process seems to have occurred in most areas, since it was relatively easy for interested groups to "pack" meetings with their supporters or to choose a method of selection to favor already seated delegates. It is not surprising that most of the interim EOC representatives were openly hostile to Potts and favored more autonomy for the area boards. The EOC executive charged that Mexican-Americans and left-wingers pushed through their candidates; however, criticism of Potts also stemmed from moderates and right-wingers, who also pushed through their candidates in some cases. With few exceptions, all factions seemed in favor of restricting EOC control over the ASCs.

At the same time, the *ad hoc* committee was recommending a more complex set of procedures for the selection of the permanent representative of the areas. These were finally adopted on December 16, 1965. These rules also influenced the procedures for the election of representatives of the poor to the service center boards, most of which were already expanding themselves into the three-section model promoted by OEO. The election guidelines provided that each area was to be divided into sub-areas or target areas on the basis of the concentration of potential service recipients. Each sub-area was to be canvassed by semiprofessional aides, who would inform residents of the nature of the EOC program and the

[24] Griffenhagen-Kroeger, Inc., *Management Organization of the Economic Opportunity Commission of Santa Clara County, Inc.*, San Francisco, California, November, 1965, p. 8.

forthcoming election of a permanent representative and alternate to the EOC, as well as a representative of the poor to the area board. The former were to be elected by an "electoral college" of at least 25 or more representatives of the poor in the target area. Although the elected representatives of the poor to the EOC or area board did *not* have to be poor themselves, voting was restricted to those with an annual income of $4,000 or less for a family of four or $3,000 for a single person.[25] To insure conformity with these rules, voters had to sign rosters certifying that they met these income criteria.

Although Skillicorn had proposed that the representatives of the poor meet the criteria for being low-income persons themselves, the EOC, including all of the minority and interim representatives of the poor, voted against this overwhelmingly. Subsequent efforts to insure that representatives of the poor to the EOC themselves had low incomes came from the more conservative members of the EOC, who sought in this way to curb attempts to extend the power of the Mexican-American groups.

As a result of these procedures, the elections extended for many months in 1966 and finally resulted in four of the Area Service Center boards' having more than 50 per cent poor people, while the rest had at least one-third of their membership who were defined as poor. The system of combined elections whereby the sub-areas elected representatives to the area board when they voted for delegates to the electoral college insured that most of the directors who represented the poor themselves had low incomes, although no such provision was included in the bylaws. Different election procedures were formulated by the various Area Service Center boards pertaining to the percentage of representatives of the poor who must themselves be poor. Only two areas (3 and 5) required that all representatives of the poor on the area board must themselves have low incomes, whereas other areas provided for a given number of representatives to be elected by town meetings or councils, in which a fixed proportion had to have low incomes.

Yet, both the elected representatives of the area to the EOC as well as the representatives of the poor to the area boards had a rather ambiguous constituency to whom they were accountable because of the character of the electoral system. In addition, elections in three of the areas were contested and in numerous cases had to be rescheduled owing to the small number of voters. In retrospect, the elections appear to have been expensive and time consuming and to have produced much less participation than expected. In one area, for example, a board member charged that the election cost $42 per vote cast.

[25] EOC, *Report on Selection of Permanent Area and Group Representatives to the EOC*, December 13, 1965.

These area elections were part of the process whereby a new 27-member Commission was to be created, with seven representatives from local and county government, public, and voluntary social agencies and educational institutions and eleven from labor, business, agricultural, religious, and minority organizations. The remaining third—the representatives of the poor—were to be from the nine ASCs, and all but the poor were to be selected by those sectors of the community designated by the *ad hoc* committee.[26]

The EOC passed several resolutions designed to expedite the transfer from the old to the new Commission within a month. One measure provided that the transfer would be considered complete when one-third of the new members were seated, thus allowing the interim area delegates to continue sitting until permanent representatives were chosen but requiring that the present agency and organization representatives leave the EOC until the new representatives were chosen. Another resolution changed the number of votes needed on important policy questions from a two-thirds to a simple majority. Both of these measures enhanced the likelihood of the area delegates' dominating the new EOC. Their control of the Commission was further aided when at the January 20, 1966 meeting the delegates from the County Taxpayers' Association and the San Jose Chamber of Commerce resigned from the EOC. In his letter to Skillicorn, Dale Scott, who had chaired the special grievances committee, spelled out his reasons for urging the Taxpayers' Association to withdraw from the EOC. First were the alleged "efforts by certain politically motivated unrepresentative pressure groups to change the Commission to a group controlled by certain parties who seek only political ends rather than a real and sincere program designed to aid the poor." He also objected to the OEO's role in intervening in the affairs of the EOC and said he felt there was "an absolute disregard for truth and fair play in their actions by accepting as fact statements that actually had no basis in fact and by actually refusing to hear both sides of the dispute." Essentially the same reasons were given by Jay Gibson of the San Jose Chamber of Commerce in his letter of resignation (January 19, 1966). Gibson added the criticism that the "lack of effort and ability of the local EOC to involve the community has resulted in the take-over of the Commission by a small group of politically ambitious opportunists." Although Potts and Skillicorn urged both men not to resign, Scott and Gibson obviously felt their presence would only legitimize rather than prevent the actions of the Mexican-American groups, and they were unwilling to risk their reputations in the political and personnel clashes about to erupt.

[26] EOC Manual: Bylaws of EOC, February 1, 1966.

The "Takeover"

One of the immediate consequences of Scott's and Gibson's resignations was to enable Potts' opponents on the EOC to force the Commission into executive session at the end of its January 20 meeting to discuss "the conduct of an employee." During the session, the possibility of dismissing the executive director was discussed, but after 55 minutes the meeting ended inconclusively.

While the Commission was in executive session, a mild commotion arose among spectators when Dr. Edgar Cumings, a member of the EOC central staff, held an informal press conference. He admitted his authorship of an unsigned letter that had appeared in the afternoon papers, accusing Potts of diverting funds meant for ASCs to other programs, failing to fulfill a promise to modify staff recruitment procedures, burying numerous worthwhile program suggestions, and generally maligning the Mexican-American community. Dissatisfaction with Potts, which had been brewing among several of his own staff members for several months, was thus dramatically thrust into open view.

Tensions between the executive director and some of his middle level staff members stemmed largely from ideological differences and policy disagreements regarding the manner and pace of organizing the ASCs, all of which were aggravated by personality factors. Cumings, a former college president in charge of ASC organization on the EOC staff, became convinced that Potts was harming the program through his autocratic manner of administration and lack of sensitivity to the demands of the Mexican-American organizations. Included among those who shared this belief were several staff members who were affiliated with various Mexican-American organizations and active in the Roundtable. They, along with five or six others, were sounded out by Cumings late in November about meeting with Mogulof to discuss their grievances. A detailed five-page list of objections to Potts' administration was prepared, but the meeting with the OEO official never took place.

Early in January, Cumings and another dissident staff member met with spokesmen of the Mexican-American organizations and offered to cooperate with them in a joint effort to secure Potts' resignation or dismissal. At this point, however, the Mexican-Americans seemed to be fairly satisfied with the progress being made toward shifting control of the Commission into their hands, and they were willing to work within the framework of the Commission for modification of program and hiring policies. Even though their personal dislike of Potts had not lessened, they were not very enthusiastic about pushing immediately to oust him. For one thing, they were not convinced they would have a workable majority on the new EOC, since its formal structure provided that delegates from the service centers would be only a third of the Commission. The election of a San Jose manufacturer and John Birch member, Raymond Gurries, from Area 5 indicated that all the area delegates might not accept the direction of the Mexican-American leaders. Also, in early January, the Mexican-Americans did not anticipate the withdrawal of the business community representatives from the EOC and the consequent increase in voting strength for representatives of minority groups and target areas. The Mexican-Americans may also have feared the loss of OEO support, which so far had been invaluable, should they insist on Potts' dismissal. Whether intentionally or not, a copy of Cumings' statement was "leaked" to a San Jose *Mercury* reporter by an EOC staff member and appeared as a front-page story on the day of the January 20 EOC meeting. In his remarks to the press while the Commission was in executive session, Cumings claimed the letter had been released without his consent and declined to name the other staff members who endorsed it.[27]

Potts told the press several days after the disclosure of Cumings' letter that he "did not answer letters that are unsigned, statements that are unsigned or other items that are not documented." As for the author, Potts said, "There will be no reprisal without adequate consideration. This is not a punishment situation. I want to find out what these people have on their minds." [28] On January 28, however, Cumings was fired for "insubordination."

Whatever reluctance the Mexican-Americans or other critics of Potts had felt about pressing for his dismissal was swept aside when Cumings was fired. Organized by a CSO leader and a well-known local labor official, a large group of pickets, including many Spanish-speaking persons, marched that afternoon in front of the EOC offices in protest of the firing. Three ASC boards called for an immediate investigation of the charges against Potts. One of them, the board from Area 3, hired Cumings as their director two weeks after he was fired. In informal meetings during the next few days, Potts' opponents decided that his removal should take precedence over their other objectives with respect to increasing the involvement of the poor. If the anticipated transfer from the old to the reorganized EOC made it possible to fight Potts through legitimate channels, so much the better. If not, they were willing to resort to more unauthorized means.

Strategy meetings were held all over the county as the dissident EOC staff members met with various social agencies, religious organizations,

[27] San Jose *Mercury*, January 22, 1966, p. 1.
[28] *Op. cit.*, January 26, 1966.

and area service boards informing them of their grievances. They found widespread sympathy for their position, and they were aided by the failure of those department heads on the central staff who, although privately backing Potts, were unwilling to express their opinions in public. Commissioners favorable to the ouster also contacted their fellow directors in an effort to win their support, and ways were sought to overcome the obstacles expected from the chairman of the EOC and those commissioners who did not want to vote against Potts publicly.

The Ousting of Potts

If Potts' decision to fire Cumings had been based on the belief that Cumings was part of a well-organized conspiracy against him and the entire EOC program, he had certainly miscalculated the response to Cumings' dismissal. What he did not anticipate was that Cumings' firing proved a catalyst for his hitherto unallied staff and outside opponents.

In the two weeks between January 20 and the EOC's next regular meeting, Potts did make some efforts to appease both the Mexican-Americans and his own staff. On January 21, he announced that applications for deputy director were being processed; about ten days later he appointed Mark Guerra to the long vacant post. The forty-seven-year-old Guerra had been a dean of students and guidance director in the San Jose high school system before taking a job as head of EOC's Neighborhood Youth Corps program. Guerra was also vice-president of the San Jose Chapter of MAPA, whose president, Aguilera, was a close friend. Rodriguez, as spokesman for the signers of the October protest, was less enthusiastic, since some of the Mexican-American leaders regarded Guerra as an "Uncle Tamales" who had allowed himself to be bought off. Furthermore, Rodriguez complained about the procedure used to select the deputy director.[29] His group had solicited applicants from all over the county, five of whom filled out the forms but none of whom were included in the list of finalists who were interviewed by a panel also chosen by Potts. Potts claimed he asked one of the Mexican-American leaders to serve on the interview panel, but that he refused. The EOC executive director denied that he appointed Guerra to appease his critics who were demanding that he himself be fired, and that regardless of the circumstances, a deputy director would have been appointed in January.

On January 31, Potts spoke to his staff at some length, assuring them of his devotion to the objectives of the antipoverty program and reminding them of their responsibility to provide continuous feedback from the

[29] *Op. cit.*, February 3, 1966.

community. He made no specific references to Cumings' dismissal, but his remarks were designed to reduce any ill-feeling generated by this action. He reviewed the history of the EOC since early 1965, stressing that although the establishment of Area Service Center boards was behind the schedule set forth in June, significant progress had been made in three areas: Gilroy, Gardner, and East San Jose, and at least four others were close to receiving final approval for their contracts. He defended the use of central EOC staff to assist the area boards in developing programs, hiring staff of their own, and contracting with local service agencies. He also reiterated his commitment to involving the poor "continuously and progressively . . . in the planning, operation and evaluation" of service center and county-wide programs. Potts noted he had urged "an adaptation to a new principle;" namely, that one-third of the persons on the EOC should be selected by the poor, one-third by agencies, and one-third by organizations including those with large minority group constituencies. He rejected Cumings' charge that the EOC had buried a hundred program proposals, by insisting that local groups submitted fewer than sixty proposals, many of which were incorporated into the basic service center plan.

On EOC personnel procedures, Potts noted that the EOC considered and approved on three different occasions the central position roster and the value of using a "near civil service procedure" for eligibility so as to eliminate the likelihood of political factors' determining the selection of personnel by the service centers.[30] In a letter to the editor of the San Jose *News*, which appeared two days before the staff meeting, Robert Barela wrote that he was "a proud American of Mexican descent" and that in his department alone "at least twenty conscientious staff members" had no inclination to fire Potts. He added that "the influential Mexican-American organizations of San Jose do not represent all of the Mexican-American thinking of Santa Clara County."[31]

Meanwhile the OEO had pulled back somewhat from its apparent earlier support of Mexican-American grievances. During January, the press reported Cutler as saying that despite poor relations with the Mexican-American community and delays in bringing the number of representatives of the poor up to federal standards, the Santa Clara EOC easily ranked among the top ten of the 200 antipoverty programs in the southern and western states.[32] In this and other public statements, the regional OEO seemed to be providing a gloss of praise for its behind-the-scenes efforts to secure some modifications in the administration of the EOC.

[30] Typescript of remarks of Potts to EOC staff meeting, January 31, 1966.
[31] Robert Barela's letter to San Jose *News*, January 29, 1966.
[32] Sunnyvale *Daily Standard*, January 26, 1966.

Mogulof wrote to the EOC on January 28 and indicated the OEO's expectation that all working committees of the Santa Clara antipoverty program include adequate representation of the people being served. However, he added a note of praise for the "very careful consideration" given to the inclusion of such representatives on the reconstituted EOC.

Later on the day of the staff meeting on January 31, the Mexican-American leaders met and drafted a resolution demanding Potts' immediate resignation. They charged that he had thrown the service center proposals at them on a "take it or leave it basis" and had done little since their October protest to repair his standing in the eyes of the poor.[33]

Potts' public response to the latest blast from the Mexican-Americans was to admit a "share in the burden for the lack of dialogue . . . but I won't accept the entire responsibility." He called for a "cease fire" and a negotiation session between the Anglos and the Mexican-Americans to salvage the antipoverty program. He said his critics "never really attacked" his idea of creating ASCs, but that they objected to his eagerness to organize them rapidly without extensive attempts at grassroots involvement until after at least a year's worth of funds were assured from the federal OEO.[34]

The Mexican-Americans' reaction to the cease fire call was, to say the least, cool. Rodriguez complained that the basic issue was not between Anglos and Mexican-Americans, as Potts had phrased it in his press release, but between "the poor and Arthur Potts." The signatory organizations could no longer be put off from their determination to remove the executive by a promise of informal negotiations.

A special meeting of the EOC was held February 3 and attended by an overflow crowd of 400 people, many of them Spanish speaking. At the start of the meeting, the anti-Potts forces saw that they did not have enough votes to win. Part of their strategy depended on the replacement of interim representatives by the recently elected delegates from the areas known to be opposed to Potts, and when these were seated after a recess, the likelihood of victory increased. After a heated debate marked by complex parliamentary maneuvers and several votes, it was decided to suspend the executive director, with pay, for a 30-day period during which OEO would investigate Potts and his relationship with the Santa Clara EOC program and staff. Although Potts did not ask for a formal hearing, he was not granted any procedural safeguard usually extended to public officials before they are dismissed. Guerra was appointed acting executive director during Potts' suspension.[35]

[33] San Jose *Mercury*, February 2 and 3, 1966.
[34] Sunnyvale *Daily Standard*, February 3, 1966.
[35] EOC, minutes of meeting number nineteen, February 3, 1966.

One of the immediate reactions to Potts' suspension was an investigation by the District Attorney to see if the entire procedure violated the Brown Act.[36] Both the San Jose City Council and the Board of Supervisors decided to defer selection of new representatives to the EOC, which deferment no doubt increased the strength of the anti-Potts forces.

Potts tried to rally support for himself among the commissioners by pointing out the extent to which Mexican-Americans were actually involved in the EOC programs. He claimed Mexican-American families were receiving 95 per cent of the county's share of OEO funds, and that there was a large employment of Mexican-Americans on the agency staff: 15 people or 22 per cent of the total professional and clerical staff, 8 people or 33 per cent as teachers in EOC projects and 63 people or 84 per cent as semiprofessionals. He claimed these proportions were especially large in view of the fact that only 4,133 of 24,373 families considered in the poverty category in Santa Clara County (16 per cent) had Spanish surnames.

When Skillicorn attempted to enlist OEO aid in making up an investigative committee, the OEO took a "hands off" position. They refused federal funds for Potts' salary during his suspension, but allowed him to be paid as a consultant.

The regular EOC meeting on February 17 was almost as crowded as the special meeting two weeks before. After considerable debate over granting Potts a fair hearing, the meeting moved on to seat the new Commission, including seven newly elected area representatives. Tension began to mount among the crowd, and shouts of "Potts has to go" were heard. By a vote of 11 for, 7 against, and 2 abstaining, the motion to dismiss Potts was passed. Most of the votes for dismissal came from six of the target area representatives and representatives of labor, Mexican-American organizations, and the Negro community. A significant exception to those lined up against Potts was Aguilera. One of the original critics of the executive director, Aguilera made several strong public statements expressing dismay with his peers and voted at both the February 3 and 17 meetings with those who opposed the dismissal.

When the vote was tallied, Skillicorn muttered, "Cruelty comes in many forms." A reporter noted that there was "a lynch party ugliness in the applause with which the crowd greeted the results of the voting."[37] One of the Mexican-American leaders was heard to say, "Well, we sure assassinated that Anglo so-and-so!" and one of their labor allies referred to the vote as a victory over the establishment.

[36] Sunnyvale *Daily Standard,* February 4, 1966 and February 7, 1966.
[37] San Jose *Mercury,* February 19, 1966.

The Commission adjourned after authorizing Skillicorn to call a special meeting in two weeks to hear Potts' appeal and to appoint a selection committee for a new executive director should the appeal be denied. Guerra was authorized to exercise the full power of the executive director's position until a new one was officially hired or Potts reinstated.

Potts did not attend the February 17 meeting; when contacted by the press later that evening, he said that he was not sure he would appeal his firing, and would do so only "if there is any good purpose to be served by an appeal." Within the next four days he tried to rally support for himself. Since four of the six new commissioners who were not seated as of February 17 were representatives of business and government, Potts may have hoped they would support him. He complained that there were no formal charges and that he was the "victim of a personal vendetta." He warned that without an impartial investigation "any executive who replaces me will be working in a state of limbo."[38]

At the EOC special meeting on March 1 only one of the new commissioners was seated, and Potts may have decided an appeal would be fruitless. At any rate he decided to tender his resignation. He said nothing, but his attorney, Robert Blake, read a prepared statement. Following this statement, Supervisor Della Maggiore moved that Potts be reinstated as executive director and that his resignation be accepted with regrets. The motion passed unanimously.[39]

Skillicorn defended Potts in an open letter to the citizens of Santa Clara County, dated March 2. He spoke out against "a movement which started out as a well-motivated concern for constructive and developmental change in the local EOC program [and] has now deteriorated into a political power struggle oblivious to the needs of the poor and designed to usurp the program." Skillicorn supported Potts, who, he said, within one year had helped develop a program "considered by experts to be one of the best in the entire western United States," and who had tried to offer a middle ground among varying interpretations of how to implement an antipoverty program. The EOC chairman had been particularly upset with the manner in which Potts had been made a scapegoat, the victim of a plan hatched by a few individuals, and he subsequently defended the succeeding executives when he felt they were unjustly attacked.

Another expression of regret at Potts' firing was made by William Fernandez to the Inter-City Council on March 3. He claimed the new Mexican-American and Negro minority control of the council wanted to obtain more autonomy for the ASCs, particularly in hiring, fiscal, and

[38] Los Gatos *Times-Observer,* February 18, 1966.

[39] EOC minutes, Special Meeting, March 1, 1966, with Potts' letter of resignation.

policy-making matters. Fernandez, however, urged that the Inter-City Council stay within the Commission.[40]

On the other hand, the Rev. John Emerson replied to Skillicorn's letter that "a watchful community of responsible, concerned citizens [will not] permit such a takeover by any extremist of either camp for ulterior purposes." Furthermore, he believed that the loss of confidence in Potts

> arose out of an essentially inflexible bureaucratic concept of programming and a patronizing approach to the poor which does not grasp the unique idea—the real genius of the program—of permitting the poor to analyze their own needs and determine their destiny. It was at the point where the administration failed to accept this principle that its executive director was considered no longer effective . . .[41]

The actual process of firing Potts seems to have been more the result of chance and haphazard planning than of careful calculation and involved, among other things, the unexpectedly rapid shift in control of the Commission to the Mexican-Americans and their NAACP, religious, and labor allies; the resignation of Scott (Taxpayers' Association) and Gibson (Chamber of Commerce); the unanticipated catalytic effect of Cumings' firing on Potts' critics; and the feeling among both influential Mexican-Americans and social service professionals throughout the country that Potts was not the best man for the politically sensitive job of executive director. Because of the temper of the times, it was also possible for the Mexican-American spokesmen, together with some of their political allies, to exploit the strong antiestablishment feelings prevailing in the community. Finally, the failure of Potts to co-opt his opposition and the reluctance of his supporters to develop countervailing power also contributed to his fall.

Aftermath: A New Administration

Guerra's stint as acting director was hampered by the lingering aura of mistrust of the previous executive. Guerra created an administrative cabinet to advise him, but the area personnel and many central staff members resented the cabinet because it was composed entirely of division heads and therefore excluded all those with anti-Potts sentiments.

On April 13, the ASC directors submitted a list of 16 "Practical Questions, Suggestions, and Recommendations" to Guerra, stressing the need

[40] William Fernandez, speech to Inter-City Council, March 3, 1966.
[41] Emerson, letter to Skillicorn, San Jose *Mercury*, March 15, 1966.

for greater emphasis on the service center segment of the entire program and better communications between the EOC and the areas. In particular, the document recommended the elimination of all new EOC central staff positions, the abolition of the cabinet or its expansion to include area directors, the provision of monthly financial reports to the ASCs, the holding of bi-monthly meetings between ASC directors and the executive director of the EOC, and the elimination of disparities between salaries at the ASC and EOC levels. Guerra's reply to the ASC directors' memo was rather noncommittal and indicated no change in fundamental philosophy. At the same time, Guerra was also having serious problems with areas 7 (Sunnyvale and Santa Clara), 8 (Alviso and Agnew), and 9 (Palo Alto, Mountain View, and Los Altos) over contract and personnel matters.

Indicative of the new mood on the EOC was the final denouement of the "Potts orientation" and the beginning of the movement to assign more power to the ASCs, from which programs were expected to emanate. On April 21, 1966, the Commission rejected six programs that had been developed during the preceding six months under Potts' aegis. Funds saved by this action were to be set aside for programs to be developed by the ASCs when they were fully activated. In addition, the central administration budget was reduced by $146,000, and it was proposed to allocate a half million dollars of the next year's budget to ASC programs. By June, however, it was learned that OEO would reduce the over-all allocation to the EOC by more than two hundred thousand dollars regardless of any EOC action.

The Commission then established procedures for the hiring of a new executive director in March and April, and on May 21 it hired Philip Buskirk for the position after receiving 150 applications. One of the original, finalist candidates for EOC director, he had been active on the Commission until May, 1965. He was a pacifist who was active in the American Friends Service Committee and had worked with the AFL-CIO's Community Services Committee and with the local United Fund.

Buskirk began work on June 1. Immediately his position was placed in jeopardy when it was rumored that he had made various deals concerning the deputy director's position, but he apparently answered all charges at the June meeting of the EOC satisfactorily, for the attacks ceased.

Buskirk contrasted sharply with his predecessor in personal manner, administrative style, and philosophy. Soft-spoken, a good listener, and an enabler, Buskirk helped implement the formation of various program and policy committees on the EOC originally recommended at a July conference of the entire EOC and ASC board and staff members at

Asilomar. Buskirk had a strong belief in the value of decentralized administration and emphasized program development and greater resident participation in the areas. In addition, he supported the reduction in the number of positions on the central staff recommended by the budget committee and stressed the importance of getting local institutions rather than EOC to operate programs such as day care in the ASCs. In this way, he functioned primarily as an agent of the new majority bloc on the EOC composed of the nine ASC representatives allied with the six members from religious, labor, and minority organizations.

A significant change occurred in the role of the EOC as it moved from its original ratifying role and became much more assertive, reestablishing a division between policy making and administration between itself and its executive. Skillicorn remained as chairman, and Pinon was elected as the vice-chairman. Numerous subcommittees were appointed, and during the remainder of 1966 they considered a host of policy, program, and administrative matters, notably personnel and budgeting issues. Many of the EOC deliberations were concerned with the changing pattern of its relationship to the ASCs, as efforts were made to decentralize programs such as Head Start and to give the centers more autonomy. Gradually the function of the central EOC was increasingly seen as the performance of common tasks, the setting of standards, and the servicing and facilitating of the program of the ASCs.

The Emergence of the Area Service Centers

Although there was considerably less discontent with the new regime than there had been with the old one, there was still some continuing strain between central EOC and the ASCs. There were frequent complaints about the lack of communication, particularly about budgetary decisions; the maintenance of the central roster system of hiring, which required the areas to employ only those certified as eligible; the top-heavy character of central staffing; and the lack of funds for program. Combined pressures from the ASCs and OEO cutbacks resulted in some staff reduction in the EOC, but despite the proposed elimination of the research department and other economies, the ASC budgets were drastically reduced by almost one-third in the fall of 1966, thus seriously limiting their program development.

The persistent struggle for service center autonomy was reflected, for example, in the attempt of Area 9 to bypass the EOC in seeking non-OEO funding for its program. After several months of debate, it was finally resolved, on December 10, 1966, that the ASCs must obtain EOC approval of all proposals and programs for funding outside of OEO, in return for which EOC staff would assist the area in securing funding for the approved program. Failure to secure EOC approval would subject the area to a reprimand and/or the loss of its delegate status and suspension of all funding by the EOC. Any fund raising within the geographical limits of the area was solely the province of the Area Service Center board.[42] Thus the EOC asserted its primacy as the fiscal agent for the ASCs, as well as standard setter for employment and personnel policies.

Similarly, another source of tension between the ASC boards and the EOC concerned the status of the commissioners from each area who had been elected by the representatives of the poor. Not only were these area commissioners *not* required to be members of the area boards, but the EOC took steps to insure that the commissioners from the area could not serve on the two boards at the same time, by defining such dual service as a conflict of interest. This met with the objection of one area board in particular, which felt that it was not represented adequately, because the area commissioner was presumably the representative of the poor and not of the entire board! A similar attempt of Area 6, largely at the instigation of one board member, to require prior consideration by area boards of any EOC policy and administrative change also failed to gain support. Thus, the ASCs continued to be represented only indirectly on the EOC.

The pattern of communication between the area commissioner and the area service board varied, and there was no consistency in the degree to which the area boards were informed and involved in EOC matters. The bylaws were changed in March, 1967 to prevent a person from serving as a *voting* member on two boards, although they might service ex officio on one of two. Although the reason given was the wish to avoid interposing another organizational layer between the elected representatives of the poor and the EOC, this position, which assumed the validity of a rather questionable elective process, probably reflected more the continuing distrust by the EOC board members of the area service boards than a democratic concern for authentic, direct representation from the poor.

As a result, these EOC representatives of the poor were not responsive to nor responsible for any organization, group, or delegate body. Two or three of the nine area service commissioners were themselves poor, although the fact that most of them had Spanish surnames seemed to be additional validity for their spoken roles. Often the position of ASC commissioner was unfilled, owing to the long delay in holding elections as well as the ambiguity and complexity of the election process. Further

[42] EOC minutes, December 10, 1966.

attrition took place through the resignation of five commissioners from the areas because they got jobs in the EOC or obtained other forms of employment. As a group, these commissioners varied considerably in expressing a particular point of view and there was no consistent pattern in their voting.

Nevertheless, by the end of the second year of its existence, through conferences, workshops, and staff meetings, central and area board and staff members seemed to have agreed on a basic philosophy of the relationship between them, although explicit operating procedures were still unformulated. The spirit of this understanding is found in the following policy statement developed by the ASC directors in December, 1966:

> While we do not regard the problems of autonomy as serious, there is nevertheless a need for further clarification in the form of specific guidelines . . . but we do not foresee any serious conflict in this area. The centers are clearly bound to the Commission and to the EOC headquarters by contractual and financial consideration.[43]

Among the nine ASCs there was great variability in organizational character, although all shared in this continuing strain in their relationship to the EOC and the limitation on funds available for programming.

The extended character of the struggle to oust the first executive and the implementation of the election process by which the area boards were reconstituted was so prolonged that it was June, 1966, before all but two of the centers were in actual operation. It was several months more before all of the permanent boards were elected, and two of the areas (4 and 6) were so torn by internal dissension that they did not employ directors until September and October. A host of organizational and administrative problems similar to those faced by the EOC in its early stages confronted every area service board as the former began to make program decisions with exceedingly limited funds and available staff. Stringent budgets, which were further reduced by OEO action, permitted only sparse and primarily self-help projects in most of the service centers. There were classes in sewing, cooking, English, and auto repair and programs of child care, recreation, study halls, tutorials, and tool lending and fix-it-up. During the summer and holidays most of the centers sponsored recreational and social activities for children that were in many ways reminiscent of the traditional settlement house activities. Information and referral services for welfare, employment, health, housing, and personal problems were offered, and hundreds of persons were seen each month. Most of these

[43] EOC, inter-office memo, "A Policy Statement of the Area Service Centers," December 10, 1966.

programs were staffed by semiprofessionals employed by the area director through use of the central EOC roster. In none of the areas was there any continuing organizational infrastructure in the neighborhoods beyond that developed on an *ad hoc* basis for election purposes. Each ASC had only two or three community development specialists, together with several semiprofessional aides who were assigned a wide variety of tasks, few of which involved community organization. Five of the ASCs did, however, have a "council" or loosely construed membership body that was convened either monthly or, in the case of several, a few times during the year.

Supplementing these area-based services were such EOC county-wide sponsored programs as Head Start, Neighborhood Youth Corps, literacy and other classes offered through the various school systems, and Small Business Development Assistance.

Most ASCs, then, did not operate in the mold originally planned for them. Instead of bringing centrally designed programs to the neighborhoods, they began to create their own programs, such as day nurseries and tool loan arrangements. Many of the ASC staff members were unhappy with having to provide these programs, but regarded it as temporary until existing agencies could be persuaded to take them on. Furthermore, the areas had much more control over the entire EOC program than was originally anticipated. They obtained veto power over all "package" programs that were to be offered throughout the county, and all such plans had to be discussed and acted upon by each Area Service Center board before the EOC could authorize them. The majority of the ASCs were also successful in developing a greater sensitivity to the minority groups in their areas. At least five of the centers had directors who spoke Spanish, although the board leadership was not always Spanish speaking.

Participation of the Poor

The restricted scope and content of the programs may have contributed to the turnover and disillusionment of board members, particularly those who were elected as representatives of the poor. In an effort to get out the vote, evidently, the potential of the antipoverty program may have been somewhat exaggerated and oversold by the semiprofessionals assigned to the elections. When faced with the factionalism that prevailed in several boards or the predominately middle-class character of the representatives of organizations, agencies, and others, the representatives of the poor on the area boards (of whom over half were low-income persons themselves) tended to drop out. If they did attend, they did not take a very active part.

The pattern of the participation of the representatives of the poor not only varied considerably between the areas but also shifted over a period of time. For example, a change in director resulted in a gradual deterioration of what was earlier a substantial low-income participation in Area 1, but produced much greater involvement in Area 9, where there had been negligible activity for almost a year. The pattern in areas 3, 5, and 6 persisted for almost two years with practically no resident participation in the latter. In Area 8, a much more effective involvement of the poor took place outside the Area Service Center board, for example, in the Alviso CSO, which became the most militant of four chapters in the county. In Area 8 the elected representatives of the poor, all of whom were themselves poor, usually failed to attend the board meetings. When present, most of them were silent, intimidated by the other directors who were quite hostile to the area director and extremely conservative. This situation contrasted with the situation in Area 7, where the representatives of the agencies and government were much more supportive of the representatives of the poor, one-third of whom were previously unaffiliated and yet were quite vocal and active. Generally speaking, those representatives of the poor who themselves had low incomes tended to be less active than the representatives who were not poor.

The most consistently active patterns of resident participation were found in areas 5 and 3 and to a lesser extent in 7. In each of these areas there was a previous history of organization based largely on ethnic grounds, together with a strong commitment to resident participation on the part of the area director. Because of the structure of the EOC program there were only a few advisory committees on which residents could serve, and more often than not the members were also semiprofessionals who were employed in the ASCs. There was also a paucity of indigenously developed projects, since most of the self-help programs were operated by semiprofessionals under the auspices of the ASC because there were no funds for new projects.

Perhaps the majority of the Area Service Center board members, particularly in San Jose and Gilroy, consisted of Spanish-speaking persons, most of whom were affiliated with organizations. Nevertheless, there was a tendency to elect as a chairman either the most assertive person or someone who could function best in a mediating role and thus be acceptable to both the representatives of the poor and the other organizations. For this reason, the social or ethnic status of the chairman did not necessarily reflect the dominant character of the leadership clique or the membership as a whole. It is surprising that only two out of the nine area service boards in 1966 elected Mexican-Americans as chairmen, although all but two of the nine area commissioners to the EOC had Spanish surnames.

In actual operation, the area service boards were about equally divided between those with pluralistic and those with elitist decision-making systems. Three were sharply split along factional lines, but the other six tended to be more cohesive. The more assertive boards were found in those areas where there was relatively greater participation of the poor, and these included two of the three boards that were more involved than the others in various forms of social action. Area 3 in Mayfair was perhaps the best example of a vocal board with a majority of low-income members that attained considerable success both in involving the poor and in achieving some neighborhood improvements and social policy objectives through conventional pressure group tactics.

In the initial organizational stages, approximately fourteen thousand persons were contacted in the Mayfair area, and more than eight thousand questionnaires were returned with information regarding community needs. The population consisted of 50 per cent Mexican-Americans and 10 per cent Negroes, representing the largest ghetto in Santa Clara County. Although most of the poor were white, 90 per cent of the participants in Area 3 board and committees were Mexican-Americans, a pattern found in most of the other areas. Over fifteen thousand people were involved in 26 group meetings during 1966, in addition to almost one hundred participants in mothers' clubs, tutoring classes, and the first Welfare Rights Organization in the county. The latter flourished for several months; it aroused the ire of the Board of Supervisors before it dissolved, owing mainly to an internal struggle for power. Similar Welfare Rights Organizations were established in two other areas, with mixed results.

A series of neighborhood improvement measures involving collaboration with city and county officials culminated in the adoption by the city council of San Jose of a unique model cities proposal to provide $1.2 million, with full self-government and decision-making power to be assigned to a council elected by the residents.

The area director, Dr. Cumings, was successful with the backing of his board in bringing pressures on the County Board of Supervisors, Planning Commission, Welfare Department, San Jose Police Department, and Human Relations Commission. Residents of Mayfair were taken by bus to attend eight meetings of the Board of Supervisors and, together with all but two of the area service boards, persuaded the San Jose City Council to adopt a rent subsidy program in January, 1966 for 900 units and also influenced the County Board of Supervisors to establish a public housing authority. The city council of San Jose also approved annexation of Mayfair, appropriated $62,000 for a community service and recreation center to be built by local residents, and also made such improvements as installing 21 street lights.

Additional community organization efforts were undertaken in the area by church and other political and social activists. For a brief period membership in CORE and CSO increased, but it eventually declined. Efforts were initiated by the San Jose Human Relations Commission and a Police Community Relations Committee to establish liaison with Mayfair citizens. Following a riot between 150 Negro youths and police on August 18, 1966, local residents, many of them active in the service center, established an unofficial "Citizens Police Review Board" to investigate charges of police brutality.

In addition, two day-care centers were established, tutoring, sports, tool workshops, and mothers' clubs were organized, and assistance was given each week to hundreds of persons in obtaining jobs, getting registered as voters, completing income tax forms, and receiving information and referral services regarding medical, dental, welfare, family, housing, educational, and employment problems.

Critics of the EOC

Part of the price for some of this social action was continuing criticism from various conservative elements in the community. Former EOC representatives of the Chamber of Commerce and Taxpayers' Association continued to attack the EOC before service clubs and other public meetings. Charges of a "left-wing revolution" within the EOC were made by a Congressman who asked for a federal investigation of possible subversive elements in the EOC. A three-part newspaper series appeared, in which the "radical" backgrounds and connections of various area board members were delineated.[44]

During the summer of 1966, EOC Commissioner Fernandez addressed the Inter-City Council proposing changes in EOC operations that would severely limit the EOC. His recommendations were later endorsed by representatives of 13 of the county's 16 cities. In his address, Fernandez described the

> revolution which has caused seizure of the local EOC . . . by Mexican-Americans . . . by which they could establish their own power structures within our community in order to successfully combat the existing order and the existing establishment . . . A new power structure was created in 1966 from the de facto leaders of the Mexican-American minority. Inevitably the program suffered.[45]

[44] San Jose *Mercury,* March 7 and 8, 1966.
[45] Fernandez, speech to Inter-City Council, July 7, 1966.

The unity achieved by these "de facto" leaders of the Mexican-American minority was somewhat short-lived. Brought together for the first time by their opposition to Potts, their solid front gradually broke up after the EOC was reorganized. There was also little evidence of their political influence; the incumbent Democratic candidate for the State Assembly, whom they backed, lost to a conservative Republican in a district heavily Mexican-American and with a 65 per cent Democratic registration. In addition, a new threat to their position arose as younger, more militant men, some of whom were employed in the Area Service Centers, began to question privately and even on occasion to challenge publicly the leadership claim of these spokesmen for the Mexican-American community. There were differences in both age and ideology between these two groups. The "young Turks" were not only more aggressive in seeking to organize a power base for themselves among unaffiliated Mexican-Americans (it was estimated that fewer than three hundred Mexican-Americans belonged to all of the signatory organizations and other voluntary associations), but they were also more willing to collaborate with Negro activists. Although the pre-EOC Mexican-American power structure was not substantially altered, its position became somewhat less secure and its legitimacy was no longer uncontested.

A five-member "blue ribbon" citizens' committee was appointed by the Board of Supervisors in May, 1966, to evaluate the EOC. After about five months of hearings it submitted both a majority and a minority report. The latter was issued by one of the two attorney members on the committee who disagreed with the majority that had criticized the reconstituted EOC because of its "control" by the poor on the basis of the coalition between the six representatives of minority organizations and the nine area service representatives. Because the poor are inexperienced in policy making and budgeting, the majority report stated, "many sessions of the Commission have been examples of bungling, contradiction and lack of understanding of programs." On the grounds that while the EOC majority represented the poor, 85 per cent of the residents of the county were not poor, it was recommended that the Commission "should be restructured to adequately represent the community whose tax dollars are being spent and who are the beneficiaries of the funds expended." [46]

Although the EOC was criticized for busying itself with administration and leaving policy making to the staff, the supervisor's committee claimed that the greatest source of difficulty was OEO and its deadlines for reconstituting the EOC. The committee's hearings were enlivened by a series of "documented abuses" of OEO policy and charges of conflict of interest against EOC staff members who belonged to Mexican-American

[46] Palo Alto *Times*, December 22, 1966, p. 9.

organizations. Buskirk issued statements defending its staff, and some of the accusers were charged with libel by one of the maligned employees. The report seemed to have had little effect on the work of the EOC, which had been quietly proceeding with the review of its program and policies in the face of Congressional reductions in OEO funding for 1967.

Organizing the Poor—Again!

In May of 1967, at the initiative of Dr. Skillicorn, who was concluding almost three years of service as its chairman, the EOC made an about-face on its policy regarding participation of the poor. In his farewell message, Skillicorn concluded that the EOC was incapable of providing adequate social services to the poor, nor would its budget and structure permit meaningful job development programs. These orthodox and traditional methods for attacking poverty rightfully belonged to the established community agencies, who had the resources for a long-range effort, and they should be stimulated to undertake this. The EOC, on the other hand, should eschew conventional service programs and become a demonstration endeavor, seeking to "recruit, train and support community organizers of the poor, and to assist them in seeking their goals once they *are* organized." [47] A second objective was to "establish a county-wide voter registration of the poor." Earlier in the spring, Dr. Skillicorn met with the nine chairmen of the Area Service Centers, who soundly rejected these concepts. Undaunted, he went ahead and presented them to the EOC, where they were adopted by an 11 to 4 vote after an emotion-charged meeting. After offering a perceptive critique of the failure of the EOC to organize the poor, he pointed to the "exciting and instructive feature to the joining of disadvantaged people for the purpose of competing and bargaining in the arena of community action and . . . development," and added that the affluent segments of Santa Clara County ought to be eager to support such an experiment. He cautioned against panicking at the mere mention of organizing economically disadvantaged groups and stated:

> I really don't think we can afford to neglect this much longer. There is a growing sense of restlessness all about us. The possibility of a militant explosion is not just a delusion; I think the fuse is already burning.[48]

[47] S. A. Skillicorn, "Sharing in the Action," EOC President's Report—1967, May 18, 1967, p. 4. See account of this speech in the San Jose *Mercury*, May 19, 1967, pp. 1 and 2.

[48] *Ibid.*, p. 3.

This was indeed a remarkable change in philosophy, particularly because it was originated independently by one of the most widely respected, influential men in the community, one who could conclude:

> The real challenge facing this Commission is not so much a matter of bringing the poor into *our* arrangements as it is a necessity for changing the arrangements.[49]

In considering how to implement this policy, the EOC had to face the same dilemmas that had confronted San Francisco and Oakland: who should organize the poor and how? Should a new, independent, countywide delegate agency be formed for this purpose, or should the task be undertaken by each Area Service Center? In either case, the EOC would be required to reallocate drastically its diminishing "versatile" funds from OEO and overcome the vested institutional interests in current programs that had developed during the preceding two years.

Thus, the Santa Clara EOC had come full circle: from its original policy of extending social services to a new commitment to organize the poor, a strategy that was initially rejected and that served to spur and justify its eventual reorganization, decentralization, and transfer of decision-making power. These changes also coincided in June, 1967 with the departure of its executive director, Buskirk, who resigned because of a health problem, and the election of Albert Pinon to the chairmanship as the EOC moved into this new phase.

Summary

In Santa Clara County the participation of the poor originally had a lower priority than the rapid organization of ASC boards and the development of program within the framework of a strong centralized Community Action Agency. The professional commitments and style of the executive director soon clashed with two sets of demands: greater influence for the Mexican-Americans and more autonomy for ASCs. The pressures generated by the Mexican-Americans, who subsequently invoked the slogan of maximum feasible participation, together with those of OEO, which insisted on speedy compliance with new directives on representation of the poor, brought about the reorganization of the EOC. Mounting Mexican-American enmity against the executive director, together with a staff revolt, resulted in a successful campaign to oust him as newly elected area representatives took their places on a reconstituted and enlarged EOC.

[49] *Ibid.*, p. 5.

Elected by a small number of low-income residents, the area commissioners, few of whom were themselves poor, together with the representatives of labor, religion, and other minority organizations, became the new majority on the EOC.

A new executive was employed whose philosophy and practice contrasted sharply with those of his predecessor. He implemented a process of decentralization. Tension between the EOC and the areas diminished somewhat, but limited funds, budget cuts, and the prolonged process of structural reorganization involving innumerable elections greatly restricted the scope of program development. The elected representatives of the poor constituted at least half of all members of area service boards but had little accountability, and their participation was significant in only several areas. Together with the EOC, some of the areas engaged in mild forms of social action and were successful in influencing some major policies in public housing.

Under continued criticism and attack by the more conservative elements in the community, the EOC became another center of power in Santa Clara largely representative of the interests of Mexican-Americans and some of the poor. Toward the end of its third year, largely at the instigation of its chairman, the EOC revised its policy and committed itself to giving community organization of the poor first priority.

4

COMMUNITY CASE STUDY OF THE OAKLAND ECONOMIC DEVELOPMENT COUNCIL

There is a certain movement in Oakland to contain the social revolution. But where it can't be contained, grudging concessions are made.[1]

Gray Area Origins

An "all-American city" in 1954, Oakland had another claim to fame through its designation by the Ford Foundation in December, 1961 for the first "gray areas" grant, amounting to $2 million. This grant launched the Oakland Interagency Project (OIP), out of which the Community Action Program evolved. Located in the office of the city manager, Wayne E. Thompson, the OIP's professional staff of three was responsible for planning, coordinating, and evaluating an extensive series of projects in the Castlemont area of East Oakland. These projects involved the collaboration of the schools and the employment, public health, recreation, and probation departments, along with several voluntary agencies, over a period of three years.[2]

Because of this experience, early in June, 1964, Mayor John C. Houlihan and City Manager Thompson assigned the OIP staff to the task of developing a CAP under city auspices even before the legislation had been approved by Congress. Oakland had evidenced for several years a

[1] John D. George, chairman, Ad Hoc Committee for Quality Education, as quoted in interview, *San Francisco Examiner,* August 25, 1966, p. 6.

[2] For the history of the Oakland Interagency Project and its significance see Jack Regal, *Oakland's Partnership for Change,* Oakland Department of Human Resources, 1967, and Peter Marris and Martin Rein, *Dilemmas of Social Reform: Poverty and Community Action in the United States* (New York: Atherton Press, 1967), pp. 18, 56-58, 157-58.

readiness to utilize federal funds to help it cope with the social and economic problems stemming from the deterioration of its central city area, and its officials were quick to perceive the possibility of bringing in additional federal funds if they built on the base established by the OIP. In addition, there were pressures from the Ford Foundation, as well as from OEO, for Oakland to move ahead as quickly as possible so it could be among the first to receive an antipoverty grant.

The staff initiated a series of discussions among the OIP's executive, technical and citizens advisory committees, resulting in an agreement to develop projects as soon as possible that would be suitable for funding under the Economic Opportunity Act of 1964. During the summer of 1964, numerous meetings were arranged by the OIP executive director, Dr. Norvel Smith, and his program director, Edward P. Dutton, with the leaders of six Negro and Mexican-American organizations wherein these official spokesmen served largely as a sounding board for program ideas and priorities.[3] A mayor's *ad hoc* committee consisting of 15 influential citizens and minority representatives also met twice for informational purposes, while the OIP staff devoted most of its time in stimulating the preparation of project proposals by the school and public health departments.

As a result of this head start, a preliminary package of proposals was submitted to Washington by October 10 and formed the basis of the principal changes and appointments that were made during the next two months. In November and December a series of intraorganizational transformations took place in which the 15-member citizens advisory committee of the OIP was expanded, mainly by the addition of minority representatives appointed by the Mayor, to become the 29-member Oakland Economic Development Council (OEDC). The OIP executive committee was augmented by some voluntary agency executives and became a technical advisory committee to the OEDC, while the OIP staff was transferred to a newly established Department of Human Resources (DHR) in the city government. In this way, quietly and without con-

[3] The several Mexican-American organizational leaders later repudiated the assumption that these consultations constituted endorsement of the proposed program. In January, 1965, just after the OEDC was appointed, they sent a telegram to OEO claiming that they had not been involved sufficiently. They also demanded that funds be stopped because of the disproportionate amount of funds going to the Oakland schools, which had for many years been regarded by Mexican-Americans as unresponsive to the special needs of Spanish-speaking children. On the history of the prior involvement of the Mexican-American community in planning, see OIP memo on this subject from Norvel Smith, Coordinator, to City Manager Wayne E. Thompson dated January 13, 1965. The memo also notes that the Spanish-surnamed community constitutes 7 per cent of the total population of Oakland, with less than half residing in the target areas.

troversy, the city of Oakland created a Community Action Program and thus retained control over this new organization.

Twenty-five members of the OEDC were appointed by Mayor Houlihan for two-year terms on December 3, 1964. These included a rather broad cross-section of the community, consisting of representatives from labor, management, minority groups, and civil rights and religious organizations, most of whom were professionals and experienced participants in community affairs. The Mayor served as chairman pro tem for the first two months, after which he was succeeded by Judge Lionel Wilson of the Alameda County Superior Court, a highly respected Negro civic leader. Norman Nicholson, a vice-president of Kaiser Industries, was elected as vice-chairman, and the director of the Department of Human Resources, Dr. Norvel Smith, was named as secretary.

The OEDC was initially convened by Mayor Houlihan on December 23, 1964. In the course of this first meeting, questions were raised about the authority of the city council over the program and budgeting decisions of the OEDC, since apparently the city had the right to approve the release of funds for any project, thus retaining veto power. This matter was not clarified at that time and considerable ambiguity persisted regarding the respective prerogatives of each body. Two decisive actions were taken, however, that set the tone of developments for the next 18 months. The first package of 14 program proposals, amounting to $810,181, was approved with only the NAACP president dissenting. Over 75 per cent of the funds were to be allocated to the Oakland schools for various compensatory and remedial educational programs, but also included were provisions for the staffing of the first two of four neighborhood service centers with legal, health, family counseling, and homemaker services. In connection with these service centers, City Manager Thompson recommended the establishment as soon as possible of "four target area liaison committees to provide grass roots liaison with the client population to be served."[4] The original OIP proposals in 1964 had called for the establishment of four target areas where there was the greatest concentration of unemployment and low-income residents: in the East, West, North Oakland, and Fruitvale districts. These areas included some 150,000 people, of whom approximately 80,000 were considered to be poor, although one-third of the low-income persons lived outside of these target areas. Residing in this 10-mile strip, running through the heart of Oakland, were over 75 per cent of the total Negro population and 60 per cent of the Spanish-surnamed groups. Only Fruit-

[4] OEDC minutes, December 24, 1964. Note the ambiguous reference to the "liaison" function.

vale had more than half of its population classified as white, but the unemployment rate in all four areas was approximately three times the city's average.[5]

Despite the designation of these areas, few efforts were made to secure the involvement of representatives from them during the summer and fall of 1964, because of the determination of the OIP professional staff and the city manager to submit a set of proposals at the earliest possible date to meet OEO deadlines. Thus, there was considerable truth to the allegation made later that the decision to organize the OEDC was made without direct involvement of target area or low-income groups themselves. Evidently it was assumed that the consultations with the officers of minority organizations and other ethnic "leaders" provided sufficient sanction. In these early days of the antipoverty program, there were no OEO guidelines regarding what was meant by "maximum feasible participation," and it was not until the end of March, 1965, that the OEO regional office stipulated that one person from each target area should be on the policy-making body of the CAP. Accordingly, it was up to each community to interpret what was feasible, and obviously there were widely differing opinions among the OEDC members and subsequently in the target areas regarding the role of the groups to be served.

Toward Resident Participation

Four months elapsed before the OEDC adopted a policy on resident participation (on April 7, 1965), largely in response to some of the unanticipated consequences of staff efforts to convene the initial meetings in the neighborhood. While there was general recognition of the necessity for some kind of advisory group of from 10 to 25 members in each target area with whom the OEDC might consult, there was much less agreement and clarity on permitting representatives from these committees to serve as voting members of the OEDC, even though there were

[5] "Profile of Target Areas For Economic Opportunity Program," Oakland Interagency Project, October 9, 1964. Additional data on the socioeconomic characteristics of the target areas can be found in Regal, *Oakland's Partnership for Change*, chapters 2 and 8; also, *Alameda County Population 1965*, Human Population Laboratory, Series A, Number 7 (California Department of Public Health, April, 1966), pp. 28-29. A later report of the Department of Human Resources, Research Division, "Preliminary Estimate of the Distribution of the Poverty Population of Oakland from Data Provided by the 701 Survey," May 11, 1967, showed an approximately equal number of whites and nonwhites living in poverty in Oakland, with about one-third residing outside the target areas.

still 15 vacancies on the Council. Yet, nowhere in the brief two-page statement of OEDC purposes and responsibilities adopted by the city council by resolution on February 9, 1965, was there any mention of the existence, let alone purpose, function, or proposed organization, of advisory committees in the neighborhoods. When the subject of resident participation was raised at the February and March meetings of the OEDC, several of the middle-class Negro representatives commented that the OEDC already contained representatives of organizations with largely low-income constituencies such as the churches and the NAACP; hence, there was no need to delay approving programs until target area committees were established. Few were responsive to the somewhat premature request in February from a Fruitvale meeting that at least 50 per cent of the OEDC membership should consist of target area residents. Although some members of the professional staff disagreed, Dr. Smith's view, which was shared by his chairman, Judge Wilson, and most of the OEDC members, was that the new target area committees should only provide advice regarding program implementation and feedback regarding impact, unmet needs, and priorities.[6]

Meanwhile, despite the absence of specific agreement on the role of the target area committees and lack of criteria on their organization, structure, and composition, DHR staff members were authorized to convene meetings in the four neighborhoods. Presumably these matters would be decided by the citizens in attendance. In these initial and generally unplanned efforts to organize some sort of town meeting that would elect representatives to serve on a Target Area Advisory Committee (TAAC), the DHR professional staff and OEDC members who presided underestimated the degree of opposition to a city-sponsored antipoverty program. Lacking agreement among themselves as to how many, if any, voting members of the OEDC would come from the target areas, criteria for election, and qualifications of those who would comprise the TAAC, the staff found themselves at a serious disadvantage when the first two meetings in West Oakland in February were "packed" by members of the East Oakland Parish, together with numerous other social action groups that sought to prevent the organization of a neighborhood link with the OEDC. Instead, these activists, consisting largely of young clergymen, students and other militant persons, tried to mobilize a city-

[6] Memo to OEDC from Dr. Norvel Smith, Director, Department of Human Resources, "Staff Recommendations for March 6 Workshop" (March 1, 1965), p. 2. Subsequently, Dr. Smith declared: ". . . there is no mandate in the law that there be advisory committees. There is only the mandate that among other groups to be included in this so-called coalition of the community were representatives of the poor, if not the poor themselves." Unabridged minutes of the Community Forum on Representation, Westlake Junior High School, Oakland, November 30, 1965, p. 2.

wide citizens' association on an antiestablishment platform, but the meetings ended in confusion.[7]

As a result of these experiences and the increasing pressures for direct representation from the target areas, Judge Wilson appointed an OEDC subcommittee on target area relationships headed by Father Clarence Howard, a Negro priest whose parish was in West Oakland and whose report on April 7 served as the basic OEDC policy on resident participation for over a year. The report, which was unanimously adopted, stipulated that "the advisory committee should be selected through a democratic process" with residence in the area as the only requirement for voting.[8] The total number of members was to be determined by each TAAC, which was expected to be "truly representative of the indigenous poor of that particular area." The committee report added that it thought that the "majority of the members of each advisory committee should be persons who qualified for the benefits of the Economic Opportunity Act," although a subsequent summary of the criteria changed this to read "at least 25 to 50 per cent direct beneficiaries." Furthermore, it suggested as an "optional guideline" that membership be ethnically balanced in keeping with the character of the target area and that three or more positions be kept open for the unorganized poor who might not be reached in the early stages of the program. The staff for each TAAC was to be a CAP field service coordinator in charge of the service center and each committee was encouraged to make use of "local resources such as social workers, public health nurses, school children (*sic*) to contact the indigenous poor so that a greater number of those who qualify for the benefits of the Economic Opportunity Act will be present at the target area meetings." Also approved was the subcommittee's recommendation that the TAAC serve as the screening and certifying body whereby two representatives from each target area would be appointed only when the committee was satisfied that these individuals were truly representative of the poor in that area. Again, a later version stated that at least one of the two nominees had to qualify as a direct

[7] Earlier, the East Oakland Parish, in addition to some Mexican-American groups, had protested to OEO regarding the manner in which the OEDC had been organized and its subsequent composition. Shortly afterwards the EOP tried to submit its own program proposal to OEO directly, but was told to work within the OEDC. In contrast to the situation in San Francisco, there was no attempt to form a coalition; instead, some of the more militant young clergymen such as the Rev. Brad Bryant, the Rev. Les Larson and the Rev. Robert Olmstead joined the TAAC and provided much of the leadership in the struggle to obtain greater representation for the target areas on the OEDC.

[8] "Report of the Committee Appointed to Study the Problem of Forming Target Area Advisory Committees and Their Representation on the OEDC," April 7, 1965. All subsequent quotations in the paragraph are from this report.

beneficiary of the antipoverty program. In spite of these stipulations, the membership committee consistently endorsed all representatives selected by the TAAC even though increasing doubts were expressed that the committees reflected the ethnic distribution found in their target areas. For example, no Mexican-American delegates were elected from Fruitvale for almost a year, and no white delegates from East Oakland for several months.

While this report represented the first attempt to impose some order and direction on the development of resident participation, it failed to define many of its key terms, omitted any mention of the function of the TAAC, and their relationship to the OEDC, authority, and scope of responsibility as well as the duties of their delegates. In addition, the subcommittee underestimated the measures required to implement any program aimed at securing representation from all sections of the target area to the extent that perhaps half would be low-income persons.

Nevertheless, adoption of the report signified a recognition that a new constituency—the TAACs—would have to be taken into account in all future OEDC actions. Awareness of this modification in its policy-making pattern was demonstrated on April 7, 1965, when the OEDC was being pressured by staff to meet one of the innumerable, successive OEO deadlines, this time to submit the first summer Head Start Program. It was finally agreed to approve the proposal even though it had not been considered in the target areas, with the understanding that it might be reviewed if objections arose in the neighborhoods.

Initial Committee Character and Role

The first representatives of West and East Oakland were seated on the OEDC on April 21, 1965, and during the next three months a series of organizational meetings and elections took place in four neighborhoods as the TAACs developed their bylaws and emerged as part of the OEDC structure. In convening the first meetings, DHR staff had relied heavily on their contacts with existing organizations in the target areas and somewhat less on the thousands of leaflets that were distributed. Thus, many of the persons who attended had some affiliation with a neighborhood, ethnic, or religious association but rarely with the civil rights movement. Because few requirements were stipulated and most of the TAACs had some difficulty in filling 25 to 30 places, it was relatively easy to get "elected" as a member of the TAAC at one of their weekly meetings. Only in Fruitvale, with its multiethnic character, was there an attempt to consider other than geographical representation in the makeup of the TAAC. Two places each on the Fruitvale committee were designated for persons representing six types of organization: Negro, Mexican-American, American Indian, Protestant, Catholic, and PTA. In addition, there were representatives from six elementary school areas and three members at large. In contrast to the TAACs in West, North, and East Oakland, which were almost exclusively Negro, the first Fruitvale committee consisted of 10 Negroes (5 men and 5 women); 9 Mexican-Americans (5 men and 4 women); 3 whites (2 men and 1 woman); 2 Chinese women and 1 American Indian man. While most of the Fruitvale members had been nominated by persons in attendance as representing various ethnic and institutional blocs, they were not selected by these interest groups, nor did they report back to them. Thus, they were not accountable to any particular constituency and tended to represent themselves. As a result, there was relatively little feedback between the TAAC and the Fruitvale area.

Somewhat the same conditions and processes of self-selection were at work in the other target areas, where an open door policy on membership resulted in the domination of the TAAC by predominantly working class or lower middle-class persons and relatively little involvement of low-income individuals. The latter category rarely comprised more than one-third of the membership, and these people were generally referred to as "they." The TAACs were aware of this anomaly, although few made any concerted effort to secure more low-income members or a more balanced ethnic representation. Increasingly, they regarded themselves as representative of the target area and because of their election as members of the TAAC, qualified to serve as spokesmen for the poor.

These characteristics were also found in the leadership of the TAACs, all of whom were also selected as representatives to the OEDC. In two of the areas, Fruitvale and North Oakland, young white Protestant ministers considerably more militant than their memberships were elected as chairmen. West Oakland, which elected a long-time resident of the area as chairman after initially selecting a twenty-one-year-old white student, also elected the Reverend Les Larson of the West Oakland Christian Parish as secretary, and he served as a dominant influence. In East Oakland the chairman was a Negro, but questions regarding his residence and eligibility were continually raised.

The expectations of those who were elected to membership on the TAAC were quite varied, but most seemed to have joined because they thought their participation would enable them to obtain a better job or some form of material assistance. In looking back on the first four months, one advisory committee member expressed the rather widely held belief that

> . . . most of them were misled and are still a bit misled now. Initially, they were told they would receive such services as medical care, housing assistance, welfare, food and clothing assistance, but this was not so. Even now, people still feel that there is something related to this they can get by being on the committee. Some members thought they would get paid by serving on the committee in the beginning.[9]

Still other members sought to participate as citizens in the antipoverty program and hoped to be able to utilize the structure of the advisory committee to attack the more basic economic, political, and social problems in Oakland. Most of them, however, expected to play a much larger and important role than the OEDC had evidently envisioned.

It became obvious during the summer of 1965, as the TAACs sent their representatives to the OEDC, that there were conflicting interpretations of their functions and authority. Although some of the TAAC members were antagonistic toward the OEDC and the DHR because of the program decisions made prior to the organization of the target areas, the advisory committees did not start out viewing themselves as opposed to OEDC policy. They saw themselves as an integral part of the structure but, with the possible exception of East Oakland, with a much broader function than merely "advising" the OEDC and providing them with feedback information. Some advisory committees claimed they were told that the TAAC bylaws were to be their sole concern. These bylaws all contained broad, ambiguously worded statements of purposes that permitted a wide range of meanings. In the absence of more specific clarification of their functions, the TAAC leadership increasingly referred to their role in terms of much greater authority and responsibility than understood by the OEDC and certainly by its executive leadership. Relatively little attention was given to these matters by the OEDC in its monthly meetings, which were primarily concerned with ratifying a succession of new program proposals to OEO as well as consideration of the extension and expansion of the original program components, a summer youth employment program, and a new request to the Ford Foundation for over a million dollars in development funds, half of which were to be allocated to indigenous self-help groups in the target areas.[10]

Increasingly, however, dissatisfaction developed among some of the TAAC representatives to the OEDC about the way in which meetings

[9] Interview with a member of the Fruitvale Advisory Committee, July 30, 1965. Unless otherwise indicated, data are derived from interviews with participants, observation of meetings and documents in the OEDC files.

[10] See minutes of OEDC, May 5, May 19, June 9, and June 30, 1965. The details of the Ford Foundation grant are summarized in a memo of June 25 from Norvel Smith, Director, Department of Human Resources to OEDC, "New Ford Foundation Grant."

were conducted. This was expressed by one representative, who concluded after attending his first meeting:

> We are among pros who vote their way and they don't give the people an opportunity to express themselves. They don't consider the little people there very important. The people on the Mayor's committee are going to dog the whole show.[11]

Another complained:

> They often go against our recommendations and really don't know what our needs are since they judge everything according to their own experience.[12]

TAAC members also objected to the fact that the OEDC meetings took place at 8:00 A.M. at the city hall with a pre-planned agenda about which relevant information rarely was received before a day or two prior to meetings. They felt that the meetings were conducted in a rigid, parliamentary, and often arbitrary manner by Judge Wilson, who occasionally treated members as if they were in his court. It did not take the TAAC members long to realize that most of the major decisions took place beforehand in the executive committee, on which they had no representation. Most of the TAAC representatives believed that they should have a greater role in policy-making functions and that their late admission into OEDC had cheated them of direct participation in the initial policy making, when 14 projects were approved for the first year. As another representative put it,

> City Hall can't operate unless there are advisory committees in the areas, so we don't want to be pawns. We want to know what powers we have.[13]

As a result, a first attempt was initiated, largely by the Fruitvale representatives, to unite the four advisory committees around the issue of securing greater representation and a voice in the OEDC and in its executive committee. During July, it was agreed to request that a representative from each TAAC be added to the executive committee and that the remaining eight vacancies on the OEDC be filled by adding two more persons from each of the TAAC lists. Evidently, word of this strategy reached the DHR staff, and instead of the battle that the target representatives had expected, they were surprised to find Dr. Smith proposing

[11] Reported at the Fruitvale Advisory Committee on July 1, 1965.
[12] Chairman of West Oakland Advisory Committee in interview, August 12, 1965.
[13] Interview with representative of Fruitvale Advisory Committee to OEDC.

that the executive committee be enlarged from 7 to 11 members by adding one from each of the advisory committees.[14]

Although both Judge Wilson and Dr. Smith were initially opposed to the idea on the grounds that the TAACs were being influenced by "outsiders," this concession by the OEDC may have been regarded as a means of expediting its deliberations, since the target area representatives were becoming increasingly resistant to approving various measures previously recommended by the executive committee. Perhaps it was thought that if these people were included in the executive committee, they might prove more cooperative. In any case, at its September meeting, the OEDC granted the target areas the additional representation without dispute, and the unity among the advisory committees soon faded.

The Struggle for Increased Authority and Representation

Two other issues regarding the role of the advisory committees developed shortly after they were organized: their authority over the multiservice center and their right to sponsor programs. Plans for the service centers had been approved by the OEDC earlier in the year, and although the target areas were not involved in this basic decision, the TAACs were organized before the final plans were implemented, and all of them had a share in the selection of sites. They also were consulted on the employment of several indigenous aides by some of the delegate agencies operating programs in the centers. Essentially, however, the service center program was predetermined and housed staff members from such agencies as the County Health Department, Visiting Nurses Association, Family Service Agency, and Legal Aid, all under the administration of a DHR coordinator employed by the city of Oakland. The relationship of the multiservice center, its coordinator, and its delegate agencies to the advisory committees was not clear from its inception. Did the center belong to the agencies, the DHR, the OEDC, or the TAAC? The advisory committees tended to regard the service center as theirs, and some of them sought influence over its personnel and programs by assuming a "watchdog" role. This point of view was stressed by Miss Joan Sparks, a colorful former lion tamer who operated a shelter for homeless girls. She introduced a resolution at the Fruitvale advisory committee on July 15, 1965 requesting the DHR to allocate office space in the center for any advisory committee member who could receive complaints, answer questions, or both. After two months of informal negotiations, the OEDC finally approved this first broadening of TAAC functions in September.[15]

[14] OEDC minutes of August 25, 1965.
[15] OEDC minutes of September 25, 1965.

The question of the scope of TAAC authority over programs first arose over an issue in West Oakland, where almost from the beginning the committee sought to become the sponsor for two TAAC projects originally initiated by the West Oakland Christian Parish: an educational program for high school drop-outs using VISTA volunteers, and a leadership training program. Originally encouraged to proceed by DHR staff assigned to it, the West Oakland committee was later informed that it was never intended to receive funds to operate the programs, since this would interfere with its advisory role and other program functions. No such incompatibility was in the minds of the TAAC members, who perceived no conflict between advising the OEDC on needs and priorities in West Oakland, serving as the board of the service center, reviewing the programs of other agencies, and operating some programs themselves. Their hopes for receiving funds for target area projects were also raised by the OEDC decision in July that half of the Ford Foundation's development grant for self-help programs (amounting to $600,000) would be assigned to indigenous self-help groups.[16] When, however, guidelines for self-help projects, which DHR staff prepared, were finally approved in September, it appeared that the advisory committee was excluded from setting up programs. A self-help group was defined as a nonprofit corporation, whose board consisted mainly of low-income persons, which would be required to submit a proposal to each of the TAACs and then to five successive screening committees. With such guidelines, the advisory committees could not hope to qualify, and West Oakland, North Oakland, and Fruitvale charged duplicity on the part of the DHR staff. Dr. Smith defended himself by asserting that these criteria were developed without reference to them and that the TAACs could administer programs by forming a nonprofit corporation outside their own structure. Subsequently, the Corporation of the Poor was organized, drawing most of its initial leadership from West and North Oakland, but this did not settle the issue of the limits of TAAC power. A feeling of antagonism toward the DHR staff, OEDC, and city government, at first confined to the more articulate and ideological members of the advisory committee, began to be expressed more generally. As one member expressed it:

> They first came out here and said a whole lot about controlling our own destiny and all that stuff and I believed it, but it was all a bunch of lies. DHR works for City Hall.[17]

[16] Memo from Dr. Norvel Smith, Director, Department of Human Resources to OEDC, July 25, 1965, "Framework for Use of New Ford Development Funds."

[17] Interview with North Oakland advisory committee member, May, 1966.

The gains that the advisory committees made during the summer did not suffice. Rather, they grew more assertive and increasingly believed that their concessions had been forced from an unwilling administration and that they had much further to go before they would have the powers commensurate with their roles as "representatives of the poor." In West Oakland, the inability of the TAAC to obtain $50 for mailing expenses was referred to frequently as evidence of the OEDC's refusal to cooperate. More and more members were speaking about resigning, expressing the view that since they did little, it would make no difference. The orientation of the program was questioned: Did it reflect the needs and wants of the people or did it serve the purposes of city hall? Members believed that the money was mismanaged because too much of it went to professionals and not to those who were supposed to benefit. This point was made by many of the TAAC members, who noted that the delegate agencies and the DHR consistently appointed staff members who were already working in other bureaucratic institutions, rather than the poor, who presumably knew best what needed to be done.

Much of this resentment was evident in the September 22, 1965 OEDC meeting, perhaps one of the most significant to take place. It was one of four, which were to be held in the evenings in a public school auditorium and resulted from criticisms that the OEDC meetings had served to accommodate businessmen who wanted to get to their offices by 9:00 A.M. As a compromise with the demand that the OEDC should "meet in front of the people," members agreed to meet in the evening once a year in each of the areas, beginning with West Oakland. At this meeting, Miss Sparks of the Fruitvale advisory committee launched what was to be the beginning of a bitter struggle by demanding that half of the OEDC be composed of elected representatives from the advisory committees. The matter was quickly referred to the newly constituted executive committee, on which each target area was finally to have a representative. The mood of the meeting was described in the press the next day as follows:

> The committee's recommendations last night were to stem a rising tide of discontent among target area residents who complained that they lacked a voice in program planning and in the expenditure of poverty funds. . . .
>
> Ralph Williams, Chairman of the West Oakland Advisory Committee, said the downtown poverty program thus far implemented in West Oakland has had only the effect of filling West Oakland with professionals and non-West Oaklanders. He said the program so far has failed to improve conditions in the area and the people are not being helped by it. Williams said the committee had for the past six months tried hard to work with the poverty program but the program has not worked with the people . . . The meeting was

> marked by a growing breach of distrust between poverty area dwellers and the professionals who guide anti-poverty projects.[18]

The following month was filled with increasing hostility on the part of some advisory committee members toward the OEDC. Each group became more convinced of its position and was angered by the intransigence of the other. In its October newsletter, the OEDC mentioned the demand for increased representation and then stated what it regarded as the major objection:

> However, fourteen of the 36 members of the OEDC already live in the poverty target areas. The four additional members will mean that 18 of the 40 will be poverty area residents.[19]

Clearly, the OEDC computed representation in a way quite different from the way the TAAC did. The former, by claiming that residence in the target area sufficed to make a member a representative of that area, whether or not he had been elected and regardless of his income, appeared to be trying to obtain double mileage out of some of the Negro members. That is, the mayoral appointees were construed to represent the area in which they lived *and* the poor as well.

OEDC leadership remained unresponsive to the demands of the advisory committees for increased representation and attacked the legitimacy of their representatives on the grounds that several were white and middle class, and in some cases, nonresidents of the target area. The advisory committees, on their part, began to view their complaints as a part of a whole. One specific incident helped to escalate this dispute.

In September the Legal Aid Society served notice that one of its attorneys assigned to the West Oakland service center was to be fired. Because she had been particularly zealous in her efforts to protect the legal rights of the poor, the West Oakland advisory committee came to her defense and insisted that she be allowed to continue to work in their service center. By taking this position, West Oakland became involved in a dispute with a delegate agency over who should have the final decision about the personnel in the service center. OEDC leaders were not happy with the involvement of the advisory committee, but at the same time recognized that a serious problem existed within the operation of the Legal Services program. Fruitvale and North Oakland joined West Oakland and were successful in having the OEDC hold up the funds

[18] *Oakland Tribune,* September 26, 1965.

[19] *OEDC Reporter,* Vol. 1, No. 1 (October, 1965), 1. For further elaboration of the OEDC position, see *OEDC Reporter,* Vol. 1, No. 2 (November, 1965), pp. 1, 4.

to the Legal Aid Society the next month. Subsequently the executive of the agency backed down, claiming that an error had been made.

The three advisory committees, excluding East Oakland, then began to demand complete autonomy within the target areas, not only asking control over the service center, but also talking more openly about vetoing any program that they did not approve, as well as having the power to initiate programs. At the October 30 OEDC workshop, which reviewed 14 program proposals, target area representatives participated for the first time, but their recommendations were submitted along with those of DHR staff, the Technical Advisory Committee, and the Council of Social Planning.

Growing Antagonism

By the time of the November 24 meeting of the OEDC, the tension and antagonism had reached a high point. Because of the persistence and ever growing demands of the advisory committees, it was decided to hold a special meeting of the OEDC on November 30. All advisory committee members would be invited, and the meeting would be devoted solely to the question of their role in the antipoverty program. This decision was influenced by a memorandum presented by Dr. Smith on November 9 concerning OEDC representation from the four target areas; the memo proposed a definition of "low income" which would restrict the use of the term, making it apply only to a family of four with an income of less than $4,000 a year and $500 per additional dependent, up to $7,000 annual income. Within this framework, based on OEO guidelines, he recommended that the TAACs should move toward 50 per cent of their membership comprised of such low-income persons. In addition, it was suggested again that half of the target area representatives on the OEDC should come from this low-income category. At the same meeting, the OEDC also approved the policy of reimbursement of TAAC members for expenses incurred during their participation. Because Dr. Smith claimed that more information regarding members' incomes was needed to request reimbursement from OEO, Judge Wilson ordered an income survey of all advisory committee members.

These actions in turn were a response to an eight-point program that the advisory committees had agreed upon several weeks before, which embodied their aims. These points were:

1. 50 per cent elected representation from the Action Committees [TAACs] both on the OEDC and its executive committees
2. Review of and approval of OEDC programs

3. Review and approval of each request of funds for services
4. Prior approval by Action Committees of all reports to be forwarded to OEO
5. Power to screen and approve programs with staff already in effect
6. Staff to be employed only on the advice and consent of the Action Committee
7. Periodic review of the programs and submission of the biannual public report
8. Power to screen and approve staff of the DHR, all of whom would be responsible to the neighborhood Action Committees

Also included was a request that the qualifications for all staff jobs should not be fixed to exclude the possibility of hiring people without formal education, professional training, or experience.

Further evidence of the more militant stand of the advisory committees was that they began to call themselves "action committees" for the first time during November. Shortly afterwards, all committees but East Oakland's changed their names in accordance with this usage.

In part, the stimulus to use the name "action committees" and to press the demands for 50 per cent elected delegates from the target areas came from the two representatives of Fruitvale, who attended a regional meeting called by the OEO in San Francisco on November 6. There they were confronted with their counterparts in the Bay Area, all of whom seemed to have more power than they. A telegram was sent by the Fruitvale area committee to Judge Wilson on November 7, referring to the philosophy of the OEO regional staff and, noting its agreement with this philosophy, requesting that its name be changed to Neighborhood Action Committee, which it called "a truer reflection of our intentions."

In the call to the November 30 meeting and afterwards, the Fruitvale committee announcement stated, "We represent the poor! *We are the poor!* Who knows better than we the needs of our community?"

When this eight-point statement was read at the November 30 Forum it was effectively put aside by Judge Wilson, who stated that it was a "fine start" and suggested that each advisory committee develop some "definite recommendations, and that each area decide on a definition of the poor or poverty" to be brought to another meeting. When the delegates who had read these demands protested that they had been approved by all four TAACs, the chairman replied, "We don't have evidence to that effect." Judge Wilson then closed the meeting with a statement reiterating his position that no alteration was needed in the makeup of the OEDC and defending his right to speak on behalf of the poor because of his own impoverished youth in West Oakland during the Great Depression. Since the November 30 meeting was used strictly as a forum and a means of clarifying positions, it turned out to be primarily an airing of grievances.[20]

By December, it was clear that the attitude of OEDC and the target areas toward each other was increasingly antagonistic. The TAAC spokesmen, as a result of their continual frustration and confusion regarding their real functions, came to a point where they demanded almost full control of the programs for their respective areas. They also viewed the OEDC as an arm of city hall and felt that somehow the Council was attempting to take away from them what OEO wanted them to have. In this light, the advisory committees were a "hoax"; they had no real power and were just "window dressing" exploited by the OEDC as a means of justifying their claim for funds from the OEO and the Ford Foundation. Much of the hostility toward OEDC and DHR was based on the experience of TAAC members with the field service coordinators and the executive director. In general, TAAC members did not trust these professionals, who were regarded as evasive, reluctant to provide information, and having interests that were viewed as completely opposed to those of the poor. On the other hand, DHR staff members, some of whom had originally been quite sympathetic in support of the advisory committees, in turn became more skeptical about members' motives, representativeness, and capabilities. Some staff members expressed cynicism about the professed interest of TAAC members in serving the poor, believing that many of them only joined to get jobs or funds for a project in which they were interested.

These beliefs were similar to those held by Judge Wilson and Dr. Smith, who stressed the tangible gains made by the advisory committees in exerting influence within the community coalition represented by OEDC. They reminded the advisory committees that they had three representatives each and by themselves comprised approximately a third of the OEDC. When other minority representatives, some of whom lived in the target areas, were included, they constituted the majority. TAAC members had been appointed to the OEDC's committees on program review and on education and were consulted on the selection of multiservice center sites and indigenous personnel, as well as on the summer youth program. In addition, they had been asked to review all new program proposals and submit their recommendations.

20 Unabridged minutes of the Community Forum on Representation, November 30, 1965, Westlake Junior High School, Oakland, 12 pp. (mimeographed). This transcription of a tape recording of the proceedings, incorrectly dated November 17, 1965, was prepared by the Program Division, Department of Human Resources, and provides an unusual insight into the attitudes of the members of the OEDC, Department of Human Resources, Target Area Advisory Committees, and indigenous residents.

At the same time, both Judge Wilson and Dr. Smith were critical of the advisory committees, regarding them as unrepresentative of their areas, since according to the income survey, fewer than one-fourth of the members surveyed reported incomes below the poverty line. The executive leadership of the OEDC, then, saw the advisory committees as being run by a small, articulate, middle-class minority who wanted to keep themselves in power and who made little effort to reach out to the low-income groups. Dr. Smith claimed that his staff had tried to persuade the advisory committees to become more representative, but since they did not do anything on their own, OEDC would have to set down some guidelines for them. He noted that Fruitvale had not elected any Mexican-Americans to represent them; as a result there were only two persons with Spanish surnames serving on the OEDC, both originally appointed by the Mayor. This was believed to be a result of the domination of three of the advisory committees by white middle-class clergymen.

Organizational Character

In view of these allegations and counterclaims, what was the organizational character of the advisory committees in December, approximately nine months after they had been organized? On all of the committees except West Oakland's, women outnumbered men, but the latter were usually in positions of leadership. An important exception was East Oakland's committee, which was composed almost exclusively of middle-class Negro women who were active in many organizations and who held virtually closed meetings (at noon, when most working men and women could not attend). Apart from Fruitvale, which had a mixture of Mexican-Americans, Negroes, Orientals, and whites, an average of 85 per cent of the committees' members were Negro, despite the high proportion of low-income whites in the target areas. The TAAC leadership did not always reflect the character of the membership, since only West Oakland and East Oakland committees had Negro chairmen, whereas two white clergymen were elected to head the Fruitvale and North Oakland committees. The latter, however, provided skillful and democratic leadership of their committees. While all committees but East Oakland's were relatively easy to join, the TAACs had great difficulty filling their ranks, and there was considerable turnover. The proportion of low-income members varied from less than 10 per cent in East Oakland to perhaps somewhat less than half in North Oakland, and about one-fourth of the membership in West Oakland and Fruitvale. Few of the members were radicals, or civil rights activists, or had any political experience. Perhaps this accounts for the fact that it took almost a year for the advisory committees in Oakland to reach a stage of development that was attained in San Francisco at the beginning. Although most of the members, with the exception of those in North Oakland, belonged to other organizations, there was no constituency for them to report to. It seems fair to describe the advisory committees as predominantly self-selected groups, tending (particularly in the case of North and East Oakland) to live mainly within the immediate vicinity of the service center. None of the committees made any serious effort during the first year to penetrate the neighborhoods they were supposed to represent, even though they considered themselves the authentic spokesmen of the target areas and resented the efforts of any other group to interfere with their roles.

The internal decision-making systems of the four target area committees differed greatly and were much influenced by the character of the chairmen and the DHR staff persons assigned to them and to direct the service center. The ways in which staff roles were performed were crucial in shaping the attitudes of each advisory committee toward the DHR and OEDC, and these staff styles differed markedly in accordance with the individual's interpretation of the ambiguous mandate given to him by the DHR. In West Oakland there was relatively little struggle for power; a rather shifting and apathetic membership served to ratify decisions made by a small clique of officers. The leading spokesman for West Oakland was strongly anti-city hall and anti-professional and was particularly concerned with getting jobs for local residents.

Much broader participation was found in North Oakland, where decisions were discussed at great length before the entire group, with no action taken unless there was consensus. A strong effort was made to retain an informal, friendly, cohesive group with the staff mainly taking the role of an enabler. Along with its consensual character, North Oakland, largely under the aegis of its chairman, took some of the most militant stands, such as refusing to participate in the income survey.

Fruitvale also operated within a democratic, pluralistic framework that grew out of the existence of ethnic factions that demanded inclusion in any decision-making process. Because there were relatively few opportunities for the employment of indigenous personnel in the service center or other DHR positions, the disputes that arose were about issues much more than about personalities. Fruitvale experienced two widely contrasting field service coordinators: One was controlling and manipulative, and the other was more of a technical assistant. The change in staff coincided with the committee's growing interest in neighborhood problems and more target area autonomy.

Characterized by endless, factional personality disputes, East Oakland almost always separated itself from the other target areas, was much less concerned with autonomy, and was least likely to criticize the OEDC. Its decision-making system was essentially autocratic, and participation by whites or men was discouraged by a small clique of Negro women who controlled the advisory committee. They were aligned with the field service coordinator, who continuously intervened in their deliberations.

On the OEDC, the twelve representatives of the target areas were equally divided between men and women, and Negro and white, and all but two or three were low-income persons. Only three or four played an active role in the meetings, and of these, at least two were from Fruitvale. Most of the others limited themselves to reporting the views of the advisory committees, but with the exception of East Oakland, they supported the antiestablishment stance of the more articulate delegates in their emphasis on jobs for residents in the target areas.

The Crisis Approaches

Just as many of the issues regarding the role and representativeness of the advisory committee initially arose out of the requirements of OEDC program planning, the subsequent relationships between the TAACs and the OEDC were also shaped by a series of events stemming from involvement of the target areas in a review of program proposals for 1966. The assignment of this function was a significant concession to the target areas. Informally, DHR staff spoke of this newest responsibility by saying implicitly, "the next round belongs to the advisory committees," a reference to the committees' lack of involvement in the approval of the first round of programs. At a December 5, 1965 workshop meeting of the OEDC, the TAAC representatives were pleased to find that their recommendations were at least being considered on an equal plane with those of the Council of Social Planning, the Technical Advisory Committee, and the DHR staff. At this meeting, the proposal for a police review board was first discussed. This brought out local opposition from representatives of the police department, city manager, and district attorney. This was the first public consideration of what later became one of the major controversies between the OEDC and the City Council, and it was noteworthy that Judge Wilson expressed himself unequivocally in favor of such a proposal.

At the December 22, 1965 OEDC meeting, 20 programs already in existence were approved for extension and expansion.[21] Questions were

[21] These programs, all administered by established agencies, included: legal services, family counseling, family planning, parochial school compensatory education, neighborhood organization, and remedial instruction for dropouts. OEDC minutes, December 22, 1965.

raised about the relationship between the advisory committees and the neighborhood organization program of the Council of Social Planning, as well as about the lack of programming information felt by many members of the TAAC. This laid the groundwork for the meeting on January 26, 1966, which was scheduled to pass on all of the new program proposals for 1966.

In the meantime, the position of the OEDC leadership was strengthened against the demands of the advisory committees for majority control of the OEDC. The advisory committees had constantly referred to Washington's being on the OEDC's side in the dispute, assuming that OEO wanted greater representation of the poor in the poverty program. An interview with Sargent Shriver, which was reported in the press on December 12, 1965, weakened their argument. When Shriver was asked the question, What is "maximum feasible participation of the poor?", he answered:

> We don't require any precise percentage or any precise number. We say only that if you don't have any participation by the poor that is not enough.
>
> Q: Besides the poor, what groups should be represented?
>
> A: We say ideally a community action program should have five components—the governmental people, the politicians, the business groups, the labor groups, the big philanthropic activities, the religious ones as well as the non-sectarian, and some participation by the poor.
>
> Q: Is there any basis for believing that in the long run the poor will or should control the programs affecting them?
>
> A: No.
>
> Q: Why not?
>
> A: We are talking about community action . . . the natural desire of various groups to gain control or dominate it, to me . . . is the opposite of what constitutes community action.[22]

The excerpts from the interview were printed in the *OEDC Review*, distributed at the January 26 meeting. Scheduled as another neighborhood meeting, this time in East Oakland, this meeting was attended by close to one hundred persons. It was held in a school auditorium, and therefore had an entirely different character from the usual morning meetings at city hall. Midway in the meeting, OEDC members were presented with a specially prepared analysis and a priority ranking by Dr. Smith, which was used by Judge Wilson as a basis for reviewing the new program proposals rather than using the recommendations prepared by the advisory committees. In part this action was attributed to the

[22] *San Francisco Sunday Examiner and Chronicle*, December 12, 1965, Section IV.

lateness of the hour and the need to make decisions quickly, but the chairman did not allow for much discussion, and his attempts to maintain order in the large public meeting met with disfavor.

Angered by this arbitrary decision, the advisory committee representatives reacted quickly. Achieving some unity among themselves, they were able to swing sufficient votes on the part of the other minority members of the OEDC to reject most of the staff's recommendations on funding and to accept eight neighborhood-based self-help projects amounting to $327,000. Some of these appeared to be outside the policy of the OEDC.[23] This marked the first time that the executive director's recommendations had been so thoroughly defeated at an OEDC meeting.

Immediately following the January 20 meeting, the representatives from North and West Oakland and Fruitvale came together to plan their joint strategy through a newly organized Target Area Advisory Coordinating Committee.[24] On February 8, 1966, a letter was sent to Judge Wilson from the Fruitvale action committee, which had in the interim elected Gerald Leo, a twenty-two-year-old college student, as chairman. The letter protested the way in which the meeting was handled, the lack of discussion, and the dominating role of the staff, and requested that no proposals be submitted for funding until all were reconsidered. In addition, the committee requested that all future OEDC meetings be held in the evenings and in the target areas and again demanded that a majority of the OEDC consist of elected representatives from the target areas.

The TAAC representatives went to the February 23 meeting of the OEDC determined to press their point. It was notable that this significant meeting, like the last, was also held in the evening and attended by over a hundred target area residents. Equally important was the absence of many members of the OEDC in the early part of the evening, including the chairman, who was ill. The vice-chairman presided but

[23] The eight self-help programs that were subsequently funded for 1966 included four financed by OEO: Spanish-Speaking Information Center, American Indian Community Development, Good Samaritan Home for Girls, and Corporation of the Poor Leadership Training. In addition, the Ford Foundation funded day care centers in North and East Oakland and Fruitvale, and a study center and a youth motivation project, the latter two being exceedingly small-scale ventures.

[24] Previous efforts to form a coalition or take joint action among the target areas had been short-lived. The attempt to submit a joint resolution in August on representation to the executive committee was undercut by prior OEDC action. West Oakland was able to interest only a few members of North Oakland in a citywide Corporation of the Poor as a common project for all the advisory committees. The chairmen of the four advisory committees got together from time to time and occasionally were convened by DHR staff, but attempts to coordinate their efforts had little success. They did, however, present a united front at the November 30, 1965 Community Forum in presenting their eight-point resolutions.

made no distinction between audience members and the OEDC and found himself trying to conduct a business meeting with over a hundred participants.

Shortly after the meeting began, representatives from North and West Oakland and Fruitvale introduced a resolution that essentially reiterated the requests in the February 8 letter. Amidst some confusion, they were able to secure passage of a resolution stating that the OEDC would "move as soon as possible in the direction of having a majority of its members chosen from the elected Target Area Advisory Committees." [25] This resolution passed by a vote of 11 to 7 and constituted a clear split between the TAAC representatives and other OEDC members. The tenor of the meeting was further evident in the willingness of the OEDC to approve the proposal for a Police Affairs Committee by a vote of 16 to 3, despite the known opposition of city officials.

Two days before the next OEDC meeting, which was scheduled for Saturday, March 12, 1965, the advisory committees received copies of a four-page single-spaced letter signed by Judge Wilson attacking the February 8 decision of the OEDC and defending the legitimacy of the present composition, structure, and function of the OEDC. Judge Wilson cited Sargent Shriver's support of a community coalition and also referred to the survey of the incomes of advisory committee members, which showed that "only one-third have incomes below $4,000 and less than one-fourth are on welfare." Judge Wilson further asserted that the advisory committees had not involved many low-income groups in their areas; thus, they could not be considered representative. As a compromise, he proposed that eight additional representatives be appointed by him from the target areas, a move that would give the neighborhoods a total of 20 out of 40 places on the board. Judge Wilson also underscored the advisory role of the committees by reiterating that there could be only one recognized policy-making body for a CAP, and concluded by defending the current meeting schedule of the OEDC.

The Walkout

By opening up the issue of OEDC composition again for discussion at the March 12 program review workshop, the letter, in effect, repudiated the decisions of the OEDC reached at the previous meeting. In response to this tactic, the Target Area Coordinating Committee met on the night of March 10 and planned a detailed, complex parliamentary strategy for the workshop. This consisted of a series of motions to give

[25] Minutes of OEDC meeting number 17, February 23, 1966, p. 1.

majority representation to the target areas. Essentially, the Target Area Coordinating Committee proposed a series of countermotions to increase the OEDC to 60 persons, with 8 representatives from each of the four target areas. In addition, they developed alternative proposals for each of the items cited by Judge Wilson in his letter. In considering the choices facing them, the target area representatives decided that as a last resort they would walk out if none of their points was accepted.

At the March 12 workshop, Judge Wilson dispensed with the reading of the minutes and stated that the action taken at the February meeting was only a "guide" and the matter was to be discussed again. The target area representatives then introduced their motion to obtain 60 per cent of the membership, but it lost 21 to 6. When Judge Wilson refused to let them read a statement, seven of the nine target area representatives walked out. OEDC members continued in session and accepted most of the recommendations contained in Judge Wilson's letter. These included reaffirmation of the concept that 20 out of the 40 members of the OEDC "lived in the target area," and thus the groups and areas to be served constituted more than the OEO required minimum of one-third. The remaining OEDC members declared that it was never intended that the advisory committees serve as policy-making bodies or become engaged in solving agency staff problems. Their functions were to elect representatives to the council, express the needs of low-income people, and review the progress of the programs.[26]

While the OEDC formally endorsed the advisory role of the TAACs and their ineligibility to sponsor programs, the reporters present clustered around the seven representatives in the other room and asked them what they were going to do next. There was considerable uncertainty, but finally they decided to draft a letter to Sargent Shriver justifying the withdrawal, along with a request for an investigation by OEO. Four demands were made: a simple majority of elected representatives from the target areas in OEDC; some executive voice in the operation of the center's program in the neighborhood; funds, whether used or not, set aside strictly for self-help programs; and staff assigned to the committees to aid them in serving the neighborhoods. The letter was signed by 11 target area representatives, including the chairman of the West and North Oakland and Fruitvale committees, and stated:

> We have tried in every way possible to represent the concerns of the poor people in our communities to the OEDC. In spite of this the council has followed its own course, funded agencies that are not trusted by the poor, supported programs that are not wanted

[26] Department of Human Resources, "History of OEDC," pp. 25-27.

> by the poor, and in general refused our advice and counsel . . .
> As advisory committee members we were led to believe that we would have a real opportunity to plan and review programs in our neighborhoods and now find that we are only "window dressing" for the council. After our advisory committees were formed we were told that our only function was to "advise and recommend." Even when we tried to do just that, spending long hours in review of proposals, our recommendations were ignored by council members who hadn't done their own "homework."

In addition, the letter criticized the operating system of the OEDC, with its hurry-up deadlines and crisis basis:

> . . . the council members too easily accept at face value the recommendations of Dr. Smith, who is more concerned about pleasing everyone by giving him a little piece of the pie, than with really helping people to get help from other sources or with forcing institutions to drastically re-evaluate their programs "for the poor!" [27]

This action of the representatives did not meet with complete acceptance by the TAAC membership itself. Although some of the committees were willing to accept the walkout, even though many insisted they should have been consulted before, they were much more critical of the letter sent to Sargent Shriver, in which the representatives had acted in the name of all committee members without securing approval. Some of the representatives were mildly censured, but the committees tended to side with them rather than with the OEDC.[28]

The *OEDC Reporter* for March, 1966 reprinted in full Judge Wilson's letter to Sargent Shriver replying to the charges of the dissident members. The judge reaffirmed the representativeness of the OEDC as a community action agency even without the missing members and once again attacked the lack of representativeness of the advisory committees, referring to the survey results as evidence of their not representing the poor. He denied that no self-help programs had been funded or that all funds were going to the established agencies. Finally, Judge Wilson welcomed the proposed OEO investigation.

The regional OEO position was most equivocal in the dispute and particularly disillusioned the TAACs. On March 20, the regional co-

[27] These excerpts are from pp. 1 and 2 of the mimeographed letter prepared by the target area chairman. Newspaper accounts of the walkout appear in the *Oakland Tribune*, March 13, 1966, p. 1; *San Francisco Sunday Examiner and Chronicle*, March 13, 1966, p. 13, and the *San Francisco Chronicle*, March 4, 1966, p. 1.

[28] It was later learned that several OEDC members convened meetings of the Negro membership of the recalcitrant TAACs and urged them to repudiate the leadership of their non-Negro chairmen.

ordinator, John Martin, stated in a letter to Judge Wilson that whereas the OEO did not require the OEDC to consist of 51 per cent target area representatives, it urged that the action of February 23 be implemented; that meetings be held at times and places convenient for the target area representatives; that the community organization component directed by the Council of Social Planning be used to increase low-income participation on the TAACs; and that the latter first approve all prospective programs. Three days later, in answer to a request for further "clarification," he added that the OEDC action of March 12 satisfied OEO requirements on representation.

The long-sought unity of the advisory committees was short lived, even though their coordinating committee continued to meet from March until May. Having decided to meet on Saturday mornings in a target area, the OEDC was convened on March 26. Two members of the Fruitvale committee declared that they were attending "under protest," until their demands were met. Similarly, West Oakland representatives would participate subject to completion of the OEO investigation, and even the North Oakland representatives, who had voted to continue the boycott took their seats, apparently assuming that the investigation would be resolved in their favor. Implying that the differences between the OEDC and the TAAC were negotiable, the OEDC then approved the recommendation of its executive committee to appoint a special committee "to look into the matter of OEDC structure, target area representation, and relationships with delegate agencies." Consisting of six members, three of whom were from the target area, and headed by Mr. Donald McCullum, former president of the Oakland NAACP chapter, the committee quickly achieved consensus. A month later, on April 23, it submitted its major recommendation that 51 per cent of the OEDC be composed of elected target area representatives and that 75 per cent of all TAAC membership and their OEDC representatives consist of low-income persons as defined by the OEDC. The report also discussed the relationship between OEDC and the target areas and recommended that the TAACs take over the community organization component for their areas, have the final decision on any local indigenous programs limited to their neighborhoods, and have representation on the personnel committees of the delegate agencies for recruiting both indigenous and professional personnel for programs in their area. There was considerable readiness to accept the report immediately, but because some aspects were still unclear and because the TAACs had not discussed the report, it was sent back to the committee for further clarification. The committee was also asked to take into account the requests of some spokesmen for Mexican-American groups that, principally because of language problems, they could no longer participate in the Fruitvale committee and wanted a fifth advisory committee for Spanish-speaking persons approved on a citywide basis.[29]

Reorganization Compromise

A somewhat different, friendlier mood prevailed during the March 26 meeting, at which the OEDC discussed the prospects of "task force" visits to other cities financed by the Ford Foundation, in which target area representatives were to be included; the requests for target area participation on various OEDC committees; and their administrative involvement in a summer youth employment program that would provide 900 jobs. Another factor that reinforced this emerging feeling of solidarity among the members of the OEDC was their almost unanimous agreement to seek funding for the Police Affairs Committee despite the opposition of the city council, which was threatening to invoke its veto power. A new mayor, John Reading, had been elected, who in contrast to his predecessor began to take an active part in OEDC affairs. His initial concern was to avert a clash between the city council and the OEDC on the issue of a police review board, and he was able to persuade the OEDC to appoint a committee to work with him and the city council to resolve their differences.

By the May 25 meeting of the OEDC, adoption of the McCullum recommendations was almost an anticlimax: The same persons who had firmly rejected the advisory committee demands two months earlier voted to accept many of the same proposals when they were submitted as part of a complete reorganization plan. For the first time since its inception 18 months earlier, the OEDC had a reasonably clear policy on resident participation, on which there was considerable agreement, although the advisory committees were divided in their reaction to the requirement that beginning in January, 1967, 75 per cent of their membership must consist of low-income persons. They wondered how they would achieve this objective. In addition to granting the Mexican-Americans a fifth, Spanish-speaking advisory committee, the final report provided that 20 out of the 39 members of the OEDC would be elected by the target areas and the remaining 19 would be appointed by the mayor from the following community-wide constituencies: elected officials (3), business and industry (2), labor (2), private agencies (2), NAACP (2), CORE (1), Negro business and professional people (1), Mexican-Americans (1), American Indians (1), religious groups (3), and Orientals (1).

[29] OEDC minutes, meeting number 19, April 23, 1966, pp. 2-3.

Rules were also specified regarding the number and composition of the Target Area Advisory Committees. Geographical representation was required, with at least one person to be elected from each elementary school attendance area within the target areas. In addition to the powers proposed in the original report a month earlier, the advisory committees gained the right to review and ratify indigenous personnel of existing programs and membership on an OEDC personnel committee to resolve disputes on personnel selection, performance, and replacement in the delegate agencies, although the latter still retained veto power.[30]

The action of the OEDC in swiftly approving the recommendations of its committee on structure and relationship was regarded as "the most notable policy decision during the quarter" in its official report to OEO, which declared:

> It may be concluded that the OEDC, Department of Human Resources and the target area advisory committee relationships are mutually respected and supported. We can optimistically project a lengthy period of harmonious productivity for the immediate future.[31]

OEDC leadership evidently believed that the new structure and membership policy would prevent the domination of the advisory committees by the "outside interventionists." Among the other conditions that seem to have contributed to this compromise solution was: a growing weariness on the part of the OEDC chairman, who began to wonder if the extraordinary amount of time involved in the struggle was worth it. Then, too, there was the fear of the possibility of riots in the coming summer. These anxieties were fed by continual speculation as to whether Oakland would become another Watts and the rather inflammatory stories appearing in *The Flatlands,* a newspaper aimed at the minority poor, first published in March and sold at each OEDC meeting. There was also an increase in indigenous social action and grassroots protest directed against the schools and the Bay Area Rapid Transit District (BART), together with talk about "bringing Alinsky to Oakland." [32] Opponents of the ad-

[30] "OEDC Committee on Structure and Relationships, Further Report and Recommendations," May 25, 1966; OEDC minutes, meeting Number 20, May 25, 1966, pp. 3-4, *OEDC Reporter,* Vol. 1, No. 6, June, 1966, pp. 2, 5.

[31] "OEDC Community Action Program Narrative Progress Report," April 1 and June 30, 1960, p. 27.

[32] The periodic concern with "bringing Alinsky to Oakland" expressed the belief on the part of some of the more militant elements in the Negro community that changes in the power structure of Oakland could only come about if conflict and disruptive strategies were used. Efforts to secure funds from various church groups to employ organizers from the Industrial Areas Foundation, headed by Saul D. Alinsky, did not succeed. Much of this activity is reflected in "War on the Poor," *The Flatlands,* Vol. 1,

visory committees probably realized that continuing the fight would only increase tensions in the city, and none of them wanted to see an explosion. Finally, it became increasingly clear to the OEDC leadership and DHR staff that a confrontation with city hall was near on the issue of a police review board and that unity was essential for this battle. The interest of the dominant Negro leadership of the OEDC in a police review board was as strong as that of the advisory committee representatives, and it was a common stake in the success of this proposal that helped bind the two groups together. The imminence of the investigation report from OEO also served to reinforce these cohesive tendencies; although the report was received after the McCullum report was adopted, there was a high degree of congruence between these two sets of recommendations. By demanding an investigation, the advisory committees had forced the OEDC to be more responsive to their wishes, and the OEDC in turn had forced the advisory committees to become more representative of the groups to be served.

Police Review Board

Having somewhat settled the issues regarding the future composition and authority of the advisory committees, the OEDC was also being challenged by city government. The fate of the police review board proposal, first submitted in December, 1965, gradually took on the character of a test case: It was regarded as an indication of whether the antipoverty program was willing to back up the minority poor in their dealings with the police, as well as of the extent to which the OEDC was its own master and could control its own funds. This issue constituted the first instance of a basic conflict between the OEDC and the city council, which precipitated a clarification of governmental authority over the antipoverty program in which the city council's veto power was finally made explicit. As long as the OEDC was not interfering with any of the city departments and was bringing several million dollars into the community, there was no disposition on the part of city government to assert its prerogative, particularly since DHR staff reported to the city manager, who in turn submitted all proposals to the city council, and all funds were disbursed

No. 1 (March 12, 1966), p. 3, an evaluation of the OEDC by Robert Olmstead, chairman of the North Oakland advisory committee and one of the leaders of the target area's battle for majority control. Letters sent by the Fruitvale and North Oakland committees to Judge Wilson are reprinted on page 4 of this same issue. The editorial board of *The Flatlands* strongly supported the walkout and encouraged the use of more militant tactics.

by the city auditor.[33] Because of the persistence of the OEDC in pressing this project in the face of the strongest opposition from the police department and virtually the entire city council, increasing strain developed between City Hall and the OEDC in the latter half of 1966. At the same time, the antagonism between it and the advisory committees diminished. The prolonged dispute over the Police Affairs Committee—it lasted for 16 months—was also the first of several new struggles for power between Mayor Reading and the OEDC, as he became increasingly critical of its role as a "second government."

The story of the police review board reveals some characteristic styles of community decision making in Oakland. Despite an informal reaction from the regional OEO staff that a police review board was probably ineligible for funding because its use would not be restricted to the poor, the OEDC voted to submit the proposal anyway on February 23, 1966. In part, this was done because the Ford Foundation had originally stated that it would not support any project eligible for OEO funding. A week before, Mayor Houlihan had resigned, shortly before he was indicted for embezzling a client's account, and the new mayor, Reading, who as mentioned above appeared to be sensitive to the demands of the minority groups, at first sought to mediate between the conflicting claims of the OEDC and the city council. On April 21, he had told his fellow councilmen that the OEDC would "fall apart" unless the city acted at once to establish a police review board.[34] Two days later, however, he was pleading with the OEDC not to confront the city council and force it to exercise its veto. Instead, he urged the appointment of a joint committee to explore alternatives such as a human relations commission or an ombudsman. Only one OEDC member openly opposed his suggestion for a committee, on the grounds that the Mayor really had no support for his position, and reminded him of his inability to muster sufficient votes even to get another Negro appointed to the council. The OEDC, however, agreed to name a committee to meet with the mayor and representatives from the city council and police department to work out a compromise, provided that the city council would adopt a resolution citing the need for some action.[35]

[33] Despite these procedures, a controversy erupted twice during 1965 when Mayor Houlihan rejected the one-and-a-half-page statement submitted by Dr. Smith to the city council requesting $758,599 from OEO. The Mayor contrasted the lack of detail with the 185-page line item budget for the rest of the city government and refused to submit the OEDC request to the city council. Dr. Smith contested the degree of local control over federal funds and was quoted as saying, "The city council has absolutely nothing to do with giving the money to the various recipient agencies." *Oakland Tribune,* May 21, 1965, p. 1. Further developments are discussed subsequently.

[34] *San Francisco Chronicle,* April 22, 1966, p. 1.

[35] OEDC minutes, meeting number 19, April 23, 1966, p. 5.

It also appointed a committee to investigate the severance of its ties from city government.

Meanwhile, the formal application for OEO funding rested on the city manager's desk. Several days later on April 26, the city council, with the Mayor's urging, did pass a grudging resolution requesting a review of the existing grievance procedure "to determine if our program can be improved upon." This was unacceptable to the executive committee of the OEDC, and the Mayor offered to resubmit the resolution on May 3, changing the "if" to "how." At the May 25 meeting, it was announced that the city council had passed the more acceptable resolution, and an OEDC committee was then appointed to meet with the Mayor and city council. Meanwhile, the Ford Foundation had given the OEDC the option of submitting its proposal to them even if OEO had not acted; at the instruction of the chairman, the proposal was mailed to the Ford Foundation on May 20. In the interim, the original proposal had been "refined" with the help of DHR staff and the sponsoring group was broadened to include more minority representatives. Its function was also modified and now the review board was no longer to be a review of police behavior, but a means of helping citizens present their complaints to the Internal Affairs Division of the Oakland Police Department. In addition, a representative of the police department was to be included on the hearing committee!

When the city council learned that the OEDC had submitted the application to the Ford Foundation, it requested an opinion from the city attorney and stated its intention to veto any grant by the Ford Foundation for the purpose of establishing a police affairs committee. The mayor charged bad faith and expressed his disappointment that the OEDC had sent the proposal to the Ford Foundation, because it was his understanding that no such action would be taken if a joint committee were to be set up to discuss various alternatives. Regarding the two actions as incompatible, Mayor Reading viewed the OEDC's decision as a means of forcing the city to reach a settlement. However, he continued to express his hope of using his office as a means of unifying a city divided on the issue of police brutality.

The joint committee met numerous times during the summer and well into the fall of 1966, but there was no resolution or alternative proposal forthcoming.[36] Nor were city council members added to the committee as was originally requested by the OEDC; instead they met with the city manager and representatives of the police department. When, as expected,

[36] *Oakland Tribune,* June 26, 1966, p. 3. The controversy was reviewed in the *San Francisco Examiner,* August 23, 1966, p. 1. See also *The Flatlands,* Vol. 1, No. 11 (July 30-August 13), 1966, pp. 6-7.

the Ford Foundation approved the funds, the city manager refused to release them on the grounds that such release would be contrary to public policy. Two days before the August 27 meeting, when the Mayor's memo was read, the Alameda County Grand Jury issued a strong statement opposing any sort of police review board, and the city council apparently hoped that the OEDC would take the initiative to call for dissolution of the committee. Instead, the OEDC was at pains not to be the one to break off negotiations with the city. As the matter dragged on, it became clear that the Ford Foundation was not going to involve itself in a clash with the Oakland City Council. Because the city was determined to prevent any funds for this purpose from being channeled through the OEDC, the latter suggested that the sponsors of the project apply directly to the Ford Foundation.[37]

Each side found legal support for its position. The Legal Aid Society staff prepared an opinion based on the original correspondence with the Ford Foundation in 1961 and concluded that the city had a different relationship to Ford than to OEO, and therefore the city should release the funds. The city council, however, relied on the opinion of one of the city attorneys that the council was the trustee for all funds received by the OEDC and as long as the council's policy opposing a police review board stood, the funds could not be used for this purpose.

The stalemate continued to the end of the year, and the Mayor was unsuccessful in persuading the city council even to listen to a report on the subject prepared by the city manager at their request in February, 1967.[38] It was clear that on this issue the city would not be budged. The OEDC must have realized that it lacked sufficient power to influence the city council, for it began at this time to consider seriously severing its relationship with the city by becoming an independent nonprofit corporation. It finally voted to do so on August 23, 1967.[39]

OEDC and the Mayor

Both sides became much more sensitive to their rights as a result of this controversy. OEDC members had denied the charge made by many of the advisory committee representatives that city hall controlled the antipoverty program and continued to assert their autonomy. Indeed, Judge Wilson claimed that he had accepted the chairmanship with the under-

37 OEDC minutes, August 27, 1966, pp. 1-2. The grand jury report is described in the *San Francisco Examiner*, August 25, 1966, p. 6.

38 *San Francisco Chronicle*, February 8, 1967.

39 *Oakland Tribune*, August 24, 1967, p. 2; minutes, OEDC executive committee, August 14, 1967 and OEDC, August 24, 1967.

standing that city hall would not try to dominate the program.[40] Originally the relationship between the city and OEDC, comparable to that between OEDC and the advisory committees, was ambiguous, and it evidently suited everyone's purpose to keep it that way. On December 7, OEO began pressing the OEDC to clarify its structural relationships with City Hall, but OEDC members were unsuccessful in their attempts to obtain full policy-making power and the exclusive right to hire and fire its senior employees, and thus modify the new ordinance, which would continue to be in effect in 1967.

A trend to reduce the scope of OEDC authority and its autonomy became more and more noticeable, particularly on the part of Reading. Although he had backed some sort of grievance procedure and had spent hundreds of hours listening to the complaints and suggestions of low-income and minority citizens in the service centers in the neighborhoods, the Mayor became increasingly critical of the OEDC and alienated most of those who had originally regarded him as sympathetic and possibly supportive of the interest of racial minorities and the poor.[41] Earlier, the OEDC complained that the city was bypassing the target areas in preparing its application for a Model City Planning Grant and that it was obstructing the OEDC's efforts to secure approval of a proposed model service center in West Oakland. At the OEDC meeting on May 24, 1967, the Mayor denied that he was attempting to gain further control, but at the same time he acknowledged requesting OEO to channel all communications to the city manager's office instead of directly to the DHR or OEDC. In addition, he was able to secure the transfer of the research department of the DHR to the city manager on the grounds that it could make a more independent evaluation of OEDC and other programs.[42] The Mayor was clearly at odds with the OEDC's program emphasis on social services and neighborhood organization, and expressed his belief that only education and job development would eliminate the unemployment that was responsible for poverty in Oakland. Accordingly, he viewed

[40] In spite of these "understandings," Mayor Houlihan was quoted as declaring: "We don't have machine politics in the west like they have in the big eastern and midwestern cities, so we haven't had the problem of control of the poverty money for the purposes of political patronage. Nevertheless, we control all the money. We [city hall] must approve all the policies made by the poverty program." *Ramparts*, Vol. 4, No. 10, February, 1966, p. 37. This issue also contains a long and somewhat notorious indictment of Oakland entitled "Metropoly," pp. 25-50, in which the city is portrayed as a hopeless "powder keg," with a white power structure blind to its problems, that can only be saved by a revolutionary awakening in the slums.

[41] For a good account of Mayor Reading's earlier public image, see "Millionaire Mayor Helps 'Have Nots,'" *San Francisco Examiner*, August 26, 1966, p. 1, the last in a series of five articles by Norman Melnick.

[42] OEDC minutes, May 24, 1966, pp. 2-3.

the composition of the OEDC as inappropriate for these economic tasks because of the absence of business men and the disproportionate number of ethnic minority members "elected" by neighborhoods and not really responsible to anyone.[43] The OEDC was sensitive to this charge and was at pains to make clear that the fear that "the poor" had engineered a "takeover" was groundless. It noted that although Oakland was one of the few cities where the poor comprised the majority of the policy-making body, the target area representatives never voted in a bloc and besides, city hall had the final word on release of funds. It also denied that the composition of the OEDC meant it was in conflict with city hall; rather, it argued, the OEDC sought to "supplement" the city's efforts.[44]

The Mayor, however, had appointed his own Manpower Commission. Although he was not completely successful in steering a $4.5 million grant for a Concentrated Employment Program to it, he was able to force the OEDC to share some of its authority over this federally financed project. Two of the major job training projects in Oakland, the East Bay Skills Center and an on-the-job training program, were also operated outside the structure of the antipoverty program, although the DHR executive staff had been involved in their establishment.[45]

Claiming that there were "two governments" in Oakland, the Mayor continued to argue for a direct relationship between OEO and city government, but with the latter delegating responsibility to the OEDC so that it would be no different from any other commission such as those governing the library, planning, or parks and recreation. Finding no difficulty in getting support for this position, the Mayor and the city manager

[43] This summary of Mayor Reading's views is based on his formal presentation and response to the questions of U.S. Senate Labor and Public Welfare Subcommittee on Employment, Manpower and Poverty, May 10, 1967, in San Francisco. The subcommittee consisted of Senators Joseph P. Clark (D), Pennsylvania, George P. Murphy (R), California, and Robert Kennedy (D), New York.

[44] *OEDC Reporter,* Vol. 7, No. 5 (April, 1967), p. 2. The defensive tone of this reply also reflected the inherent lack of political strength of the OEDC and the target areas, owing in large measure to the character of Oakland's city manager form of government with its citywide, nonpartisan elections that minimize the impact of minority and neighborhood votes.

[45] Because of its designation as an economically depressed area, Oakland received substantial federal assistance over and above the usual grants-in-aid, which amounted to close to $100 million per year and involved over 125 federal programs, including 30 separate manpower projects! Among the most significant of these special projects approved for Oakland during 1966, which were related to the war on poverty but administered outside of the OEDC, were: the East Bay Skills Center, a $4.5 million project to provide job training for 1400 persons, which opened in April, 1966; Mayor's On-The-Job Training Program for 800 persons; Adult Minority Project of the State Department of Employment, financed by the Ford Foundation; and a Concentrated Employment Program costing $4.5 million, jointly administered by the OEDC and the Mayor's Manpower Commission; and a Demonstration Service Center in West Oakland costing close to $1 million.

took a "hard line" on the OEDC's request to have the final authority over the selection of a new director of the DHR when Dr. Norvel Smith resigned in June, 1967 to accept the position as deputy director of the OEO regional office. They were also unwilling to modify the city's veto power over the OEDC. When it became evident after almost eight months of discussion that there was no way of resisting these encroachments on OEDC autonomy, the OEDC on August 23, 1967 approved its executive committee's recommendation to sever its relationship with the city, "with no hard feelings," and moved to reconstitute the OEDC as an independent nonprofit corporation.[46] At the same time, it was expected that the DHR would continue to staff the OEDC, thus maintaining this somewhat ambiguous relationship.

Out of this experience in fighting city hall, the OEDC became a more cohesive and unified body, as the middle-class professionals and less affluent Negroes from the target areas who together comprised 70 per cent of the Council membership joined in the attempt to maintain the prerogatives of the OEDC. There was a progressive narrowing of the differences between them and a development of consensus regarding the use of OEO funds to develop programs and to promote employment and job training for minorities. Relatively little interest was expressed by either group in trying to organize the poor to change community institutions. Their philosophy was perhaps best expressed in the oft-stated belief of the executive of the DHR that a CAP must "help the poor enter the middle class." It was therefore not surprising that most of the record number of 67 programs funded by the OEDC during 1965-67 were sponsored by established agencies such as the Oakland schools, County Health Department, and Family Service Bureau on the assumption that in this way the poor could best obtain those social services needed to help them become self-supporting.

Target Area Trends

Meanwhile, significant changes had taken place in the composition and character of the advisory committees, as they became somewhat less interested and involved in OEDC affairs. They began to turn inward, expressing greater concern about neighborhood issues and problems, and conceiving of themselves more and more as central community councils

[46] See fn. 38. The attitudes toward the "divorce" of the OEDC from the city of Oakland are described in the *Oakland Tribune,* September 15, 1967, p. 2.

for their areas. All of them, for example, were deeply involved in administering the summer youth employment program in 1966 by sponsoring neighborhood improvement jobs for 66 youths in their areas.[47] Some of their members had resigned because they were able to obtain jobs in this program or as nonprofessional staff members in the County Health Department, schools, legal aid, Family Service Agency, and several other delegate agencies.[48]

Others served on advisory committees of these delegate agencies, and in the case of those working for the Oakland schools and County Health Department and to a lesser extent, legal aid, were regarded as making a valuable contribution to and having some influence on policy. Still others became members of the boards of the five indigenous nonprofit corporations whose programs were funded by OEO or the Ford Foundation.

In the latter half of 1966 there was considerable turnover in both the leadership and membership of the target area committees as plans were made to take over the neighborhood organization program from the Council of Social Planning and to reorganize the committees to comply with the new requirement of 75 per cent low-income membership by the end of the year. Efforts to formulate a unified plan for the five target areas met with considerable resistance, as each one sought to advance its own program. For example, West Oakland alone proposed a budget of almost $1 million. A conference held in August revealed considerable confusion and disagreement regarding the purposes of the neighborhood organizations, but eventually a formula was negotiated whereby West Oakland received $60,000; North and East Oakland and Fruitvale $30,000 each;

[47] The Summer Youth Employment Project, which provided jobs for 300 youths for 10 weeks at a total cost of $209,000, was the first time that the advisory committee members were involved in developing a work program, recruiting, screening, and selecting the youth and their adult supervisors. This experience constituted the most tangible evidence of their changed status and role within the OEDC. Some of the details can be found in the *OEDC Reporter,* Vol. 1, No. 6 (June, 1966), pp. 1-2. A surprisingly favorable account of the project appears in *The Flatlands,* Vol. 1, No. 11 (July 30-August 13, 1966), pp. 1-3. The experience in West Oakland is also glowingly described in the *Oakland Tribune,* September 14, 1966.

[48] OEO regulations prevented a person from serving on a board or committee if he was employed on a project receiving OEO funds. Ostensibly this was done to avoid a traditional conflict of interest, on the assumption that employees should not be policy makers. This was a most unpopular rule—some feared that it would result in a leadership drain as the most able of the indigenous target members would get jobs in the antipoverty program, but this did not occur to the extent anticipated. Close to 270 subprofessionals were employed by OEDC-funded programs over a two-year period, but a majority (171) were part-time teaching aides in the Oakland schools. The relatively small number of jobs, their brief duration, and low-income prerequisites all tended to mitigate any significant impact on advisory committee participation.

and the Spanish-speaking committee $15,000 for this program in 1967. Each target area committee established a separate board, which was essentially a subcommittee of the board to administer the program. They soon became embroiled in many of the personnel issues that had plagued similar indigenous groups in other communities.

Procedures for the election of "eligible recipients" were approved in October, and during November and December leaflets were distributed and publicity released about the elections, which were scheduled in school auditoriums in each area. In three of the target areas, West, North, and East Oakland, the election process was carried out more or less as intended, and a total of over two hundred votes was cast. In Fruitvale there was a very poor response, and the committee qualified by reducing its over-all size, thus keeping constant the number of low-income members. The Fruitvale committee, more than the others, had deteriorated considerably after the departure of its chairman in August and several others who had given major leadership. It fell prey to factional squabbling among the Negro members who remained after the Mexican-Americans withdrew to form their own committee. In general, however, reorganization of the advisory committees to increase the proportion of low-income members was associated with positive results in all areas but Fruitvale. Although they lost half of their "over-income" members, the advisory committees expanded in size, and even that in East Oakland became more assertive and less dominated by its staff; these trends were noticed before reorganization, however. Thus an election process in Oakland, coming almost two years later than those in San Francisco and Santa Clara County, reemphasized the ethnic character of the advisory committees. For the first time, all of the chairmen and all but 7 of the 20 representatives to the OEDC were Negro. Four of the target area committees were almost completely Negro, including for the first time the chairmen of the North Oakland and Fruitvale committee, both of whom were women.

The reconstituted advisory committees, which included representatives from schools and improvement clubs but very few churches, became quite ingrown and increasingly developed a vested interest in their programs and "their" service centers. Bypassed by other city departments, which sought out their own constituencies, the advisory committees, whose purpose and responsibilities were still somewhat unclear, operated more as separate, neighborhood ethnic associations rather than as representative constituents of a citywide organization. Typically, each utilized the neighborhood organization program primarily for social service information and referral rather than to organize groups around issues. Equally characteristic was the prevalent factionalism, the subordinate role of the low-income members, and the dominance of small cliques of the more middle-class women participants.

Neighborhood Organization

The decision of the OEDC to assign the neighborhood organization function to the advisory committees also came about as an unplanned concession, since there was relatively little pressure from the advisory committees to take on this responsibility. One of the requests of the March 15 walkout had been for more staff to assist the advisory committees in their work, but this was more an expression of dissatisfaction with the field service coordinators than a desire to organize the poor. As noted earlier, most of the advisory committees were more interested in receiving funds to administer social service programs of their own than in reaching out and involving a larger number of low-income persons. When the Council of Social Planning announced in April, 1966 that it would not seek renewal of its contract for neighborhood organization, the McCullum committee saw this as a compromise possibility whereby the advisory committees might be responsible for a function that at the same time would not conflict with its review of similar programs. Accordingly, with some reluctance and considerable confusion, the advisory committees found themselves in late 1966 planning to take over a program with which they had relatively little connection.

Originally the neighborhood organization process was supposed to include the formation of the Target Area Advisory Committees, but when the DHR decided to form them by themselves, two separate and parallel structures for resident participation with considerable distrust and suspicion between them had evolved in the four target neighborhoods. The advisory committees were so preoccupied with their struggle with the OEDC that they tended to neglect many of the neighborhood problems, which became the concern of the 12-member staff of the Council of Social Planning. Two professional community organizers and two indigenous aides were assigned to each area; in varying ways, they sought to bring residents together around a common set of neighborhood interests that required group action. Over twenty groups, including new and previously existing but moribund block clubs and parent and tenant associations, were aided in such neighborhood self-help projects as securing improved lighting, traffic signs, and one-way streets, sponsoring anti-litter campaigns, blocking permits for pool halls and liquor stores, and so forth. Relatively little of their effort went into recruiting new members for the advisory committees or stimulating attendance at their meetings. In two areas, West and North Oakland, there was considerable antagonism toward this program, which involved expenditures of over $100,000 a year.[49]

The Council on Social Planning claimed that over six hundred persons were involved in these neighborhood groups, but very few of them had low incomes. Most of them were employed, many were home owners, and many were affiliated with other political, religious, and social groups and belonged to the working class and lower middle class. The council recognized that its strategies resulted in the organization of neighborhoods and not the poor; that the poor had dropped out owing to the concern of the neighborhood councils with projects that were of peripheral interest to them. This was not surprising, since a survey of target area opinion revealed that low-rent housing and job training were regarded as having the highest priority. These needs were not used by staff as issues around which to organize, nor were they part of any OEDC-sponsored program.[50] Other factors enumerated by the staff for the low participation of the poor were: the lack of incentives for participation, i.e., insufficient jobs and other sources of income; lack of backing from the sponsoring agency and its professionals; indifference and recalcitrance of the established agencies, and the attitudes of the poor themselves—apathy, fear, and misperception of the war on poverty and their need for quick action.[51]

Apart from encouraging participation in neighborhood improvement projects, the council staff was directly involved in only one major attempt at social action, Job Opportunities in Bay Area Rapid Transit (JOBART). After foundering for almost a year as a loose coalition of human rights and civil rights leaders, Negro ministers, and NAACP members from San Francisco, Richmond and Oakland, the organization was assisted by one of the neighborhood aides in its goal of securing jobs for minorities and adequately compensating residents who had to be relocated. These efforts

[49] The neighborhood organization component was subject to the most intensive level of evaluation by the Research Division of the Department of Human Resources. Their findings reveal a rather dismal record, in which few of the community development goals were approximated and a negligible portion of the poor were involved. See *Evaluation Analysis of the Council of Social Planning's Neighborhood Organization Program, plus four Appendices* (Department of Human Resources, December, 1966).

[50] Survey data derived from interviews with 2,623 households, May-July, 1966, by the 701 Project, a demographic survey directed by Sheldon Siegel for the city of Oakland. The same survey found that fewer than one-fifth of the persons in the target area knew that there was a service center located in the neighborhood.

[51] Council of Social Planning, *Report on Component Twelve, Neighborhood Organization to OEDC*, Report Number 88 (Oakland Area, December, 1966), particularly pp. 25-28. Opinions of the eight community aides regarding their experiences can be found in Harold Nawy in collaboration with Martin Thimel, *The East Bay Community Action Program; Part II, Strategy or Stratagem* (University of California School of Criminology, February, 1967).

produced little, and negotiating sessions were broken off after four months when it was concluded that BART was not acting in good faith.[52]

Some of the more active advisory committee members were also involved during 1966 in other forms of social action organized outside the framework of the antipoverty program in such groups as: the Ad Hoc Committee for Quality Education, which sponsored an abortive boycott of the Oakland schools that was not supported by the advisory committees; Blacks United to Motivate Progress (BUMP); Corporation For The Poor; Alinsky Committee To Integrate Oakland Now (ACTION); the Oakland Direct Action Committee; and in the recurrent failures to organize a working coalition of minority and low-income groups in Oakland.

Perhaps one of the most significant events was the launching of *The Flatlands*, a newspaper directed at the poor, whose editorial board consisted of some of the most articulate members of the advisory committees, together with several other militant leaders of grassroots groups. Providing a new and important medium of communication among the diverse ethnic elements of the target areas, the paper identified issues in a flamboyant, tabloid style, attacking police brutality and discrimination in housing, education, and employment.[53]

The radical posture of *The Flatlands* was, however, not in keeping with the enduring character of the participants from the target areas. While increasingly more ethnic in their perspective and more sophisticated about their right to be involved in community decisions affecting them, the members were still basically moderate in their perspective. The growing polarization between the members of the OEDC and the TAAC and the rising militancy of other groups in the ghetto was illustrated by the leaflet distributed by the OEDC during the summer of 1967 urging neighborhood residents to keep cool and not get involved in any disorders because the jobs of hundreds of youths might be endangered. Furthermore, the message went on, if there were no disturbances, there was a good chance the community would be rewarded with even more summer jobs next year.

Growing out of the OEDC reorganization, an alliance had been forged by middle- and lower-class ethnic minorities who controlled the OEDC, which, at the same time that it asserted its independence of city govern-

[52] A detailed analysis of JOBART is found in Appendix III, *Evaluation Analysis of the Council of Social Planning Neighborhood Organization Program* (Oakland Department of Human Resources, Research Division).

[53] See fn. 31. The paper received its original support from the Oakland Project of the University Extension, University of California; East and West Oakland Parishes, United Presbytery of the Bay Area, The American Friends Service Committee, and the Sunday Evening Discussion Group. The biweekly issues of *The Flatlands* featured profiles of many of the key leaders of the Target Area Advisory Committees and numerous feature articles dealing with low-income and minority groups in Oakland.

ment, had become increasingly institutionalized. A new director of DHR was appointed in October, 1967. With a markedly different philosophy than his predecessor, he sought to change the direction of the OEDC and shift its resources from support of existing social service agencies to the development of indigenous, autonomous, functional corporations in the low-income community. As it started its fourth year, the OEDC was readying itself for a test of the viability of the alternative approach that it had originally rejected: the organization of the poor into a power bloc.

Summary

Originating out of one of the first gray area projects, the OEDC had members who were appointed by the Mayor of Oakland and consisted of a cross-section of community interests, but no elected representatives from the target areas. Capitalizing on the previous experience of its predecessor organization, the OIP, the OEDC approved 14 projects at its first meeting and expressed its intent to establish four liaison committees in the neighborhoods. Specific policy on resident participation was not adopted until four months had passed, and initial attempts to convene organizational meetings in the target areas resulted in unexpected opposition. Because of their manner of recruitment and the vague criteria for membership, the four advisory committees attracted relatively few poor persons, but rather upwardly mobile working-class persons, predominately Negro, and for a long time their leadership did not reflect the ethnic character of the membership.

Three of the four advisory committees conceived of their function as much broader than providing feedback and advice to the OEDC, and they began to press for membership on the executive committee, from which they had been excluded, and for more than the eight places that had been assigned to them on the OEDC. Out of their frustration at the OEDC meetings and their encounters with DHR staff, which seemed to result in confusion, ambiguity, and constraints on a more active role, several advisory committee members began to demand majority representation on the OEDC. After a coalition of Target Area Advisory Committees was formed for the first time, membership on the executive committee was conceded to each of the committees.

This still did not satisfy some of the more militant members, who continued to demand majority control by the target areas, the right to administer and propose programs, and a greater measure of authority over the service centers. Although the advisory committees regarded themselves as the authentic spokesmen for the target areas and entitled to be the dominant voice in the CAP, their representativeness was consistently questioned by the leadership of the OEDC on the grounds that neither their leadership nor membership reflected sufficiently the low-income residents in the neighborhood.

Antagonism between the two groups was heightened at a critical OEDC meeting, when the recommendations of the advisory committees for the second year's programs were subordinated to those of the executive director. Drawing together, the target areas were able for the first time to vote down the executive's recommendations and to form a coalition that succeeded in forcing through a resolution the next month that committed the OEDC to grant them 51 per cent of the membership. This action was subsequently repudiated, and when the OEDC refused to consider their alternatives, the target area representatives walked out and requested an OEO investigation. Within a month, a compromise solution was negotiated, giving the target areas 51 per cent control and a larger role in the service centers, but requiring them to have 75 per cent low-income membership. In addition, a fifth advisory committee on a citywide basis was created for the Spanish-speaking groups, and all five committees were given responsibility for community organization in their areas. An earlier program of neighborhood organization had failed to involve the poor, and this was also true of the community organization efforts of the reconstituted advisory committees, which became increasingly ingrown and preoccupied with their internal problems.

Part of the impetus to settle the dispute over representation came from the need for unity in facing up to the city council's challenge to the authority of OEDC to receive funds from the Ford Foundation for a police review board. The city finally invoked its long-dormant veto power, and this action was followed by other attempts by the new Mayor to curb the autonomy of the OEDC. Eventually the OEDC concluded that it could no longer maintain its organizational integrity in the face of greater city control, and it severed its relationship with the city to become a nonprofit corporation.

5

BERKELEY AND CONTRA COSTA COUNTY

The CAP, daring and original, demands community responsibility, empathy and basic democracy.[1]

Berkeley Case Study

The case studies of Berkeley and Contra Costa County are presented in summary form because neither developed target area organizations comparable to Oakland's, San Francisco's, or Santa Clara County's. The abbreviated accounts that follow focus primarily on the origin of the CAPs and their response to the inevitable pressures for increased representation of the poor. In both Contra Costa County and Berkeley, the organizational vehicles for resident participation functioned on a community-wide level rather than in the neighborhoods.

In contrast to most of the other communities, Berkeley displayed almost from its inception considerable readiness to accommodate itself to the demands for increased representation of residents from the target areas. This reaction was in keeping with its liberal tradition as a university community and manifested in a series of efforts to deal with the problems of discrimination against Negroes in housing, employment, and education. Despite the fact that the proportion of Negroes in its population doubled from 1950 to 1960, the extent of residential segregation actually decreased in Berkeley in this decade.[2] The Berkeley City Council was one of the

[1] "The First Step . . . on a Long Journey," OEO Congressional Presentation, April, 1965, p. 47.

[2] While the proportion of Negroes in the population increased from 11.7 percent in 1950 to 19.6 per cent in 1960, Berkeley had the fourth largest *decrease* on a national index of residential segregation. Karl E. and Alma F. Taeuber, *Negroes in Cities: Residential Segregation and Neighborhood Change* (Chicago: Aldine Publishing Co., 1965), p. 40. Although 88 per cent of Berkeley Negroes live in 7 out of the 28 census tracts, they are still better off with respect to education, employment, income, and housing than the nonwhite population of the Bay Area. For example, the proportion of professionals among Berkeley Negroes approximates the percentage of professionals among the total employed population in the San Francisco Bay area. Thomas W.

first to enact an antidiscrimination ordinance in 1962, although it was later defeated in a referendum. Nevertheless, whereas only 26 per cent of the Berkeley electorate were in favor of a fair housing ordinance in 1959, four years later 47 per cent wanted to keep it.[3] Voters in Berkeley opposed repealing the state's Fair Housing Law, Proposition 14, by the largest proportion in the San Francisco Bay area, 64 per cent. The Berkeley City Council assigned the field of human relations to its welfare commission, and a social planning consultant was employed in the city manager's office who subsequently devoted much time to strengthen communications between city hall and the Negro community. The Chamber of Commerce, in response to pressures largely from CORE, created an Equal Opportunity Committee and made some efforts to remove discriminatory barriers in employment. The board of education demonstrated a strong commitment to end *de facto* segregation in the schools by employing as school superintendent Dr. Neil Sullivan, who was nationally known for his courageous stand against segregated education. The failure of an attempt to recall the school board and the election of Negroes to the city council and to the board of education were further indications of a community climate in which racial injustice was at least recognized by a substantial number of Berkeley citizens.

Even before the Economic Opportunity Act had been passed, numerous social agencies and community groups had discussed its implications for Berkeley, and a large public meeting was convened by the Council of Social Planning—Berkeley Area around the end of September, 1964, to consider what steps might be taken. An eight-member study committee was appointed to recommend the form of a Community Action Program for Berkeley. It consisted of representatives from city government, the Council of Social Planning, the board of education, the state department of employment, the Chamber of Commerce, and the NAACP. They rejected proposals whereby Berkeley would become part of a county-wide CAP or receive staff service from the Council of Social Planning. Instead, they obtained approval to form a new, independent, nonprofit corporation, the Economic Opportunity Organization—Berkeley Area (EOO-BA), which would include official participation by city government and the Berkeley Unified School District. This interim planning committee incorporated itself in January, 1965 and served as a board of directors for the next few months as it deliberated on a more permanent form of organization.

Casstevens, *Politics, Housing and Race Relations: The Defeat of Berkeley's Fair Housing Ordinance* (Berkeley, Calif.: Institute of Governmental Studies, 1965), pp. 5-6.

[3] Casstevens, *op. cit.*, pp. 80-83.

At a public meeting on March 10, 1965, sponsored by the interim committee, objections were raised to this committee's proposal of an 11-member board consisting of six representatives of established agencies and five delegates from human relations organizations. The critics were mainly some white spokesmen for CORE and some Negro PTA leaders, whose recommendations were rather quickly accepted by the interim committee. It was agreed that only four places on the board should go to the original initiating groups—the Council of Social Planning, the schools, city government, and the Chamber of Commerce. The remaining seven places were to be selected by the city council from nominations of persons living in the low-income areas or representing organizations whose memberships resided there. No mention was made of such representatives being poor themselves.

The interim committee then asked CORE to draft a letter, which was then sent to almost one hundred organizations asking them for recommendations of persons to serve on the EOO-BA. A three-member nominating committee from the city council, including Wilmont Sweeney, its sole Negro member, then selected four Negro women from each of the four elementary school districts whose boundaries were coterminous with those of low-income census tracts. In addition, representatives of the Mexican-American Political Association and NAACP, instead of CORE and the council of churches, were also appointed by the city council.

When the board met for the first time in May, 1965 it elected John R. Lipscomb of the Chamber of Commerce as chairman. Dominant roles were played by Wilmont Sweeney, representing the city of Berkeley, and Dr. Samuel Schaaf, a member of the Berkeley Board of Education. Despite efforts to secure representation from the poor, it subsequently turned out that only one of the four target area representatives was a low-income person, and all of them played a rather negligible role in the deliberations. In this early stage of organization, the EOO-BA was seen largely as a vehicle for the funding of projects sponsored by the Berkeley schools, and the major influences were those of the professionals and elected officials from city government and the schools. The board of directors early asserted itself as the policy-making body and viewed its newly employed executive director, Scipio Porter, as distinctly subordinate to it.

THE CREATION OF THE CITIZENS ADVISORY COMMITTEE

One of the promises made by the interim committee in response to earlier criticisms from CORE regarding participation of the poor was that as soon as the new board was seated, a citizens' advisory committee would be created as a formal part of the structure. Pressure to appoint this supplementary vehicle for the participation of target area residents had increased as a result of a large number of board nominations submitted to the city council and the resentment over the council's initial selections. Apart from the possibility of co-opting indigenous leadership and defending the EOO-BA against any charge of elitism, other reasons for the establishment of the citizens' advisory committee (CAC) may have been the belief of several board members that target area residents who might benefit from the programs could not, because of a conflict of interest, serve as board members of a nonprofit charitable corporation.

The first discussion of the formation of the CAC occurred in the second meeting of the board of directors on May 13, 1965, when Chairman Henry Poppic, representing the Council of Social Planning and chairman of the By-Laws Committee, announced that CORE's suggestion for an advisory committee was under consideration. At the next meeting, on May 27, Chairman Sweeney of the board's nominating committee recommended the creation of a Citizens' Advisory Committee consisting of 60 members, one-third of whom should be residents and potential beneficiaries of the poverty program, one-third agency representatives with a substantial demonstrated interest in poverty, and one-third interested citizens. He further indicated that he had prepared a list of 49 possible nominees who could be contacted to serve on the committee. The motion to create the CAC was carried, and Mrs. Mary Jane Johnson, an NAACP activist, was selected by the board as chairman. By July 12, Sweeney had nominated the last 16 individuals to complete the roster of 60.

THE FIRST REORGANZATION

After the CAC was authorized and while its nominees were being recruited, the EOO board of directors spent most of the summer of 1965 in a prolonged process of developing the first set of bylaws. These meetings, which eventually centered on the size of the policy-making body, quickly involved the CAC leadership, and the changes that were eventually adopted on September 13, 1965 reflected the rising influence of the CAC.

Early in June, the By-Laws Committee of the board proposed a relatively minor change in the size and composition of the EOO—increasing its membership from 11 to 13 by adding a representative from the University of California and the chairman of the CAC. The CAC leadership, however, supported by two neighborhood councils in South and West Berkeley, pressed for larger target area representation by requesting a 17-member board that would include 9 instead of 4 representatives from the target areas.

While this debate was going on and four sets of bylaws were successively reviewed, the CAC, which was originally conceived as an advisory body to the board of directors, began acting as if it were the appropriate source of project proposals. Subcommittees were appointed by Mrs. Johnson, the chairman, to consider suggestions and project proposals in the fields of education, health and welfare, and housing. Members of the educational subcommittee met with Berkeley school administrators on the details of the Head Start program funded by the EOO. Out of their dissatisfaction with the personnel policies in these projects, CAC leaders were able to get support from Dr. Schaaf, representing the board of education on the EOO, to agree to consider only those educational programs that were initiated by the CAC. From this delegation of authority it was only a small step from the CAC to assume, informally and without effective opposition from the board, responsibility for the planning of all projects.

The struggle for a greater voice by the CAC was reflected in part in the personality and ideological conflicts between its chairman, Mrs. Johnson, and Councilman Sweeney, who represented a more conservative approach to problems of race and poverty. Mrs. Johnson presented herself as an indigenous spokesman for the poor, and it was also rumored that she might challenge Sweeney for his city council seat. The growing power of the CAC was clearly evident on September 13, 1965, when the board adopted the new bylaws. While providing for a membership larger than that proposed by the CAC, these still gave those purporting to speak for low-income groups an effective majority. The new board was to consist of 21 members, including 9 elected representatives of the target areas and delegates from at least six organizations with low-income constituencies, such as CORE, NAACP, West and South Berkeley neighborhood councils, welfare rights organizations, and the Mexican-American Political Association, in addition to representatives of the city schools, labor, churches, the University and the Berkeley board of supervisors. In addition, CAC members would comprise 20 out of the 41 members of the new corporate membership of the EOO.

BYLAW IMPLEMENTATION AND PROGRAM CONCERNS

In the fall of 1965, with a new set of bylaws, the EOO-BA began to turn its attention to more substantive aspects of the war on poverty. Still pending, however, was the implementation of the new bylaws pertaining to the composition of the board. The new representation created a unique arrangement whereby members appointed to the new board sat side by side with the old board members. It was stipulated that the first 4 of the 11, the original initiating groups, would serve until July, 1966 and the other 7 would remain in service until July, 1967, completing the transition to the new plan. This meant that until July of 1967 the 9 resident participants would not be fully represented, because the interim membership would be holding a portion of those seats.

The redirection of attention from procedural matters, which preoccupied the board during most of 1965, to the more substantive elements of project proposals coincided with a noticeable decrease in attendance on both the board and the CAC. The board continued to meet semimonthly, but the CAC reduced its meetings to once a month. The attendance at the board meetings fell off to little more than half its total membership, as four of the original members resigned, and the CAC, despite its increased power, experienced a decline in attendance from 30 or 40 to 10 or 15, of whom less than half were active members. Most of the nontarget area residents dropped out of the CAC in the early part of 1966, and it became more and more a small clique of Negro residents who were split in their support between Sweeney and Mrs. Johnson.

In program development the trend continued toward increasing responsibility for the CAC. Although neither body had delineated its responsibilities, the CAC continued to assume chief responsibility for the initiation of project proposals and the determination of priorities. This left the board acting more like a review body than a policy-making group. Despite a strong effort by a small group of board members to stop the power drain, a slim majority conceded the propriety of CAC initiation of proposals.

The creation of the CAC and its subsequent activity changed the complexion of the EOO from an organization originally dominated by the four initiating organizational interests to a community agency increasingly responsive to the spokesmen for the recipients of the programs. In the early stages, the program orientation of the EOO-BA was primarily educational, reflecting the influence of the Council of Social Planning and the school board, but as the CAC influence increased, the board was forced to accept not only the new members representing ethnic minority interests but a new list of program priorities consisting of employment and small business development, with education last. Thus, although their constituency had declined, the CAC leadership won a victory for their point of view by numerical default and by virtue of access to information. The CAC emerged as the most influential body of the EOO-BA.

THE EMERGENCE OF NEW LEADERSHIP

During the first part of 1966 the relationship between the board and the CAC remained generally unchanged. The board continued to defer many matters to the CAC, and the chairman of the CAC continued to press for more power over programs. Attendance remained at a relatively low level in both organizations during the four months from February to June, 1966. During this period the CAC convened only three times. Of these meetings two were joint meetings with the board of directors. The board did not do much better; on two occasions, less than a quorum attended and no action could be taken. There were numerous resignations from the board, and five vacancies were unfilled for over five months. The replacements were increasingly sympathetic to the positions taken by the CAC.

Among the proposals dealing with resident participation that were approved by the board in 1966 was one calling for a Neighborhood Service Center and a Community Adult Participation Program, both of which were eventually implemented later in the year. These projects involved 37 nonprofessional jobs for residents and were awarded primarily to women in the target areas who carried out information and referral tasks as well as some community organization. The operation of these service programs gradually diminished the informational role of the CAC, and a number of its members received jobs in the programs. Fifteen block clubs and improvement associations were staffed in West and South Berkeley, and some conflict developed between them and existing neighborhood councils in the area. Controversies also occurred around the use of this staff for voter registration, resulting in a conflict between the CAC and the board over this assignment. Fearing the use of staff for partisan purposes, the CAC opposed their assignment to voter registration, but in contrast to its usual practice, the board stood fast against the CAC and continued the project.

It was during this controversy that the professional staff emerged as an important policy-making element. Originally subordinate to the board and distrusted by the CAC, the staff became a more cohesive and powerful group of professionals and nonprofessionals with the ability to shape policy more effectively than either of these two deliberative bodies. During the latter part of 1966 and into 1967 the three components—the CAC, the board, and the staff—became involved in a three-way struggle, each group seeking to maintain its particular powers, to the end that most of the participants became suspicious, hostile, and weary.

The CAC, which had acquired broad program authority, seemed to lose its esprit during the conflict; interest waned and attendance dropped to as low as five at one point. The board sensed that much of its power had been lost to the professional staff and the staff in turn was also demoralized because of this struggle.

Toward the end of March, 1967, the EOO-BA director tendered his resignation and was quickly followed by three key staff personnel from April to June. These resignations including those of Mrs. Johnson, the CAC chairman, and Wilmont Sweeney had a serious effect, because both the programs and board lost leadership and began to fail.

At the June, 1967 meeting of the corporation, the board completed the transition to the new membership plan adopted in September, 1965; they secured a new executive director, appointed a new CAC chairman and enacted another set of bylaws that provided for the first time that target area representatives would be elected by their respective target areas.

SUMMARY

The Berkeley EOO was organized as a nonprofit corporation, although it enjoyed close working relationships with city government and the schools. Initiated by an interim committee representing four established interests the EOO was quite responsive to the demands by CORE to increase representation of the low-income neighborhoods. This was in keeping with Berkeley's tradition of being liberal and relatively more sensitive to the needs of minority groups than other communities. An original board of 11 persons, including 4 nominees from the elementary school districts selected by the city council, was incorporated and approved the first series of school-sponsored projects. It also created a Citizens' Advisory Committee of 60 persons, one-third of whom were from the target areas. Although it had only advisory powers, the CAC quickly became an important force and began taking on program planning functions, beginning with education. The board eventually served as a review and ratifying authority for project proposals developed by the CAC.

Increased representation of target area residents was achieved by the process of bylaw revision in which the CAC was able to gain sufficient support for its position, which was subsequently adopted by the board. Enlarged to 21 members, the board was effectively controlled by those sympathetic to the idea of resident participation. The CAC and its supporters continued to dominate the priority-setting and policy-making processes of the EOO at the same time that they were declining in numerical strength. Despite these shifts in power, interest in the EOO waned as board, CAC, and staff members resigned. Their resignations resulted in considerable turnover, reorganization, and a rather desultory community program.

Contra Costa County Case Study

ORIGINS OF THE EOC

Contra Costa, like some other Bay Area counties, was once an agricultural county but has in recent years become more heavily populated and industrialized. Pockets of poverty have grown up in the new industrial regions of Richmond and Pittsburg, and also persist in the still largely agricultural East County where the county seat, Martinez, is located.

In the spring of 1964, rumors of the possible passage of a federal Economic Opportunity Act began to reach public and private agencies in the county. Particularly interested in the possibilities of such a program for the county was the Council of Community Services, a social planning body under voluntary auspices whose president, Dr. Henrik Blum, was the public health officer for the county. At the time, the council was deeply involved in two large-scale, federally financed demonstration projects in Negro neighborhoods in Richmond and Pittsburg. In March of 1964, the council's executive, Richard Sax, took the initiative to sound out the county administrator regarding the Economic Opportunity Act, but found little interest. With the passage of the Act there was more receptivity to the formation of a Community Action Program, and in August, after some informal discussions between members of the Health and Welfare Subcommittee of the Board of Supervisors, representatives of the Council of Community Services, and the Taxpayers' Association, the Board of Supervisors finally accepted the council's offer to convene an advisory committee.

Staff members of the Public Health Department and the council then prepared data for a series of meetings with representatives of schools, public housing, city government, employment, and public welfare to acquaint them with the Economic Opportunity Act and to urge them to prepare specific proposals that might be funded. Meetings were held in quick succession in Richmond and Pittsburg, in which some low-income persons known to the council were involved.

In short order, the council convened an "Economic Opportunity Council" of 162 persons by extending an invitation to several hundred organizations throughout the county. Three meetings were held, and 50 specific proposals including provision for 800 new jobs and amounting to over $5.5 million were approved by approximately 75 persons who designated themselves the Contra Costa Economic Opportunity Council. The various projects were first screened by a steering committee of 21 persons, including seven representatives from low-income areas in the county and seven each from governmental agencies and other community interests. There was a great emphasis on completing this work as soon as possible; later, Contra Costa claimed it was the first California county to submit a comprehensive proposal.

It was also proposed that this Economic Opportunity Council function as a nonprofit corporation, contracting with the Council of Community Services for staff services with the county serving as the fiscal agent. There was, however, considerable ambiguity in the description of the relationships between these three bodies. While the Board of Supervisors did approve the projects as submitted to it, it modified the proposal and lodged the administrative responsibility in the county government. This was done largely because of the advice of a seven-member advisory committee consisting of the mayors and at the instigation of the representative of the Taxpayers' Association and other county and school representatives, who strongly opposed the plan for staffing the EOC by the Council of Community Services.

After several weeks, word leaked out that OEO had rejected the proposed CAP and instead funded several separate projects that had been included in the county program package, including a very substantial community development demonstration project sponsored by the Council of Community Services in Richmond.

Furthermore, the regional OEO office had serious reservations about the Board of Supervisors' acting as the CAP with only a committee of seven members as an advisory group and recommended that a nonprofit corporation or some joint agreement be worked out that would broaden the role of the advisory committee. Somewhat reluctantly, the Board of Supervisors agreed to continue as the official Community Action Agency and to enlarge its advisory committee to 28 with the addition of the members of the original 21-member steering committee as a reconstituted Economic Opportunity Council. The county administrator's office was asked to serve as staff, and Contra Costa thus became the only Bay Area county government to assume administrative and fiscal authority for the CAP.

Slowly, efforts were resumed to encourage public and private agencies to submit their proposals through the Contra Costa EOC for ratification, and an application was subsequently made for a program development grant.

Almost five months passed before the actual size of the EOC was stipulated. During that time, membership was open to both organizations and individuals with an interest in poverty programs. In contrast to other CAPs, this one placed no limits on the number of representatives from various sectors of community life. As a result, the membership in the EOC progressively expanded from 28 in January of 1965 to 60, established as the limit in May, 1965, and then again to 100, the number authorized on September 29, 1965. Members were elected by the council and subsequently approved by the Board of Supervisors.

In March of 1965, bylaws and rules of procedure were adopted, in which the purposes of the council and its advisory powers were described as providing "policy coordination for all aspects of the War on Poverty in Contra Costa, reviewing new and continuing programs submitted under the Economic Opportunity Act of 1964, and recommending amendments, modifications, approval or disapproval." It was further "intended that membership in the Council shall be broadly representative in order to reflect both geographical and social economic factors and shall specifically include adequate representation of the target groups." [4] Also in March, the mayor of Martinez was elected as the first chairman of the council.

During the first few months of the council's operation, it tended to be dominated by a relatively small number of city and county officials and other governmental agency representatives, who constituted over half of its membership. A full-time director for the EOC staff, Eugene Brusatori, a former social work supervisor in the welfare department, was not employed by the county until the end of May. The small staff was subject to civil service regulations and assigned by the county manager to the Office of Economic Opportunity of Contra Costa and to serve the EOC. Finally, in April, a first set of eight program proposals was approved by the EOC and ratified by the supervisors.

CORE LEADERSHIP AND THE CHANGING CHARACTER OF THE COUNCIL

During the formation of the council, an important role was played by the CORE representative, James Vann, even though action on CORE's application for membership was delayed almost six months. On May 16, 1965, largely under Vann's direction, CORE wrote a long letter to the council that constituted a significant effort to examine the basic organization and future plans of the EOC. In the letter, CORE complained that its members had not been admitted to council membership and attacked the council structure as inadequately representative of those people being served, and in particular, overloaded with city and county officials. They pointed out, for instance, that there was no spokesman for industry and only one for labor. They charged that no effort had been made to determine specific target areas, short of using census tracts, or to determine the problems existing in depressed areas. It was felt that program proposals were simply extensions of existing programs espoused by public agencies.[5] CORE called for further involvement of the poor in planning, and in particular, they asked for the dissemination of information, hopefully by area offices more conveniently located than the county seat, Martinez, which was remotely situated in regard to the poor areas of the county. They challenged the council proceedings by specifically objecting to the Board of Supervisors' reserving the final authority on all matters, the electing of officers and committees by the council before it expanded membership, and various other parliamentary procedures. Finally, CORE expressed disenchantment with a number of programs being proposed

[4] By-laws and Rules of Procedure, Contra Costa County EOC, March, 1965.
[5] CORE letter to the EOC, May 16, 1965.

by the welfare department and the Richmond Community Development Demonstration Project, another OEO financed program.

Subsequently, CORE was admitted to membership, and its representative, James Vann, became a member of the seven-member rules committee, which then took the leadership in bringing about structural changes in the council. In addition, the rules committee was the seat of power in the EOC because it controlled the nomination of council members. The members of this committee included representatives of business, education, labor, Greater Richmond Parish, and CORE, and a Negro minister from the newly organized Council for Community Advancement in Richmond. It usually had two or three members, though, to represent groups in the target areas or the "poor."

During June and July, 1965, the influential liberal, white community members in the council began to drop out, and they were replaced by the growing number of ethnic minority representatives, largely from the Negro neighborhoods in the communities of Richmond and Pittsburg. Although on a county-wide basis the Negro community could be regarded as relatively insignificant politically, this was not necessarily true in Richmond, the largest and most industrialized city. In Richmond, a Negro had been elected mayor and was subsequently appointed to a judgeship. Negroes were involved in Democratic party politics, and the NAACP and CORE had had active memberships for many years. The North Richmond Neighborhood House had attracted widespread attention because of its programs for Negro parents and youth. The Richmond Community Development Project, an OEO demonstration project, with its "new careers" programs and the organization of a new Negro civic group, "Advance," also gave impetus to and opportunities for a more assertive role for Negroes. In Pittsburg, the Council of Community Services and the Social Service Department had sponsored a Concerted Services project in which substantial federal funds were going into a few census tracts in which Negroes lived. The county supervisor from that district, who was in close touch with this project, was considered to be sympathetic to the program and reputed to be available and receptive to communication with Negroes who lived in Pittsburg. Thus, the Negro community in Contra Costa had tended to make its influence felt by playing an active role within some of the existing private and public agencies. This also became true in regard to the affairs of the EOC.

On July 15, 1965, under Vann's leadership, the rules committee recommendations for changes were adopted, providing for open meetings of the council, and restricting group and organizational membership to two-thirds of the total council and individual membership to one-third. Within the affairs of the council itself a voting split became noticeable along agency-resident lines. Perhaps the most important action of the July meeting was to establish an executive committee of six persons, including two target area representatives.

These changes emphasized the "open" character that the council was acquiring. Meetings were held at various locations in the county, with bus transportation and car pools provided to increase participation by different segments of the community. The EOC emerged with a highly diverse membership wherein delegates from the county departments and the neighborhood councils and representatives of the poor sat side by side, each with one vote. Programs were reviewed by the Program Application Committee, with the council passing on them. Meetings assumed a town meeting character with membership attendance of about 30 to 40, and with 50 to 100 persons in the audience.

GROWING REPRESENTATION OF THE POOR

The principal and most radical organizational change grew out of the rules committee recommendations, which were debated at the September 30 meeting of the council. It was proposed by the rules committee that the total membership of the EOC should be set at 100, with 40 elected representatives of the poor who were poor themselves, 30 members from agencies and organizations giving direct services to the poor, and 30 members-at-large and representatives from agencies and organizations having a contribution to make to the economic potential development or climate of the community. Although Vann had been unable to get more than 40 per cent representation of the poor, elected representation was suggested for the first time.

In the rules committee deliberations, Vann had suggested that 75 per cent of the EOC consist of elected representatives, and he now decided, together with other neighborhood representatives, to carry his battle to the floor of the council. Prior efforts were successful in insuring a large attendance of target area residents, and it was arranged that a motion calling for 75 per cent representation be introduced. This was initially opposed by agency, labor, and government representatives. After a lengthy, heated, and complex debate, however, the council, 37-1, adopted a compromise of 60-20-20. At this same meeting, the businessman who had served as head of the rules committee resigned. Shortly thereafter, Vann took his place, and the committee was charged with formulating the details of the election procedures; that is, deciding who was qualified to vote, who could be elected, the balloting process, and so forth.

In October, CORE again addressed a letter to the council, in which they sought to call the council's attention to several matters. In particular, they called for an executive committee consisting of a majority of indigenous representatives with the elected delegates in each target area electing from among them one representative to the executive committee. They suggested that advisory panels with representatives of the poor be set up to review proposed programs during the development phase, and they once again asked for regional information and service centers. Further, they emphasized that program priorities must be established, with more attention given to job and direct service programs.[6]

By December, a subcommittee was set up to conduct elections. It included Craig Randall of the Contra Costa Council of Community Services, James Vann, and the staff of the EOC office. The December 16 meeting of the council agreed that 56 seats would be filled by election and 4 held open for future poverty areas. The debate centered around suggestions that elections be conducted under the auspices of existing neighborhood groups, such as the Neighborhood House Project and the Community Development Project; however, Vann pointed out that competing groups might arise, impeding the free nature of the elections. The council answered the CORE letter by agreeing that participation of the poor in program planning and implementation was important and that jobs and neighborhood service centers would be given priority in existing and future projects. Perhaps because active neighborhood programs existed in some areas, separately funded by the OEO, the EOC never did succeed in decentralizing and establishing neighborhood centers.

In January, E. P. Stephenson, executive director of the North Richmond Neighborhood House, again called for conducting elections through the existing neighborhood organizations, pointing out that representatives elected through such organizations would have a constituency to whom they would be accountable, and also a means of staying informed about problems in their areas. The rules committee, however, continued with their independent election plans, scheduling the election in 21 census tracts in May. At this point, the council consisted of 73 members, 18 of whom were believed to be poor themselves. Twenty-six of the members were Negro and six came from Spanish-speaking groups; one of these, Primo Ruiz, was elected as council chairman.

Criteria for the election were established as follows: Each candidate must have resided in a census tract or voting district or adjoining census tract or voting district for at least one year and meet the income criteria for poverty as previously established by the council. These criteria were: single person, $1900 yearly; couple, $2400; family of three, $3450; family of four, $4100; family of five, $4850; family of six, $5300; for each dependent over six in a family, $600 was to be added. Each voter had to be a

[6] CORE letter to the EOC, October 21, 1965.

resident of the census tract, qualify as a member of a low-income family, and show evidence of qualification if challenged by another resident of the same census tract. The term of membership for elected representatives was to be two years except that for the first election, one-half of the terms would expire on June 30, 1967; the remaining one-half on June 30, 1968. In addition, no elected council representative could be impeached before the end of the first six months in office.

In March, 1966, the OEO declared that further funding of programs through the Board of Supervisors would be contingent upon their passing a resolution expressing their willingness to appoint anyone to the EOC who was duly elected, and the board subsequently agreed to this. The OEO, however, did not approve the use of any federal funds for the costs of the election, and the lack of adequate support and manpower severely limited the effectiveness of the election campaign. According to the conservative estimates of the election committee, only some 40 per cent of the county's poor were too widely scattered to make their candidacy or voting practical. When the elections were actually held, approximately 11 per cent of the eligible voters in the voting districts turned out.[7] Thus for the first time, 60 elected representatives of the poor took their place upon the 100-member council. Vann was subsequently elected chairman of the EOC and served during 1966-67; the elected representatives assumed a dominant role in the policy-making processes of the EOC under his leadership.

SUMMARY

In Contra Costa County the Board of Supervisors somewhat reluctantly agreed to serve as the CAP's sponsor and functioned mainly as a ratifying body for the EOC. Originally established through the interest of the Council of Community Services and some county agencies, the EOC had an early history marked by the progressive enlargement of its size and increased representation of the poor. These changes were achieved over a six-month period by means of a parliamentary process and occurred principally because of the forceful leadership assumed by the representative of CORE, who later became the chairman of the EOC.

[7] Election memo from Ruth Anderson to Craig Randall, President, Bay Area Social Planning Council, June 22, 1966.

II

COMPARATIVE ANALYSES

6

TYPES OF COMMUNITY CONFLICT RESOLUTION: WHO SHALL CONTROL THE CAP?

The controversy was inevitable; what is being attempted is a fundamental change in the way government responds to the needs of the poor.[1]

A comparison of the five communities reveals three different types of CAP responses to the external and internal pressures to increase the representation of the poor on the governing board and to grant greater autonomy and policy-making power to the neighborhood organizations. These patterns of community decision making or more accurately, conflict resolution can be classified as a *debate, game,* or *fight.*[2]

In both Berkeley and Contra Costa County the progressive enlargement of representation from low-income groups came about through a process of bylaw revision that extended over a period of three to four months. In Berkeley this process also coincided with the informal assumption of planning responsibilities by the CAC, and similarly in Contra Costa County, the EOC became the major planning body for the antipoverty program. Represented on these bylaw committees, although in the minority, were persons who identified with and defended the interest of the poor and who pursued this cause with great persistence.

The claim of the low-income groups for a greater voice was regarded as quite legitimate and no strong opposition developed either in government or on the part of the professionals. In Berkeley, it will be remembered, the issue was the size of the board, and the final compromise was an even larger governing body than the CAC had proposed. In Contra

[1] President Lyndon B. Johnson, Message on Urban and Rural Poverty, March 15, 1967, p. 3. (90th Congress, 1st Session, House of Representatives, Document No. 88.)

[2] Anatole Rappoport, *Debates, Games, Fights* (Ann Arbor: University of Michigan Press, 1961). These distinctions are applied to the field of international relations. Their use in describing community decision-making patterns is discussed in this chapter.

Costa County, the debate was whether the target areas should have 40 per cent, 55 per cent, or 75 per cent of the places on the new board; the compromise was 60 per cent.

Thus, the response in these two communities can be characterized essentially as a *debate* in which different points of view were eventually resolved over a relatively short period of time through the formal parliamentary procedure of committee and board meetings. The proponents of resident participation were either able to persuade their opponents or to obtain enough votes to win when the matter came before the CAP board. The gains in resident participation were achieved through the skillful and diligent use of rather similar resources for influence by CAC members in Berkeley and by the CORE representative and his allies in Contra Costa. These resources consisted essentially of strong commitments, a demonstrated willingness to work, political skills, and knowledge, which helped these people impress the other members with their competence. In addition, the sanction given to maximum feasible participation by OEO reinforced the pressures generated by these ethnic representatives.

Some other similarities in the debates that took place in Berkeley and Contra Costa County were: the initiation of the process in both communities by CORE, which had considerably greater influence in Contra Costa than in Berkeley; the enabling and facilitating rather than the assertive role of the executive in both communities; the provision for eventual area-wide public elections in the target areas; and the extremely slow pace in decentralizing programs, particularly in Berkeley.

Because of their greater complexity and conflictual character, the community responses in Oakland, San Francisco, and Santa Clara County will now be analyzed in more detail.

During most of 1965 and continuing into the early months of 1966, these three CAPs were embroiled to various degrees in a struggle for power with the neighborhoods that ended largely in substantial victories of the target areas, which achieved their goals of "control" and the decentralization of authority. In order to understand better the dynamics of this process, we shall first identify the *contestants* in these community conflicts, some *predisposing and precipitating* factors, and the *pattern of issue emergence;* and then examine the *process of conflict resolution.*

The Partisans

The antagonists in these three communities consisted of two groups. On one side, opposing the transfer of power to the target areas, were the executive leadership systems of the CAP. In San Francisco, this consisted of the Mayor, who had appointed the original EOC himself and, apart from OEO, appears to have had relatively little support. A former Democratic congressman with a background of many years' service in the labor movement, he fought bitterly to maintain control over the program, often asserting that city funds were involved for which he was politically accountable. In Oakland, the chairman of the Economic Development Council and the director of the Department of Human Resources usually worked together almost as a team, and they had the backing at least of the business representatives on the OEDC. Both of these men were upper middle-class Negro professionals who saw the poverty program as providing an opportunity to help even the chances for Negro competition in the job market. In Santa Clara County the executive director of the EOC, a former social worker, also stood almost alone, although he was backed by his chairman and representatives of government and social agencies on the original EOC. Both the executives of the Santa Clara and Oakland CAPs placed a high value on administrative efficiency, merit system hiring, and a nonpolitical process of social service program development.

Arrayed against these officials in San Francisco and Santa Clara County were ethnic-based coalitions led by relatively young, militant, politically astute spokesmen of minority organizations. In San Francisco, most of the leaders came from the civil rights movement. They saw an opportunity to organize the poor, most of whom were Negro or Spanish-speaking, with federal sanction. Essentially, they sought control of the program in order to promote the interests of their respective ethnic groups. In San Francisco, the leadership who spoke for the target areas in the name of the poor was largely Negro, although few of them were either elected or impoverished themselves. Maximum feasible participation was given the strongest political interpretation by this new generation of ideologues, who saw the poverty program not only as a means of obtaining power over some new social service resources, but also as a way of obtaining leverage on other community institutions by building a political base of power in the target areas.

In Santa Clara County, the Mexican-American coalition secured allies among labor, religion, and the NAACP. In contrast to the emphasis on maximum feasible participation of the poor in San Francisco, in Santa Clara, low-income representation was promoted more by OEO than by the Mexican-American spokesmen, who were more interested in obtaining additional power for their own ethnic group. Only much later did they raise the issue of maximum participation. On the Area Service Center level, the issue was more one of local autonomy than participation of the poor; although in four Areas there was also a strong concern with securing low-income representation. Other groups aligned against the Santa Clara

EOC, in addition to the persons in Area Service Centers seeking full autonomy, were several governmental and voluntary welfare agencies as well as several dissident EOC staff members.

In contrast to San Francisco and Santa Clara, however, leadership in the target areas in Oakland was provided primarily by a group of young, white, Protestant ministers identified with the three parish organizations that had been organized to work among the poor. They failed in their initial attempt to secure target area control over the program and later joined forces with the other spokesmen for the advisory committees to seek increased representation on the executive committee and the board of directors of the OEDC. Ultimately, they sought majority control, together with the assignment of planning and program sponsoring functions to the advisory committees. The Oakland coalition was perhaps the weakest of the three, even though it did enjoy for a time the support of some of the central staff members. Contrary to the trend in San Francisco and Santa Clara, where it was possible for both Negro and Spanish-speaking groups to unite in the CUAP, there was a strong separatist move among Mexican-American spokesmen in Oakland.

Both in Washington and in the regional office in San Francisco, OEO must also be considered one of the partisans. In Santa Clara, OEO intervention, whether intentional or not, served to strengthen the position of the Mexican-Americans. In San Francisco, the Mayor was able to get support both from Washington and the regional office, but it did not prevent the ultimate victory of the target areas, which received little support from Washington. In Oakland, the OEO investigation, which both sides claimed they wanted, seems to have had little influence on the final outcome. The forces at work that produced the changes in composition of the OEDC seem to have been more or less independent of the OEO investigation, even though there was considerable similarity between the two sets of recommendations. In general, the OEO regional office took a "hard" line and stressed the maximum participation of the poor as early as the summer of 1965.[3]

Notably absent from the ranks of the partisans in this community decision-making process were the customary economic influentials. They seem to have abdicated in both San Francisco and Santa Clara; in the latter, their resignation from the EOC gave the opponents of the executive director the necessary votes to dismiss him. In Oakland, the few representatives of business and industry comprised a minority that more or less consistently supported the chairman. In both San Francisco and Oakland,

[3] Evidence of the official position and high expectations of the regional office can be found in regional CAA Bulletins, Number 11, July 2, 1965; Number 12, July 26, 1965; Number 15, October 5, 1965 and in particular Number 16, October 29, 1965.

the mayors deplored the lack of participation of employer groups and regarded this as a major deficiency of the CAPs.

There were also some notable differences in the character of the influence systems that were pitted against each other in these communities. San Francisco was the only community where government was directly involved, in the person of the Mayor, who as the chief executive of the city and county had appointed all the members of the original EOC. In Santa Clara, where the EOC was also in the form of a nonprofit corporation, the Board of Supervisors did not seek to control the antipoverty program and did not intervene in the contest between solidary and bureaucratic power, the latter manifested in the person of the executive director. Oakland stood midway between Santa Clara and San Francisco in the degree of political power opposed to the target areas. As in Santa Clara, the power that the Oakland advisory committees faced was bureaucratic, wielded by the OEDC chairman and the executive of the Oakland Department of Human Resources. As far as is known, the city council in Oakland refrained from involving itself in the conflict over representation, in contrast to its intervention in the issue over the police review board. In Oakland and Santa Clara the struggles over representation were intramural, that is, within the CAP, whereas in San Francisco they were between the Mayor and the EOC.

In all three situations, the contest became highly personalized as the two sets of antagonists fought over control of this new social service and political resource.

The Process

In addition to the similarity of the contested issues and the character of the partisans in each of the areas, some of the factors predisposing and precipitating the struggle between the CAPs and the neighborhoods were also very much the same. For example, each community made a series of crucial decisions regarding the *priority of program development over community organization.* This meant that the grassroots participation of residents would be sought *after* the planning or approval of programs by the board of directors or the organization of some official structure in the target area. This approach was justified on the grounds of expediency: OEO funding deadlines precluded any extensive involvement of residents because of insufficient time. This action was opposed by many of the target area organizations that were subsequently established by the CAP and was used as evidence that the CAP was not sincerely interested in carrying out the objectives of the antipoverty program.

Although these decisions started from somewhat different premises and conditions, their consequences were essentially the same. In San Francisco, an attempt was made to interject target area ideas into professionally designed projects, but these opinions were secured through an unsystematic sampling of households conducted by agency staff members rather than as an expression from organized neighborhood groups. This type of client consultation was rejected by the CUAP, as was the rather casual and token involvement of some of the traditionally ascribed minority spokesmen in Oakland by the Interagency staff in the summer of 1964. Subsequently, three major sets of decisions regarding submission and funding of proposals for the first year were made by the OEDC before representatives from the advisory committees were seated.

In Santa Clara County, priority was assigned by the executive director to the development of Area Service Center structures and programs *before* community organization would be undertaken. The emphasis on the speedy creation of functioning organizational structures encouraged the use of existing organizations and led to jurisdictional disputes between groups seeking official recognition as the legitimate representative of the EOC. In addition, there was opposition to resident participation in four other areas, which was eventually directed against the executive himself.

There was also a common element in the event that seemed to precipitate a more overt form of conflict between the neighborhoods and the CAP; namely, the reluctance of the executive leadership of the CAPs either to pay sufficient attention to the demands of their antagonists or to try to co-opt them. In San Francisco, Mayor Shelley ignored the first requests by CUAP on February 28, 1965, and the matter was not even discussed at EOC meetings. This action served to provoke CUAP to send a telegram to OEO demanding the cessation of funds until the Mayor met with them. The Mayor's intransigence made him an extremely convenient common target for all of the groups comprising the CUAP and helped draw this loose coalition together.

Similarly, in Santa Clara County the refusal of the executive director to accede to the Mexican-Americans' demand for greater representation and the appointment of a Spanish-speaking deputy director greatly angered them and led to their request for OEO intervention. This resulted in the official request from the OEO regional office for reconstitution of the EOC, which subsequently made possible the dismissal of the executive. The director's failure to make concessions to the Mexican-Americans regarding the position of deputy director or approval of the CSO project, his difficulties in delegating authority and tolerating opposition or even differences also served to antagonize many staff members and professional colleagues and made it easier for the Mexican-American leaders to secure allies.

In Oakland, however, the willingness of the OEDC gradually to make small concessions and compromises during 1965 probably prevented any severe rupture in their relationship and, at the same time, also retarded the development of a coalition between the Target Area Advisory Committees. Some of the demands from the target areas were anticipated and concessions were made by the OEDC without its being formally pressed to do so. It was only after the advisory committees, having had a taste of participation in a program review process for the first time, saw their recommendations ignored that they "revolted." The arbitrary rejection by the OEDC chairman of the February, 1966 decision to move toward majority control by the target areas was also a strong impetus in bringing together the coalition of the advisory committees that planned the strategy leading to the walkout on March 19.

What is illustrated in all these precipitating events is that a strong show of force produced an equally powerful response in the antagonists; that is, power called forth power when the cause was legitimate and there was belief in the sufficiency and appropriateness of resources for success. What the CAP executive systems accomplished by their refusal to listen or act was to strengthen the determination of their opposition, pushing them closer together and provoking them into an adversary role.

The pattern of issue development varied. In San Francisco, the question of control of the CAP emerged early; it was explicitly acknowledged by both sides, and it persisted for eight months as CUAP consistently and progressively enlarged the extent of the power it demanded for the target areas—from increased representation to majority control of the executive committee and the EOC and, finally, to administrative authority over all programs. Along with the escalation of their demands came an increasingly personal attack on the mayor, who reciprocated in kind.

In Oakland and Santa Clara County, the goals were more emergent and they shifted. After several false starts and premature demands, the Oakland neighborhood advisory committees became more informed and assertive, although the demand for 51 per cent control of the OEDC was usually in the background and pressed only sporadically. This issue did not become a unifying bond among the advisory committees until six months had passed. The uneven pace and gradually expanded scope of their demands reflected a general lack of militancy and a weak constituency, as well as the effects of the compromises and concessions granted, which served to "cool out" some of the activists. Whereas the white middle-class ministers who were the advisory committee chairmen in Fruitvale and North Oakland may have wanted to move more aggressively, they were constrained by their less militant constituency and their white middle-class status, of which they were frequently reminded by the OEDC leadership.

In Santa Clara County, once the question of Mexican-American representation was raised, it became more and more important and within three months was resolved in their favor, although even here there were a number of false starts. The issue of Area Service Center autonomy was fought out in the nine different areas over a 10-month period and finally settled when the reconstituted EOC and its new executive were in agreement regarding the policy of decentralization. There was in Santa Clara County a succession of issues; one rode on the next, and they eventually culminated in a single controversy over the executive. His dismissal represented a victory for both the Mexican-Americans and those in favor of decentralizing power in the Area Service Centers.

In all three communities, despite their disparate patterns of issue emergence, the antagonists all accused each other of essentially the same "crime": an illegitimate "power grab."

The pattern of conflict resolution in San Francisco and Santa Clara County can be characterized as a *fight* from start to finish, while in Oakland the struggle was primarily a *game* that spilled over into a fight for a period of somewhat less than two months. In San Francisco and Santa Clara, there was an either/or choice: either the position of Mayor or that of the CUAP would prevail; either Potts was going to be the executive director or he was not; power would either be centralized in the EOC or decentralized in the Area Service Centers. In San Francisco, the final showdown came about because the ethnic-based coalition persisted unrelentingly and was able to mobilize a broad and impressive expression of community support. The victory of the neighborhoods was also commensurate with the intensity of the fight, since they achieved a measure of autonomy and power greater than that of any other community.

In Santa Clara County, the combination of OEO requirements and a staff revolt, together with the persistent pressure of the Mexican-American coalition, ended in the dismissal of the executive and a victory for those in favor of a decentralized program. Walkouts, boycotts, picketing, demonstrations, personal attacks, staff conspiracies, and packing of meetings were some of the organizational weapons used. The executive CAP leadership in Santa Clara and San Francisco as well as in Oakland used such tactics as delay, denial, obfuscation, discrediting the opposition and its leadership, insults, and appeals to OEO.

In Oakland, however, the issues were not so mutually exclusive. The process stretched out for almost a year and was eventually resolved by means of persuasion, committee debate, and negotiation in a manner similar to that by which Berkeley and Contra Costa County gave additional representation to the poor. In the course of the year, concessions and compromises were slowly but consistently made by the OEDC to avoid conflict and perhaps to discourage a coalition. The muted character of the conflict in Oakland was further evident in the manner in which the OEDC eventually severed its relationship to the city after eight months of discussions. Both sides sought to avoid the separation, which was mutually regarded as regrettable, and the Mayor announced that he would continue to recognize the independent OEDC as the official CAP.

This pattern contrasts with the unwillingness of the San Francisco Mayor and the executive of the Santa Clara EOC to negotiate until virtually coerced to do so. In the case of the latter, the negotiation was delayed too long to be effective. Thus, while Oakland co-opted and compromised with the opposition, San Francisco and Santa Clara County did not do this. By underestimating the determination and strength of the coalition, the antagonistic actions of the San Francisco Mayor and Santa Clara executive helped promote solidarity and a will to fight among their opponents. In addition, they were unable to develop sufficient additional support for their position to countervail the newly emergent power of the ethnic coalition.

Despite the varied character of the routes they took, all of the CAPs expanded their governing boards and executive committees to permit greater numerical representation of the target areas. In addition, the neighborhoods acquired greater autonomy and policy-making authority. Another important aspect of these changes was the method of selection of the representatives of the poor. Instead of being appointed by some governmental body or official, they were to be elected by a duly recognized target area organization. Thus, their representative status was modified from being merely token or symbolic to constituting from one-third to a majority of the CAP board members and being accountable to a particular constituency.

The quantitative increases in low-income representation depicted in Figure 1 may not, however, reveal the full measure of this shift in power since several other types of CAP board members were usually in full support of the target areas. These allies usually represented various ethnic and minority organizations (NAACP, CORE, Urban League, MAPA) and church groups, and these sources of support more than compensated for the bare, precarious majority won by the target areas.

At the same time, the number or percentage of low-income members is not a reliable guide to their actual influence. For example, Contra Costa County, which had the largest proportion (60 per cent) of elected target area representatives, had one of the most centralized programs. In San Francisco and Santa Clara counties, and later Oakland, where the target areas did in fact control the program, their elected representative comprised 51 per cent and 33⅓ per cent, respectively, of the board members.

In any case, a transfer or at least a redistribution of power took place from the CAPs to the areas to be served. What was done with this newly acquired power will be analyzed subsequently in chapters 7-10.

How can these different community responses be "explained"; that is, what factors might account for the occurrence of a debate in Berkeley, but not in San Francisco? A fight in Santa Clara, but not in Contra Costa? First, a *caveat*. The list of variables that might influence the particular pattern of conflict resolution is probably as long and indeterminate as those aspects of a community's social structure assumed to favor a monolithic or a pluralistic power structure.[4] The inconsistent and inconclusive character of these studies is as discouraging as Banfield's conclusions about a similar effort to link comparable sets of variables that might explain patterns of community decision making:

> From very different starting places (economically, culturally, and otherwise), the large central cities seem to come to very similar outcomes. And this in spite of differences in the form and style of their governments and in the content of their policies.[5]

Although the critical independent variables in this study are difficult to isolate, it is still possible to note the presence and even the extent of certain characteristics of the politico-ethnic community associated with the three types of CAP responses.

In Berkeley and Contra Costa, the community "climate" was more conducive to consensual modes of decision making, as manifested in their greater sensitivity and responsiveness to the relatively mild pressure exerted on behalf of the low-income population. This climate was influenced by the previous pattern of community efforts to deal with ethnic minority problems, which tended to be relatively liberal and rational.

In Berkeley, the lack of opposition to and support for the position of the target areas on the EOC board reflected to a large extent the significant sector of enlightened attitudes in a university community relatively sympathetic to the Negro, with whom the antipoverty program was clearly identified. The community representatives on the EOC came from the

[4] Much of this research is summarized and critically analyzed in Bert G. Swanson, ed., *Current Trends in Comparative Community Studies,* Public Affairs Monograph Series, No. 1 (Kansas City, Missouri: Community Studies, Inc., 1962).

[5] Edward C. Banfield, *Big City Politics* (New York: Random House, Inc., 1965), p. 11.

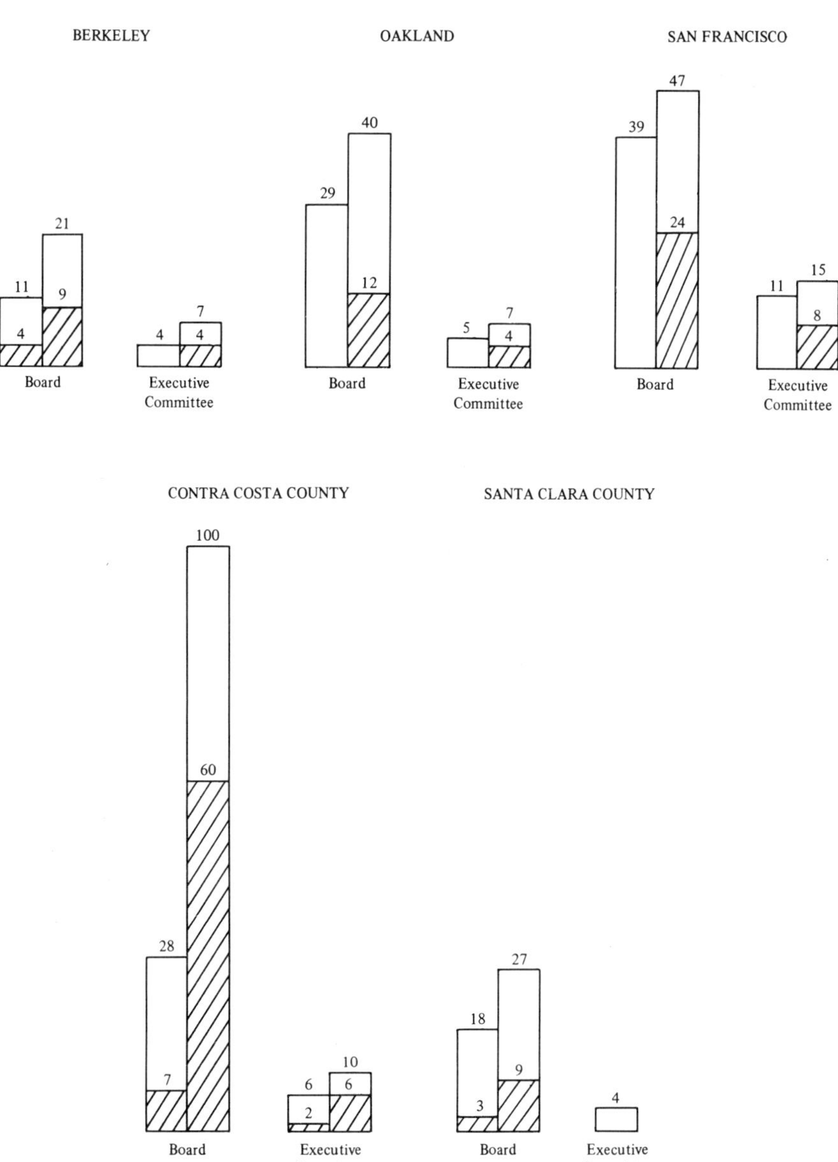

KEY

SHADED PORTION: Representatives from the target areas.

LEFTHAND COLUMN OF EACH PAIR: Number of members at inception, 1965.

RIGHTHAND COLUMN OF EACH PAIR: Number of members in May, 1966.

FIGURE 1. Changes in CAP Board and Executive Committee Size and Composition, 1965-66

schools, the Council of Social Planning, city government, and the Chamber of Commerce and expressed the attitudes of the more liberal elements in the community. Over the last ten years, there were many indications of Berkeley's awareness of the increasing proportion of Negroes in its population, and growing recognition of the legitimacy of their claim to improved opportunities in housing, education, and employment. For example, a majority of Berkeley voters had supported anti-discrimination legislation, had elected Negroes to the city council and the board of education, and had accepted the steps taken to combat *de facto* segregation in the schools.

In Contra Costa County, the Negro settlement was confined to two cities, Richmond and Pittsburg. In both of these communities, and to a much greater extent in Richmond, previous partisan political activity and social service projects over a 10-year period resulted in the emergence of indigenous participants ready and able to promote minority interests, as well as a nucleus of white liberal supporters in the community.

Of major importance was the fact that there was relatively little political power at stake in either Berkeley or Contra Costa, where the poverty program was not perceived by the legislative bodies as a political threat nor as a new resource that might disturb the current balance of power. In Contra Costa the program was clearly under the authority of the county, and in both of these communities, political power was highly diffused.[6] The more liberal elements held a slight majority in both the city council and board of supervisors. In both places, typically, nonpartisan politics prevailed, with relatively little structure in the political systems.[7] Because the dominant community groups that organized the CAPs in Contra Costa and Berkeley did not reject or even strongly oppose the claim for greater representation of the poor, it was not necessary for the minority groups or target areas to organize the fighting coalitions found in the other communities.

Unlike in Berkeley and Contra Costa County, the growing sense of ethnic power in San Francisco and Santa Clara County was mobilized by civil rights activists and minority politicians and directed against the CAP

[6] A comparison of the CAPs in Chicago, Philadelphia, New York, and Los Angeles also showed that those cities *without* strong political party organizations were more likely to permit participation of the poor on the governing boards than "machine" cities. The latter were more adept at obtaining a greater share of OEO funds. J. David Greenstone and Paul Peterson, "Reformers, Machine and the War on Poverty," a paper presented at the 1966 Annual Meeting of the American Political Science Association, September 6-10, 1966, New York City.

[7] Eugene C. Lee, *The Politics of Non-partisanship* (Berkeley, Calif.: University of California Press, 1960).

in a struggle for control when their demands were not met. This struggle took place in a context in which the political stakes were considerably higher. In San Francisco there was a much greater concentration of power in the office of the Mayor; hence his understandable concern that control of the antipoverty program might get into the hands of those who did not owe allegiance to him. Furthermore, Negro votes were a contested prize because of their concentration in two assembly districts in San Francisco, where they could influence election outcomes. Negroes had also been elected to public office from San Francisco, and many were closely identified with a well-organized faction of the Democratic Party, whose congressional leader actually came to their assistance and intervened in the struggle with the Mayor.

Whereas political power was relatively unstructured in Santa Clara, with a weak commitment to the antipoverty program by the Board of Supervisors, the situation was somewhat different in San Jose, the largest city in the county, where the Mexican-American vote was believed to be an important factor in at least one assembly district. The concentration of Mexican-American population encouraged the development of numerous ethnic associations, although with a small, over-lapping membership, and the emergence of leaders who gave the impression that they had influence over this constituency. As a result, there were a cadre of young, ambitious Mexican-American organization leaders who had gained political experience within their own ethnic community and within various factions of the Democratic Party. Few of them had been co-opted, and most were resentful of their traditional exclusion from community decision-making and were increasingly alert to opportunities to utilize community institutions to benefit Mexican-Americans.

Whereas in San Francisco and to a lesser extent in Santa Clara ethnic minorities were a political force to be reckoned with, in Oakland, the Negro and Mexican-American vote could not be counted on. Minority voters in Oakland have demonstrated little political "muscle" and have been notoriously unsuccessful in pressing their grievances with the school board or the city council. Oakland's nonpartisan politics have been dominated by Republicans, and the nine-member council, elected on a city-wide basis, has been a bastion of conservatism for many years with the interests of business, industry, and homeowners receiving primary attention. Politics in Oakland has less structure than in San Francisco in the sense that there are fewer concentrated and well-developed blocs or centers of influence. This is particularly evident when one compares the power of the Mayor of San Francisco with that of his Oakland counterpart, who presides over a council-manager form of government and has no official or informal sources of influence beyond that of the other councilmen.[8]

The other distinguishing feature of the Oakland "game," in contrast to the fight in San Francisco and Santa Clara, was the superior capability of the ethnic coalition that evolved. In San Francisco a series of issues in housing, civil rights, and urban renewal in which minorities were involved led to the emergence of an indigenous leadership cadre. The latter were predominantly younger and more militant than the moderate, middle-class professionals who were usually recognized as official minority spokesmen. Although the community leadership role of the traditional leaders was somewhat threatened by the rise of these activists, a *modus vivendi* seems to have been worked out that, despite the intergenerational and ideological conflict, provided for a division of labor and mutual recognition of their respective spheres of authority. The war on poverty provided an opportunity for this younger leadership to consolidate its influence further, because the same set of coalition skills that had been developed in previous controversies over civil rights and redevelopment were called for.

Unlike in San Francisco, there was a relatively low level of indigenous involvement in political and civil rights activities in Oakland. The political process and the character of the ethnic community in Oakland operated to minimize the opportunities for indigenous leadership to emerge, develop, and acquire the experience and other resources required for participation in community conflict.[9] For example, the social action in Oakland pertaining to civil rights was initiated by outsiders such as clergymen, students, and other political activists. The paucity of indigenous minority leadership was further implied in the dominant role of white clergymen in three of the four target areas, as well as in the ineffectual character of Oakland CORE compared with the influence this organization exerted in San Francisco, Berkeley, and Contra Costa. Much of the potential ethnic leadership had moved out of the target areas in Oakland, and others had been co-opted. Thus, there was a wide and virtually unfilled gap between

[8] Some recent, useful if somewhat biased descriptions of the politico-ethnic community in Oakland can be found in: "Metropoly: The Story of Oakland, California," *Ramparts*, Vol. 4, No. 10 (February, 1966), 25-50; *The New York Times*, January 17, 1966; *The Flatlands*, Vol. 1, No. 1 (March 12, 1966); *San Francisco Examiner*, August 23-26, 1966.

[9] Demographic comparisons between San Francisco and Oakland suggest that the size and growth rate of the Negro community may be less significant than other factors influencing its political capabilities. With less than half of the total population of San Francisco, Oakland had a Negro community in the 1960 census that exceeded San Francisco's by 20,000 and had a growth rate four times as great. Yet the Negro community in San Francisco was considerably more active politically. Similarly, in Santa Clara, the Mexican-Americans, who comprised but 16 per cent of the population, were able to obtain control of the EOC.

some of the militant "Black Power" advocates and the reputational leaders of the Negro community, most of whom also had little following. The characteristic pattern among ethnic minorities in Oakland was one of apathy and longsuffering patience, as evident in their ability to tolerate inaction on the proposal for a police review board for over two years. Earlier reactions to the redevelopment program in West Oakland also contrast sharply with the militancy that similar urban renewal efforts generated in San Francisco. It is not clear to what extent these differences might be related to the fact that Oakland had proportionally twice as many low-income families as San Francisco and 12 per cent more Negro population, more widely dispersed. However, the lack of ability to mobilize around an issue in Oakland is striking. Another element was the existence of the Oakland Interagency Project, which provided the OEDC with a head start on the target areas in experience, knowledge, and skill in planning, financing, and administering social service programs. This city-backed alliance between social service professionals and bureaucrats with access to both the Ford Foundation and OEO was a formidable antagonist for any neighborhood-based, low-income groups. In San Francisco, where there was no previous history of an "umbrella" organization, the contest was strictly between solidary and political power, and strongly influenced by the character and outcome of previous struggles about civil rights and redevelopment.

A final point of contrast between the Oakland situation and that of San Francisco and Santa Clara was the relationship between the Negro and the Mexican-American communities. There is some evidence that the effectiveness of the coalition arrayed against the CAP was enhanced to the extent that the Mexican-American and Negro groups could be allied; indeed, the more ethnic the coalition was, the more militant. As noted earlier, the relationship between these two ethnic minorities was quite strained in Oakland, whereas it was possible for them to collaborate on a limited basis in San Francisco and Santa Clara.

In summary, it has been suggested that the character of the politico-ethnic community influenced the particular mode of conflict resolution of the issues around resident participation (that is, whether it was a debate, game or fight). Where political power was more concentrated and structured on a partisan basis and where minority votes had a significant impact on election outcomes, the political stakes were naturally higher and conflict more likely. A history of previous involvement in community controversies by indigenous leadership cadres capable of organizing an ethnic coalition seemed to be the other set of factors associated with a contest.

A Theoretical Note

The preceding analysis and interpretation can be a source of hypotheses and contribute to emergent theories of community decision making, conflict resolution, and planned change. There seems to be considerable overlap between these concepts, and they probably refer to the same social processes but from different perspectives. For example, the pattern of community responses to the pressures to maximize the participation of the poor that has been classified as a debate, game, or fight is quite similar to a typology of "purposive social change at the community level" recently proposed by Roland L. Warren.[10] This schema is based on a continuum of consensus–difference–dissensus, which implies either collaborative, campaign, or contest strategies respectively. These, in turn, are virtually equivalent to a classification of methods of resolving organizational conflict suggested by March and Simon: problem solving; education, persuasion and bargaining; and pressure.[11]

This convergence among attempts to order the basic processes by which changes in community policies can be accomplished, depicted below, constitutes a typology that is a first step in theory building.

	Berkeley *Contra Costa*	*Oakland*	*San Francisco* *Santa Clara*
Type of community decision-making pattern	Debate	Game	Fight
Degree of congruence of interests between partisans	Consensus	Difference	Dissensus
Type of strategy and methods	Problem solving	Education persuasion bargaining	Pressure

Several of the distinguishing features of this trichotomy of ideal types, as well as some of the conditions associated with them, will now be briefly delineated.

The following definitions are proposed for the three modes of conflict resolution (debate, game, and fight) based on the extent of goal consensus, stake or issue-salience, strategy, and resources for influence.

[10] Roland L. Warren, *Types of Purposive Social Change at the Community Level*, Brandeis University Papers in Social Welfare No. 11. (Waltham, Massachusetts: Brandeis University, 1965.)

[11] James G. March and Herbert A. Simon, *Organizations* (New York: John Wiley & Sons, Inc., 1958), pp. 129-30.

Debates are characterized by efforts to persuade or convince others within an open, formal, parliamentary framework on the appropriate means to a goal on which there is more or less consensus. There is general agreement between the partisans regarding the definition of the issue and the methods to be used to resolve it. The stakes are perceived as moderate or low and probably not worth really fighting about. The resources for influence tend to be reason, commitment, and expertise. The strategy is a rational one of *collaboration*, demonstrating good will and constructive problem solving; getting the facts, examining alternatives, and trying to persuade others in a democratic manner.

At the other end of the continuum is a *fight*, marked by an all-out, either/or contest in which the goal is the total defeat of the opposition. Capitulation is the objective, and there is no place for bargaining, debate, negotiation, or other democratic processes, since neither side can afford to compromise. There is *dissensus:* no congruence between the values and interests of the partisans, and a marked disparity between their goals. High stakes are involved, and the strategy calls for the use of coercive power, solidary resources, and combat tactics by a coalition. Other characteristics of a contest for power are the escalation of conflict in the manner classically described by Coleman, in which issues become generalized and attacks personalized.[12]

Somewhere in the middle is a *game*, which contains both elements of democratic debates and the possibility of overt community conflict. There is divergence on the perception of the issue and the goals, with relatively high stakes involved. A wide variety of resources for influence are used, such as control of communication, expertise, funds, status, legitimation, and solidary power. The strategy is one of a campaign or "cold war" in which pressures are not permitted to build up to the point of serious conflict, so co-optation occurs, concessions are made, and there is some informal negotiation.

These characteristics can be summed up in Table 2.

In a recent test of the hypothesis that collaborative strategies would occur under conditions of consensus and contests would take place where dissensus exists, Warren and Hyman found support for these propositions.[13] In analyzing 35 case studies reported in the literature, they also found that collaborative strategies tended to have task- and integration-oriented goals about equally; to occur in small communities somewhat more than large ones; to be almost exclusively nongovernmental in

[12] James S. Coleman, *Community Conflict* (New York: The Free Press, 1957).

[13] Roland L. Warren and Herbert H. Hyman, "Purposive Community Change in Consensus and Dissensus Situations," *Community Mental Health Journal*, Vol. 2, No. 4 (Winter, 1967), 293-300.

TABLE 2
Three Types of Community Conflict Resolution [14]

	Debate	*Game*	*Fight*
Type of issue or situation (based on degree and possibility of agreement)	*Consensus* Common interests, although values may differ. High likelihood of agreement on means of resolution.	*Difference* No agreement on substance or means of resolution or that there is an issue. Agreement is possible, but more than discussion is needed.	*Dissensus* No congruence on values or interests. Recognition of the issue is refused or the proposed solution is strongly opposed. Agreement not expected: an either/or situation.
Goal and extent of planned change	*Agreement* based on involvement plus increased collaborative competence. — Expected change is relatively small and incremental. No serious opposition expected.	*Support:* some agreement and interest. — Considerable change is required to overcome apathy or opposition.	*Victory* over opposition. — Great change is involved, usually a redistribution of power.
Strategy and methods	*Collaborative* Rational and democratic. Attempt is made to get the facts and reconcile viewpoints via reasonable discussion: A problem-solving model suitable for community development processes.	*Campaign* A planned effort to convert apathy to interest and moderate opposition to agreement or at least support. Use of education, persuasion, or moderate coercion and pressure although overt conflict is avoided when applied to social planning. Bargaining and negotiation may also be employed.	*Contest* Temporary abandonment of consensus efforts to further one's own side of an issue despite opposition of important groups. Involves various forms of social action, both within and outside community norms usually through a coalition.
Resources for influence	Normative appeal: "goodwill" and activism. The power of reason, expertise and persuasion.	Exchange of valued resources for concessions. Available sanctions for bargaining.	Coercive threat of disruption by solidary groups. Pressure of public support and attention.

[14] Based on Warren, *Types of Purposive Social Change.*

auspices; to involve key leadership in active support rather than in opposition; and to accomplish their goals in most cases.

By contrast, the cases within a dissensus environment tended to have task-oriented goals only; to predominate in larger communities; to have a higher proportion of governmental auspices; to involve key leadership actively in both support and opposition; and to fall short of goal accomplishment in most instances. In addition, the authors concluded that these findings may be blurred unless a distinction is made between proposed changes that generate opposition and those that do not.

This study of resident participation suggests that there may also be other attributes of what we have called the "politico-ethnic community" that may be associated with these modes of community change. If the choice of strategy is influenced by the possibilities of agreement or opposition, which in turn reflects the degree of congruence between the interests of the partisans, then the way in which power is distributed in the community and certain characteristics of the ethnic community would be highly relevant. The extent to which power is concentrated and structured along partisan and ethnic lines heightens the stake of those in whom it is vested and increases the possibility of disagreement and opposition to any effort to disturb the current distribution or balance of power. Conversely, where power is decentralized and diffused with few discernible blocs, there may be less at stake for any one group and less likelihood of a militant posture.

Within the ethnic community, this study has found, its density, organizational experience, and leadership are important variables influencing what can be called "coalition capability." That is the capacity to organize and maintain an association of minority and allied groups that can mobilize appropriate and sufficient power to countervail the concentrated power arrayed against them. This power may be political, as in San Francisco, or bureaucratic-professional, as in Santa Clara.

What is being suggested, then, is a parallel continuum to the one based on consensus-dissensus, whereby the degree of agreement or opposition expected, which is associated with one of three distinctive modes of resolution, is also related to the concentration of power and coalition capability. It is therefore hypothesized that these variables are maximized in the direction of dissensus and the use of contest strategies as depicted in the following diagram:

	Debate	Game	Fight	
	Consensus	Difference	Dissensus	
Low	Concentration of Power			High
	Coalition Capability			

This exploratory study, then, tends to support or at least illustrate the proposition that there are three distinct types of community decision making or conflict resolution and that the degree of agreement or opposition expected seems to determine the use of three related and appropriate strategies. That is, when there appears to be a high possibility of agreement because of common interests or, conversely, there is little or no opposition because of apathy, low salience of the issue, or careful selection of a homogeneous decision-making elite, a *debate* may be expected.

Where there are differences between the parties, but agreement or at least support is a strong possibility, various *game* strategies will be employed, such as persuasion, mild pressure, and bargaining techniques if feasible.

Finally, where there is a conflict of interests, no agreement on the issue or means of resolving it, and no belief in the feasibility of other strategies, a *fight* will take place in which coercive pressure and other combat tactics will be utilized.

Furthermore, the findings of this study, together with that of Warren and Hyman, suggest that associated with the degree of interest congruence would be the following conditions under which, for example, a debate rather than a fight would occur: a diffused pattern of power distribution; a low potential for coalition formation; small community size; voluntary auspices; support of key leadership, and explicit process or community integration goals.

By indicating some of the major conditions under which different forms of community decision making may occur, these hypotheses are suitable for empirical testing through further comparative community studies. Meanwhile, they appear to be useful for assessing the various possibilities of community change and choosing appropriate strategies.

Summary

Each CAP faced the same dilemma: how to make policy decisions in the face of uncertainty regarding the meaning of resident participation, the identification and selection of those who could speak for or represent the poor, and how to involve the poor in a process in a relatively brief period of time. While Community Action Programs in San Francisco, Oakland, Berkeley, and Santa Clara and Contra Costa counties interpreted the mandate for resident participation in different ways, there was a net increase in all of them in the various forms of participation of the poor and in their influence.

A comparison of these five communities revealed three different types of CAP responses to the pressures to increase the representation on the governing board of the groups and areas to be served. These community decision-making patterns were classified as a "debate" (Berkeley and Contra Costa), a "game" (Oakland), and a "fight" (San Francisco and Santa Clara counties) and can be better understood in the context of the distinctive character of their respective politico-ethnic communities. This analysis also has theoretical significance for community organization practice, and a typology is proposed for three classes of planned change with their related goals, strategies, methods, and resources for influence.

7

WHO SPEAKS FOR THE POOR? TOWARD REPRESENTATIVE PARTICIPATION

By requiring involvement of those with a stake in the welfare programs—whether or not they are actually "poor"—the local poverty programs represent a new development in participatory democracy.[1]

At the extreme this [maximum feasible participation] sets aside two hundred years of theory about representative government.[2]

Introduction

In this chapter and the two that follow, the trends and patterns in resident participation on the neighborhood level in San Francisco, Oakland, and Santa Clara during 1965-66 will be compared. These three communities have been selected for more intensive analysis because Contra Costa did not develop a decentralized program. In addition, although Berkeley eventually established a neighborhood center, the major arena of resident participation in both of these communities remained the CAP rather than the neighborhood. The comparative analysis draws on the experience of the 18 different target areas in the three CAPs as the locus of the program development, social action, and employment modes of resident participation.

Beginning with an overview of the origin and development of the target area organizations (TAO), the recruitment strategies used in the selection of a representative constituency are examined, as well as the criteria for participation and the resulting character of the membership. Chapter 8 is concerned with the distinctive character of the organizations that evolved out of the struggle for power between the neighborhoods and

[1] Roger G. Davidson, "Poverty and the New Federalism," in Sar A. Levitan and Irving H. Siegel (eds.), *Dimensions of Manpower Policy: Research and Programs* (Baltimore: The Johns Hopkins University Press, 1966), p. 75.

[2] William H. C. Wheaton, "Metro-Allocation Planning," *Journal of the American Institute of Planners,* Vol. 33, No. 2 (March 1967), p. 104.

the EOC, and their contrasting orientations and roles. The different patterns and outcomes of four types of community organization (social service outreach, organizational maintenance, community development and social action) are described in Chapter 9. Chapter 10 summarizes the effects of resident participation on the delegate agencies, minority groups, local government, and the poor in the three communities.

Recruitment Strategies and Their Consequences

The circumstances surrounding the development of resident participation in the different neighborhoods were quite similar. In the early stages of the organization of a CAP, target areas were usually designated on the basis of their high concentration of economically impoverished minority families and individuals, although other indicators of social disorganization were used, such as low education, high morbidity, and unemployment. This had the effect of fixing the geographic boundaries of any neighborhood organization in which all the residents of that target area might be eligible for membership. Each CAP then had to identify "representatives of the groups and areas to be served" and involve them as rapidly as possible in the establishment of a new organization that could become the officially recognized arm of the antipoverty program in a target area.

The CAPs were faced with an ambiguous OEO policy,[3] the pressure of program application deadlines, limited staff, and many imponderables regarding the nature of the poor and who could speak for them. As in all such attempts, the strategies chosen by CAP staff members as they tried to identify and organize a representative constituency shaped the future character and role of the participants in the TAO. Two somewhat different organizing patterns were found, both of which relied on the creation of an interim organization that eventually paved the way for the establish-

[3] OEO did not prescribe the criteria for maximum feasible participation in the neighborhood beyond stating that "residents of the areas or neighborhoods in which the program will be carried out and of members of the groups that it will serve" should be involved in "existing or new representative organizations for advice on program policy and, where appropriate, for actual conduct and administration of neighborhood-based programs." *CAP Guide*, p. 16. Three years later Community Action Memo 57, January 11, 1967 detailed how each CAP was expected to implement the 1966 amendments to the Economic Opportunity Act, which established specific legislative requirements for representation of the poor on all policy-making boards connected with the CAP. At least one-third of the governing body had to be made up of "representatives of the poor persons who are residents of the areas and members of the groups the community action program is intended to serve. Such representatives need not themselves be poor, but they must be selected in a manner that insures that they truly represent the poor." Five selection processes were suggested that seemed to de-emphasize the role of neighborhood-wide elections and the use of reverse income criteria for voters or candidates.

ment of a permanent board of directors, usually by means of some election procedure: (1) a single organization or combination of several existing neighborhood organizations was sought out and ultimately became the major source of the new, official body for target area participation in the CAP; (2) a completely new organization was created, either by means of a series of decentralized, area-wide elections as in the Mission and Western Addition, or by selecting the membership of the TAO at several public meetings, as in Oakland. The first policy was initially followed in five out of the nine areas in Santa Clara as a means of accelerating the development of a coalition type of organization that could contract as soon as possible with the EOC for the operation of the service centers. These existing organizations included indigenous groups newly organized by ethnic associations, as well as traditional social agencies and community councils. In Chinatown, a somewhat similar method was used when the EOC organizers convened a new alliance of representatives of those groups that had traditionally spoken for the Chinese community. In contrast to Chinatown, where there were neither elections nor representatives of the poor, Santa Clara reliance on existing organizations resulted in the reinforcement of pre-existing attitudes toward resident participation—both pro and con—jurisdictional disputes, and a revolt against what was perceived as an infringement on area autonomy by the EOC. In Oakland, a "takeover" by groups opposed to the OEDC was the consequence of the open and unplanned character of the initial meetings.

Regardless of which tactic was employed, all the CAPs were confronted with the task of creating a new organization. It appeared most feasible for the staff members to work with those organizations and individuals previously known to them, who were most visible, articulate, interested and "ready," rather than attempt to seek out the unaffiliated poor. As a result, there was a strong tendency to rely heavily on the members of existing neighborhood and ethnic associations in the organization of the interim or organizing committees, which then formulated criteria for the permanent TAO. In this way, organizations and individuals initially involved continued into the next stage. The only exception to this was the Mission Area Organizing Committee, which deliberately disbanded itself after proposing that the permanent board consist exclusively of indigenous, low-income members.

The manner in which these early meetings were convened in most neighborhoods could be described as the now familiar "creaming" process, whereby those persons most accustomed to participation in voluntary associations became the nucleus of the organizing committee, thus excluding most of the hard-core poor. Thus "representativeness" was a function of the recruitment policy, which in turn was largely a response to the character of OEO deadlines and guidelines.

This meant that from their inception, the TAOs did not consist primarily of the alienated underclass usually described in the sociological literature on the poor.[4] The original composition of the TAOs, which persisted even later when they were reorganized by elections, consisted less of the poor who were conceived as potential consumers of OEO-financed social service programs than of upwardly striving members of ethnic minorities—Negro or Spanish-speaking—who knew something about poverty, having recently escaped from it, or who were still living close enough to the poor to be able to identify with their plight. The primary incentives for involvement in these initial stages were the prospect of jobs, payment for participation, access to services, or political power for oneself or one's organization or ethnic group. Whereas there was considerable cynicism on the part of EOC staff members regarding such motivations for participation—"the smell of money was in the air," as one of them put it—there was also a very small idealistic, altruistic minority among the participants. The socioeconomic status of the members varied from public assistance recipients to the middle class; on an over-all basis, no more than a third had low incomes themselves as defined by OEO criteria, even though many members who earned more, such as those in the Western Addition, saw themselves as poor. In San Francisco and Oakland, there was one predominately middle-class TAO, and in Santa Clara there were two.

These community-wide generalizations, however, obscure the considerable variation in the proportion of low-income members in each TAO. For example, the Mission had a completely indigenous low-income board, and the majority of the members of the Hunters Point board were also low income, although in the Western Addition such persons comprised less than a fifth of the board. In Santa Clara at least three of the area service boards were comprised of over 50 per cent low-income persons, whereas in Oakland the poor constituted less than a third of the membership.

Most of the board members consisted of persons in the thirty-to-forty age range, although young men in their early twenties held leadership positions in both San Francisco and Oakland. The majority of the participants belonged to an ethnic minority, and low-income whites were both inconspicuous and uninfluential. With the exception of the TAOs in

[4] An excellent survey of some of these studies is found in Edwin J. Thomas and Robert D. Carter, "Psycho-social Factors in Poverty," in Mayer N. Zald, ed., *Organizing for Community Welfare* (Chicago: Quadrangle Books, Inc., 1967), pp. 195-261. One of the most thoughtful attempts to distinguish four subgroups among the poor is S. M. Miller, "The American Lower Classes: A Typological Approach," *Social Research*, Vol. 31 (Spring, 1964), 1-22.

Mission and Fruitvale, all the TAOs were dominated by a single ethnic group. In Oakland, women predominated in three out of the four advisory committees, with men and women equally divided in the fourth, although men ended up in control of most of the leadership positions. In San Francisco, women dominated the Hunters Point board. In Santa Clara, white middle-class women were active on three boards and were chairmen in two, where there was the least amount of poverty, and were a distinct minority on all of the others.

The pattern of leadership composition also varied. In San Francisco, chairmen of the three target area boards during the first year and a half were Negroes, whereas in Oakland young, white, middle-class ministers, considerably more militant than their membership, headed two of the advisory committees for over a year. It was not until toward the end of the second year that they were replaced by two Negro women. The ethnic leadership in Oakland never did approach that of San Francisco in sophistication or in militancy.

In Santa Clara County, only two out of the nine area service boards had Mexican-American chairmen, although the EOC itself was dominated by area representatives and organizational delegates who were Spanish-speaking. There was a tendency in Santa Clara and to a lesser extent in other communities to select as a chairman someone who could best function in a mediating role; that is, someone who would be acceptable to both the poor and the middle-class representatives as well as to the various agency and ethnic factions. In this way, the socioeconomic status of the chairman did not necessarily reflect the dominant character of the leadership clique or the membership as a whole. This seems to support the observation that "self-selection of the least representative residents into leadership position is especially characteristic of slum-based organizations." [5] For example, the third chairman of the Fruitvale advisory committee was an Oriental college student in a TAO consisting predominately of Negroes and Mexican-Americans. In the Mission, Spanish-speaking groups could not agree on a candidate because of their mutual distrust, and a Negro was elected, representing an ethnic minority along with the Indians. Nevertheless, discounting for the special political factors involved in each TAO, the following list of target area chairmen during 1965-66 is instructive:

[5] Harold B. Wilensky and Charles N. Lebeaux, *Industrialization and Social Welfare*, 2nd ed. (New York: The Free Press, 1966). Some of these relationships between the leadership and membership of low income organizations are explored in Louis A. Zurcher, "The Leader and the Lost: A Case Study of Indigenous Leadership in a Poverty Program Community Action Committee," *Genetic Psychology Monographs*, Vol. 76 (1967), 23-93.

Oakland

West Oakland—White student; Negro, federal blue-collar worker
East Oakland—Negro, semi-skilled worker
Fruitvale—White, Protestant minister; Mexican-American small businessman (three months); Oriental college student; Negro woman
North Oakland—White, Protestant minister

San Francisco

Western Addition—Negro minister
Mission—Mexican-American attorney; Negro student
Chinatown-North Beach—Chinese public school administrator
Hunters Point—Negro law student
Central City—White, Protestant minister

Santa Clara

1. White, "Anglo" priest
2. White, airline pilot
3. White, businessman
4. White, woman teacher
5. Mexican-American plumbing contractor
6. White, PTA and clubwoman leader
7. Mexican-American businessman
8. White, government employee
9. White, dentist

Criteria for Representativeness

Three criteria were employed in determining membership in the TAO: *residence, low income,* and *ethnicity,* with all three frequently regarded as interchangeable.

Residence in the target area was a necessary though not always a sufficient basis for voting and/or participation in a neighborhood organization; often, it was assumed that most of the residents who belonged to ethnic minorities were poor. Although the composition of the TAO was supposed to be a microcosm of the neighborhood, each CAP determined for itself the particular "mix" for the composition of the TAO. Because low income was usually not a requirement for voting and membership was not always based on a formula that would provide for equitable geographic or interest representation, the TAOs varied greatly as to the extent to which they reflected the particular demographic and socioeconomic character of their neighborhoods.

The use of income criteria was an attempt to prevent capture of a TAO by the non-poor. EOC members realized that unless specific places were set aside for the poor, they would be crowded out by those more accustomed to involvement who would speak on their behalf. Because of the election rules and the heterogeneous socioeconomic character of the target areas, these precautions were not effective in preventing middle-class domination of most of the TAOs. Reverse income stipulations were utilized only in Santa Clara County, where only the poor could vote for their representatives, and in the Mission, where the candidates for the board had to be low income. Out of this experience it was found that only a series of sub-area elections, as in Santa Clara and Mission, with specific income requirements for voters, candidates, or both assured the presence of a minimum proportion of low-income members in the TAO. Where there were no such elections, as in Oakland, the self-selected and non-representative character of the advisory committees persisted as a controversial issue for almost a year and served as a constant challenge and threat to their legitimacy.

From the very beginning, the CAP was interpreted as much more a social service and ethnic than an economic opportunity act. Shortly after the EOCs were constituted, there was a strong presumption on the part of Negro and Mexican-American groups that they could speak for the "groups to be served." In the Mission, Western Addition, and Chinatown, as well as in three areas of Santa Clara, ethnic associations took the initiative in trying to organize neighborhoods and in asserting their claim to becoming the TAO. Leaders of Negro and Mexican-American organizations quickly perceived the potential of the CAP and the TAO as a new and practically mandated means of gaining status, power, and jobs for the members of their groups. At the same time, this assumption of leadership often aroused considerable distrust by low-income persons of the minority organizational representatives and other self-appointed leaders who purported to speak in their name. This trend was reinforced by the ambiguity surrounding the concept of "representative of the poor," which, according to OEO policy, did not require that such persons be poor themselves, as long as they were elected in a democratic manner by an assemblage of the poor.[6] This meant that the term "representatives of the poor"

[6] "In the selection process, there should be maximum possible involvement of the groups and persons to be represented. A selection process should be designed to encourage the use, whenever feasible, of traditional democratic approaches and techniques such as group forums and discussions, nominations, and balloting. This will minimize the possibility that a representative does not command the support or confidence of the group or area that he represents." *CAP Guide*, p. 18. Note that in Com-

could refer to: (1) the entire TAO; (2) those members whose income was below the poverty line, regardless of whom they happened to represent on the TAO board; (3) those who regardless of income were selected in some manner by low-income residents; or, (4) those elected representatives of the poor who were low-income themselves. It is this more restrictive usage that will be employed in the rest of this chapter.

Elections and the Participation of the Poor

Traditionally, of course, the interests of the poor have been defended and supported by reformers, middle-class liberals, coalitions, and politicians dependent on their votes rather than by the poor themselves, who have been regarded as powerless and voiceless. The CAPs proposed to change this, but the extent to which elected representatives of the poor could speak for their constituency depended on the degree to which they were informed, articulate, and accountable in some way.

The numerous neighborhood elections and their aftermath in San Francisco and Santa Clara can best be described as a *pseudo-political process.* An election might appear to be intrinsically more democratic and more likely to insure a representative TAO than any other process, but its success depended on the conditions under which it was conducted, the criteria established for candidates and voters, and the extent to which the neighborhood was organized, as well as the number of persons casting ballots. As noted earlier, it was found that whereas sub-area elections took longer, they assured more low-income representation than a single election meeting for the whole neighborhood. Furthermore, even if the representatives of the poor were not required to be poor, but low income was a condition for voting, as in Santa Clara, the majority of the elected candidates were likely to have low incomes.

Although neighborhood-wide elections, which were utilized to make the transition from an interim to a permanent board of directors of the TAO, as in San Francisco and Santa Clara, produced a greater proportion of low-income members, they did not necessarily insure a more "representative" or actively involved low-income constituency. Some reasons were the

---

munity Action Memo 57, referred to in footnote 3, the fact that the representatives of the poor need not be poor themselves is made much more explicit. Part of the confusion in the meaning of "maximum feasible participation" was the reluctance of the OEO to indulge in a "numbers game" and employ a rigid percentage formula. Informally, a rule of thumb prevailed that one-third of the governing board should consist of representatives of the poor; this was later incorporated in the 1966 Amendments to the Economic Opportunity Act.

laxity with which many of the elections were conducted; the flexible criteria for candidates; the small voter turnout; and the failure to maintain sub-area constituency organizations after the election. Consequently, the elections to the TAO in San Francisco and later to the TAOs in Oakland and Santa Clara generally produced the equivalent of a process of self-selection of board members who were not accountable to any constituency and who represented only themselves, even though the representatives of the poor had proportionately increased in number.

In the search for a representative constituency, there was relatively little concern with *accountability*. Although the *CAP Guide* stressed the importance of the representatives' being responsible to a constituency and functioning as elected delegates,[7] a series of factors operated to minimize accountability of the elected representatives of the poor. The vague, *ad hoc* nature of the electorate was mainly responsible. It was not possible, in most instances because of lack of staff, to maintain some continuing form of sub-area or infra-neighborhood organizational structure after the election. As a result there was no organized group to and from which the elected representatives of the poor might report, even if they had wished to do this. There was a weak attempt at accountability in five of the areas in Santa Clara, where there were "councils" somewhat similar to town meetings or general assemblies, to whom the area boards were supposed to report periodically. However, with the exception of two of them, they did not meet frequently or function actively. Santa Clara was, of course, distinctive in the way in which it insured that the representatives of the poor to the EOC—the area commissioners—would *not* be responsible to any organized group or delegate body!

In the Western Addition, 28 neighborhood councils were organized by the end of 1966, although no more than six of them were regarded as operating satisfactorily, even though each had a staff member assigned to them. These neighborhood councils had the right to recall their representatives to the board at will, although this power was used only twice. As a result of this system, there was a strong tendency on the part of almost half the board members in the Western Addition not to convene meetings in their neighborhoods, preferring instead to act independently rather than face the possibility of being voted out of office. Only in the second year of the board's operation, during 1967, were efforts made to change the bylaws so that neighborhood representatives on the area board could not vote on issues unless they first ascertained the position of the neighborhood council that elected them. That accountability was more sig-

[7] *Ibid.*, p. 18.

nificant than the socioeconomic status of the representatives of the poor was the conclusion of the Central City area board when it became the first and only TAO to abandon the practice of geographical, mass-based elections. After eight months it found that only one of the eight elected representatives remained, so it adopted a system whereby organizations with a predominately low-income membership would be responsible for selecting delegates to the area board.

Another type of accountability was found in the Mission where, although the indigenous board members were elected at large, over half belonged to various ethnic and neighborhood groups to which they showed considerable loyalty. This contrasted to the pattern in Fruitvale, where most of the representatives were elected to the advisory committee because of their institutional or ethnic affiliations, but reported back to them rarely. At best, therefore, some informal accountability to organizational interests was evidenced. There was still very little accountability to the neighborhood electoral units, which in the last analysis were essentially a political expedient and CAP artifact. Thus, none of the TAOs really resolved the problem of electing bona fide representatives of the poor who had an organized base of power or some reasonable facsimile of a constituency to whom they reported. The significance of this condition was perceptively analyzed by the chairman of the Santa Clara EOC:

> All delegate bodies of the EOC and of Area Service Center Boards are highly organized, powerful, and representative *except* for the delegate bodies of the poor, which are *un*organized, power*less,* and *non*representative . . . because they are non-existent. Unlike other representatives, the poor have no power base from which to operate. In the dynamics of community action, this puts them at a tremendous disadvantage. It is true there are a number of people speaking "on behalf of the poor" . . . and undoubtedly sincerely so; but "behalfer" representation is merely "symbolic" representation and is not feasible participation of the poor.[8]

The election process was, however, only a means by which the poor were to be brought into a decision-making process in the target area. More significant was the degree of involvement of the indigenous persons after they were elected. How active were they? In Santa Clara the elected representatives of the poor were active in no more than three out of the nine boards and moderately involved in one or two others, with no consistent correlation between the percentage of low-income persons and the

[8] S. A. Skillicorn, "Sharing in the Action," Santa Clara EOC President's Report, 1967, p. 3.

dominance of their role.[9] The elected representatives of the poor in Santa Clara were generally less assertive than the agency and organizational delegates, who usually comprised two-thirds of the boards, and the former also tended to be much readier to accept the recommendations of the professionals. The two areas where their involvement was greatest included those with the highest concentration of poverty and density of population. An equally significant element was the previous existence of ethnic organizations in the neighborhood. The participation of the poor in Santa Clara was greatest where ethnic organizations were interested in securing their involvement and where the area director also had a strong commitment to this goal. The more ethnic the representatives were, the more militant they were likely to be; however, with but few exceptions the more active participants still tended to be those of higher socioeconomic status and not members of any minority group.

This was also the case in Oakland and particularly noticeable in North Oakland. There, although over half of the members were low income, the most articulate participants during 1965-66 were white. In Santa Clara it appeared that the elected representatives of the poor, with only a few exceptions, had relatively little impact on the deliberation on the area service boards. In Oakland, Western Addition, and Chinatown the same generalization could be made about the relatively small proportion and marginal role of the low-income members.

On the other hand, the low-income persons who comprised virtually the entire membership of the board in the Mission were an exceedingly active group, perhaps because over half were closely identified with ethnic, religious, and neighborhood groups whose interests they sought to protect. The fact that as a board they were more sensitive to the uses of power than most of their counterparts in Santa Clara might be accounted for by the more complex political and ethnic organizational structure in the Mission and the absence of middle-class persons on the board. In the Mission, however, the low-income status of the board may have been less important than its ethnic mix, which subsequently produced considerable factionalism and "politics in the raw."

The finding that the roles played by low-income persons in most of the TAOs were not particularly significant must be interpreted in the light of these facts:

[9] A distinction can be made between involvement and participation; included in the former are less intensive relationships, such as belonging, attending, and being aware or informed. In the latter are more active roles such as assenting or opposing (having an opinion); giving more active support or protesting; expressing opinions and recommending action; initiating the introduction of an issue; or giving leadership in some way. These constitute a continuum; members of the TAO, like most others, tended to cluster at one end.

1. The number of such persons was very small, and they were usually in the minority; only in Santa Clara and in the Mission were they formally "visible." At the same time, there were some low-income individuals who played important roles, even though as a group they may not have been very active.

2. The designation of "low-income member" was itself a highly arbitrary one, an artifact of OEO ideology and policy, which sought to prevent middle-class representatives from dominating the TAOs. As a distinction it merely indicated the economic status of a member; it did not imply that such a person identified with or was a spokesman for the "interests of the poor," whatever they might be,[10] nor did it imply that other TAO members, whose income happened to be above the official poverty guideline, did not conceive of themselves as poor or serve as effective spokesmen for the low-income residents.

3. The absence of a clear constituency of the representatives of the poor, as well as most of the other members of the TAO, would also temper the expectations regarding their performance.

In general, there was not much support for the active involvement of low-income members in the 12 out of the 18 TAOs where they comprised a minority. They rarely received any form of in-service training, and relatively few of the staff had a strong commitment to the participation of the poor. Inducements for their participation were also weak, since there were few tangible rewards, and no payments for meeting attendance were permitted until March, 1967.[11] Surprisingly few representatives of the

[10] This seems to involve an assumption that somehow the poor were a more or less homogeneous group, all of whose members had a high stake in the CAP. This belief disregarded the great diversity among those who happened to have incomes of less than $3,000 a year. Not only were there critical differences in age and ethnicity, but both the causes and remedies for their impoverishment varied. For all practical purposes the "groups to be served" by the CAP did not include 60 per cent of the poor; those who were employed intermittently or at substandard wages or who were elderly and/or not in the labor market. There were few program benefits that raised their income. Because the bulk of the services were aimed at the approximately 25 per cent of the poor who might have been aided by improved access to social services, it could be questioned whether, strictly speaking, these nonbeneficiaries should have been eligible to vote. They were able to vote since they were part of the "areas to be served," but this geographical rationale seemed weaker than the justification for involving the potential clientele.

[11] Since reimbursement for the travel expenses of low-income members to meetings was originally allowed only if a 25-mile round trip was involved, few qualified. These rules were somewhat liberalized by Community Action Memo 29a, February 21, 1967, which implemented the 1966 Amendments to Section 205 of the Economic Opportunity Act. Allowances of $5 per meeting, not to exceed two per month; reimbursement for travel, per diem and meal expense in connection with the official meetings; and babysitting were authorized for those persons falling within the OEO poverty-line index. This was based on an income of $3,000 for families of four, so again very few of the members who participated were eligible.

poor dropped out because of the frequency of the meetings or the expense of travel, baby-sitting, and so forth. Although there was considerable turnover among these members of the TAO, most of the reasons for their failure to return pertained to factionalism or a lack of sense of accomplishment. These forces were, of course, superimposed on those structural and social-psychological barriers to participation of the poor rooted in the realities of poverty itself.[12]

Summary

The reliance on existing organizations and the identification of ethnic minorities with the poor meant that the majority of the members initially recruited to the TAO had previous community attachments and were among the more highly motivated members of their groups. Consequently, the strategies used to organize a representative group of participants who could speak for the poor resulted in the selection of an initial constituency with low accountability and consisting less of client-participants than of persons who were much closer to the social service consumer than those who had previously made allocative decisions. Because of these recruitment policies, low-income persons *per se* were generally underrepresented in the TAO, and their role and influence were small.

[12] Some of the obstacles are reviewed in Frances Piven, "Participation of Residents in Neighborhood Community Action Programs," *Social Work,* Vol. 11, No. 1 (January, 1966), 73-80; Arthur B. Shostak, "Promoting Participation of the Poor: Philadelphia's Anti-Poverty Program," *ibid.*, pp. 64-72; and Alan Haber, "The American Underclass," *Poverty and Human Resources Abstracts,* Vol. II, No. 3 (May-June 1967), 5-19. See also references in footnote 2.

8

WHAT ROLE FOR THE TARGET AREA ORGANIZATION? THE DISTRIBUTION AND USES OF POWER

> *. . . its stunning success in building the most broadly based community decision making structure since the days of the New England town meeting . . .*[1]

> *. . . the ability of the neighborhood boards to shape their own program under the Act—and related programs, too—was even stronger symbolic proof to the embattled community that they could get "in."*[2]

Officially, in each of the communities the TAOs were to involve a group of representative residents in decision making regarding the identification of needs and the recommendation of appropriate programs. One of the principal goals was to enlarge opportunities for more effective utilization of decentralized educational, welfare, legal, employment, and health services. The TAOs were also supposed to improve the effectiveness of the social service system by influencing the allocation of new resources for the neighborhood through communicating information about needs, recommending programs, and encouraging use. At the same time, a secondary or latent purpose was to reduce the feelings of alienation and powerlessness of the poor by providing means for exerting influence on community institutions to make them more responsive to the needs of the low-income population.

In performing these service, educational, and political roles, the TAOs constituted a new organizational hybrid. They were quasi-public, non-

[1] Melvin B. Mogulof, "A Developmental Approach to the Community Action Idea," *Social Work,* Vol. 12, No. 2 (April, 1967), 13.

[2] Earl Raab, "Which War, Which Poverty?" *The Public Interest,* No. 3 (Spring, 1966), p. 50.

profit organizations, supported almost exclusively by tax funds, with a representational pattern that combined elements of both an elected membership of individuals, including some low-income persons and, as in Santa Clara, delegates from various interest groups who nominated their own representatives. In Oakland the prevailing structure was more in the form of a *neighborhood association*, with some elements of a *council* in Fruitvale and West Oakland, where specific ethnic groups or geographic areas had designated places on the advisory committees. With the exception of Chinatown, the target areas in San Francisco consisted solely of elected board members and combined the character of *representative assemblies* with that of *social service agencies* operating their own programs and subcontracting others. The most autonomous TAOs were the separately incorporated ASC Boards in Santa Clara, which were miniature CAPs for their areas, employing personnel and operating programs of their own although on a very small scale. The Area Planning Boards in San Francisco were also quite independent, although they were not incorporated.

Once the TAOs were established, whether as interim bodies as in San Francisco or as permanent organizations, as in Santa Clara or Oakland, they all sought to increase their influence by demanding more representation on the CAP board of directors and a greater measure of autonomy and policy-making power for themselves. While there were considerable differences in the original functions and powers assigned to them, in no case were the TAOs satisfied with this original delegation of authority. Most of their early efforts were devoted to enlarging the scope and content of their limited advisory powers. There were, as noted earlier, variations in the duration, intensity, and final outcome of these struggles. In this process of striving for a sense of identity, purpose, and increased power, the TAOs had numerous choices regarding the type of organization they could become. They could become a means for developing an independent base of power if the members acted aggressively, or could serve to "cool out" or co-opt indigenous leadership. They could provide a vehicle for extending the existing social service system in the neighborhood, or they could promote self-help, mutual aid, and indigenously sponsored projects or operate programs itself. They could seek the broadest type of participation as a primary goal, or they could become closed groups, the private preserve of a neighborhood elite.

The particular course "chosen" by each TAO, which resulted in its distinctive character and role, was influenced by its dominant orientation, its relationship to the EOC, and its operating system, all of which are the focus of this chapter.

Two Orientations

Whereas all the TAOs fought for more power, they had somewhat different goals and priorities, which expressed two contrasting orientations toward the opportunities presented by the war on poverty: the competent community or the competent program. In San Francisco the dominant purpose of the Area Planning Boards initially was Area Development, a concept originally promoted by the Western Addition board which involved the organization block by block of a low-income constituency whose needs and preferences were to become the basis of program plans. In this orientation, poverty was conceived of largely as a function of the social system rather than as a consequence of individual deficiencies. Hence, the San Francisco strategy was to use the limited time and available funds as judiciously as possible in the form of leverage on existing institutions through organizing the poor to pressure them. In this variation of a community development ideology, the extension of established agency programs were of secondary import: neighborhood organization rather than services was the primary goal, since in this way the TAOs could best implement their control of the CAP.

An opposing philosophy was found in Oakland, where the advisory committees sought increasing power not so much to organize the poor as to be able to influence the selection and manner of delivery of social services by various agencies. In particular, some of the advisory committees wanted to sponsor and operate service programs for the poor themselves. The dominant orientation in both the OEDC and in most of the advisory committees was to perceive the poor as persons whose major need was for jobs and specialized social services that would correct their educational and vocational deficiencies, enhancing their economic capabilities in competing on the employment market. When the advisory committees in Oakland did take on community organization functions, it was a role largely thrust upon them and resulted in little, if any, organizational success.

This emphasis on program was also found in Santa Clara, where the Mexican-American coalition wanted power less to organize the poor than as a means of influencing and operating service programs that could provide jobs for their members. In this way the TAOs in Santa Clara and Oakland accepted the original focus of their respective EOCs on program. The controversy was essentially a jurisdictional one between the EOC and the neighborhood over who should control the program. In contrast, the

San Francisco area leadership, in all but Chinatown, rejected the EOCs plan to initiate social service programs; instead they proposed a large-scale community development effort employing approximately 250 persons and involving the expenditure of almost $3 million over a two-year period.

The difference in these orientations can best be understood as a consequence of the dissimilar ideological commitments and political experience of the TAO staff leadership as well as the stage of CAP development. The Area Development plan in San Francisco was promoted primarily by the same group of Negro civil rights activists who were victorious in their fight with the Mayor over control of the EOC and who subsequently were selected for key staff positions by the area boards on which they had served. They perceived area development not only as a vehicle to implement the intent of the poverty program, but also as the basis of a potential political organization that might be used for other issues. They had been successful in withholding approval of any other programs; so there was considerable pressure on OEO to release funds for area development even though the Mayor's appointees and the executive leadership of the EOC were not in favor of this proposal. The TAO leadership both in Oakland and Santa Clara was much less "ethnic" and militant, and in the case of Oakland, entered the scene after the first year's programs had already been approved. In Santa Clara, the Mexican-American organizations had much more limited experience in working together as part of an alliance, were at an earlier stage of political development, and were more interested in the tangible possibility of staff positions and badly needed educational and job training programs than in the potential, as well as the possible competition, of new organizations for Mexican-Americans. They also inherited a set of prior program decisions by the EOC; although these were eventually overturned, the funding requirements of a broad community development effort were beyond their financial capabilities by the middle of 1966.

The orientations in San Francisco and Oakland shifted in the course of the first two years, with Oakland becoming somewhat more concerned with neighborhood organization as a result of its unsatisfactory experience with the delegate agency, and San Francisco becoming much more program oriented. The original commitment to area development proved too intangible and controversial to sustain. Under constant attack, it produced few results and encountered many obstacles both within the TAO and in the neighborhoods. Santa Clara surprisingly reversed its orientation at the beginning of its third year and made a policy commitment to organize the poor, but its implementation of this policy remained much in doubt.

Two Centers of Power

Despite their differences in orientation, all of the communities experienced a continual strain between the TAO and the EOC board and its staff, which periodically erupted into open conflict and which was only mitigated when the TAO demands were met. Some of the tensions diminished as a result of concessions, such as those made in Oakland by the OEDC when it agreed to 51 per cent representation by the advisory committees, or when the advisory committees were given the responsibility for administering the summer youth employment program in 1966. Similarly, the support by the new executive director in Santa Clara of the trend toward decentralization lessened somewhat the antagonism between the area boards and the EOC. In neither case, however, was the gap between the EOC and TAOs ever successfully bridged, as the latter continually complained about central administration staff, accusing them of employing too many professionals and keeping money from the poor. The widely shared suspicion, distrust, and hostility toward "downtown," "city hall," or "central" was one of the leading unifying forces in the neighborhoods. Some of the resentment toward the CAP, in the form of "spillover," even nourished other social action groups by serving as a source of discontent. Even when the areas had almost complete autonomy, as in San Francisco, there was continual strife between the professional staffs of the EOC and the areas. Superimposed on structural anomalies and administrative ambiguities in San Francisco were strong personal rivalries and ideological conflicts among key staff members that fed into factional quarrels in the area boards and ultimately brought about the resignation of five leading professional staff members and the complete disruption of one area board.

Just as the CAP constituted a new source of power in the community, which could affect the decision making of local government and delegate agencies, so the TAO represented another competing center of power for the EOC. As the new, sponsoring organization, the EOC was particularly visible, close, and familiar so it bore the brunt of the TAO's hostility much more so than did the "traditional enemies" of the poor such as city hall or the departments of public welfare, police, redevelopment, or public housing. Given the relatively vague character of the authority lodged in the CAP, it was not surprising that the TAO and the EOC would frequently attack each other's right to represent the poor and control the antipoverty program. By stressing the "maximum" rather than the "feasible" participation of the poor, the TAOs with few exceptions identified their fight for greater autonomy and power with the right of the poor to shape the character of the antipoverty program. Perceiving their membership, regardless of its composition, as the authentic spokesmen for the poor, the TAO regarded a victory for the neighborhoods as synonymous with a triumph of the poor.

The conditions of a cold war usually prevailed in all of the communities, but the frequency with which it erupted and the character of the strain between the TAO and the EOC, as well as their respective strategies, varied somewhat. In Oakland, despite the resentment toward the OEDC and the Department of Human Resources frequently expressed by TAO chairmen and many of the more active members, the ambiguous and frustrating advisory role assigned to the neighborhoods was tolerated much longer than in any of the other target areas. The coalition between the advisory committees was noticeably more fragile and short-lived than the TAO alliances in San Francisco and Santa Clara, and the committees were much less militant in the brief episodes of the walkout and boycott. These conditions may reflect both the pattern of concessions made by the OEDC and the relatively weak membership base on which the leadership had to rely in Oakland. There was a much weaker tradition of ethnic organization in the Oakland neighborhoods than there was, for example, in the Mission and the Western Addition.

The struggle for power between the EOC and the TAO was played out in two arenas: in the day-to-day working relationship between central and area staff members and in the EOC meetings where the target area representatives fought for the interests of the neighborhoods and the poor. The staff members had their own stakes in the outcome which, although similar to those of the TAO, were much more personalized and intense. The staff role was again different in Oakland, where the field service coordinators assigned to the target areas were employees of the Oakland Department of Human Resources. Although some of them did become ambivalent about their primary loyalties, they were usually regarded as instruments of city hall by the TAOs. In Santa Clara, where the professional staff employed by the area boards chafed under the administrative controls imposed by Central, and in San Francisco, there was little or no communication between the EOC and area staffs, with the areas functioning in a highly independent manner. Over a period of time, the Santa Clara EOC took on the pattern of a functional federation of service centers with a growing consensus regarding their division of responsibility and separation of powers, while San Francisco failed to resolve its problematic central-area relationships, which persisted into the third year of operation.

These experiences suggest that the attempt of the CAP to limit the authority of the TAO once it was established was unlikely to succeed. The demand, "All power to the neighborhoods," was an inevitable result once the target areas were designated and it became necessary to establish an official arm of the antipoverty program, or at least to give some visibility to the CAP and secure some reliable channels of communication with the neighborhoods. The distinctive ideology of OEO provided the sanction, rationale, incentive, and dynamism for the decentralization of authority that was achieved to the greatest extent in San Francisco. The anomalous relationship between the central administration and the areas meant that the former had insufficient authority to carry out its prescribed functions of coordination, evaluation, and planning, since the areas could initiate program and employ personnel. The tail did indeed wag the dog in San Francisco, where the central EOC served mainly as the official channel for OEO funds to be administered by the areas and occasionally as a broker on their behalf.

Santa Clara also illustrates the critical character of the delegation of authority; the consequences when rival centers of influence are established with needs of their own that diminish the amount of centralized power. The act of designating nine areas opened a Pandora's box of struggles for power that occurred both vertically and horizontally in nine new arenas, constituting multiple challenges to the authority of the EOC. Indeed, in the eyes of some, the EOC had given rise to a monster that practically devoured it. Perhaps if a smaller number of target areas had been delineated or if the EOC had been able to maintain an administrative pattern similar to that in Contra Costa County, delaying formal decentralization, it might not have been necessary to build up such an extensive central administrative staff and a network of service centers. Alone, the pressures of service center autonomy might not have been strong enough to challenge the powers of the EOC, but they were aided by the demand of OEO to reconstitute the EOC within 90 days, plus the drive of the Mexican-Americans to oust the executive director. Together these trends reinforced each other and hastened the reorganization of the EOC.

In Oakland, however, the other side of the decentralization process was more evident; namely, the fragmentation of power that might be used against the OEDC and which required that a coalition be formed. This the advisory committees were able to do only with the greatest of difficulties and for very brief periods of time. They, too, won a compromise victory aided by the strength of a series of external forces.

Thus, the designation of multiple target areas by itself was sufficient to bring about a major change in the power distribution only if there were other forces operating against the EOC.

Yet even when the target area became the majority group on the EOC, their representatives did not constitute a solid bloc; in San Francisco the Mayor's appointees, who comprised a cross-section of community interests, did not vote together consistently. Rather, there were shifting alliances—depending on the issues—in which different mayoral appointees secured allies from Central City and to a lesser extent in Hunters Point and Chinatown, with the Mission and the Western Addition often sticking together. In San Francisco, Oakland, and Santa Clara County, relatively few of the target area representatives played leadership roles in the deliberations of the EOC, which were usually highly formalized public meetings occurring in the presence of large and often articulate audiences. The target area representatives could almost always be depended upon to support programs and issues in which the interests of indigenous or ethnic groups were at stake and where job applicants or qualifications were involved.

A curious double standard was noted among the EOC representatives whereby those coming from the TAOs were expected to be accountable to their membership, whereas those from other sectors of the community, whether appointed by the Mayor or selected by designated organizations, usually insisted they were speaking as individuals and not for their organization. In contrast to the low accountability of the TAO members, their representatives to the EOC, while sometimes very casually selected, did report back rather consistently and were quite conscious of their delegate status. Only Santa Clara proved to be an anomaly, making a deliberate attempt to prevent the elected area commissioner to the EOC from being a member of the Area Service Center Board, thus further accentuating the distance between these two levels.

Although the belief was widespread in many Oakland advisory committees that their representatives to the OEDC had "sold out," there were surprisingly few instances where co-optation was clearly evident. This was most noticeable when several of the target area representatives in Oakland were interested in getting jobs or in getting one of their proposals funded. Nevertheless, the target area representatives were "different" from their membership in being among the more able, ambitious, and articulate persons in these groups, and their experience on the EOC often enhanced their organizational skills. Whether they were selected on a rather casual basis, as in Oakland or by means of a series of "elections," as in Santa Clara, the target area representatives to the EOC did not seem to separate themselves in any substantial way from their TAO members.

Issues and Roles

The contrasting orientations of the TAOs and their relationship to the EOC were also expressed in the issues with which they were concerned and the ways in which they performed their service, political, and educational roles. Four different types of issues were considered by the TAOs at various stages of their development and illustrate the manner in which these groups used their hard-won power. In the early phases much time was devoted to problems of *organizational maintenance*, that is, the recruitment and replacement of members, preparation of bylaws, appointment of committees, and so forth. Later agendas were concerned with *program review*, *staff selection*, and the *external relationships* of the TAOs to the service centers and delegate agencies, as well as the recurrent struggle with the EOC.

While all TAOs were continually involved with organizational maintenance and enhancement, there was more concern with program development in Oakland than in Santa Clara and San Francisco. Because of its predecessor organization—the Oakland Interagency Project—the OEDC had a head start on other cities in its ability to design fundable projects. This experience, together with the continued support of the Ford Foundation, made it possible for the OEDC to approve 67 programs and to consider 30 others in the course of three years. The advisory committees were able to obtain from the OEDC the right to review and make recommendations on all program proposals, and this activity soon took up a considerable portion of their meeting time. While initially the advisory committees were quite critical of the proposals, they subsequently treated this reviewing task in a more perfunctory way and like the other TAOs were somewhat more adept in obtaining additional power than in exercising it effectively.

Chinatown was the only San Francisco area board willing to approve programs developed by established agencies; the other three areas rejected proposals for their neighborhoods that were not developed with the participation of their board members or formulated by low-income residents. The latter criterion was utilized by the Mission, which approved only seven programs, all of which were designed by indigenous groups. The other San Francisco boards were much more preoccupied with the administration of the Area Development Program and their internal matters.

During most of 1965-66 the ASC Boards in Santa Clara were almost exclusively involved with structural reorganization, which was so prolonged and costly in time and energy that relatively little program was developed. The ASCs never did achieve the "farmers' market" concept originally intended because of the limited amount of funds available, which had to be divided in nine ways. Although they had the authority, they had very little money for area service projects.

Despite the various modes of program review found in the TAOs and the differences in their composition, orientation, and relationship to the EOC, the types of programs that were eventually approved were all quite similar. This held true for the projects developed by indigenous groups in the Mission and for Oakland programs, which also tended to be both small in scope and quite conventional in their conception. Included in the TAO programs were such social service amenities as day care, language training, youth employment, remedial education, and tutorials. The sameness of the programs, regardless of the TAO membership mix, may be due in part to OEO funding policy in which a precedent was rather quickly established whereby certain well-known types of programs were approved for funding. Rather than risk possible rejection, most CAPs and indigenous groups rarely proposed projects not cited as "examples" in the *CAP Guide*. While these constraints did not have to operate in Oakland, where indigenous projects were funded by the Ford Foundation, the grassroots programs were not substantially different in kind from those in other areas. This suggests that there may be certain basic social service needs that should be institutionalized and that until these are provided there may be little incentive to innovate.

Common to all the TAOs was the way in which *employment of the poor* was an issue. Originally one of the most powerful incentives for participation, the question of jobs in the war on poverty came to be a primary source of internal conflict in the TAOs and, somewhat less controversially, one of the most important criteria used by them in judging program proposals. Employment naturally appeared as the most tangible and logical benefit of the CAP; the acceptability of programs formulated by established agencies, the EOC, or TAO staff was greatly enhanced by the inclusion of a large number of jobs to be filled by residents. It made little difference that most of the jobs were of short duration, uncertain tenure, and low salary because of their "nonprofessional" classification. Because of the pervasive perception of the war on poverty as a source of employment, the major criticism of the CAP was that it provided so few jobs. Employment in the antipoverty program was also regarded as a source of ethnic power, as illustrated in the demand for a Mexican-American deputy director in Santa Clara and in the insistence on employment of Spanish-speaking personnel in the Mission and Fruitvale.

Because of the rather limited opportunities for patronage, there was constant pressure to lower the job qualifications so that practically anyone might be eligible. In view of the small number of jobs and the great number of applicants, the issue of employment became extremely controversial, particularly in San Francisco's Western Addition and the Mission, where the nonprofessional positions became pawns in the struggle between various factions. It was not unusual for disappointed and disgruntled job seekers to turn their resentment onto the board or staff member who had acquired a particular position, with disruptive consequences. Rejected applicants for jobs in the target area formed part of a continuing pool of persons who, as members of the audience attending EOC meetings or as board members, criticized other board or staff members in public. In some instances two or more board members would compete for the same job, as in Santa Clara's Area Service Center No. 4, when the victorious area director had to suffer the hostility of the loser, who became the chairman of the board. Because the qualifications were generally low, it was quite arbitrary which of hundreds of applicants would be selected as nonprofessional staff members. Personal favoritism, jealousies, and a host of patronage factors rooted in individual, ideological, and ethnic loyalties entered into the selection process. The struggle over who should get what job intensified internal political struggles within the TAO, particularly in San Francisco, which had twice as many positions to be filled (250) as Oakland, and deflected them from their other social service and political functions. Furthermore, in some neighborhoods such as Hunters Point, considerable envy, distrust, and resentment were generated by those who did get the jobs, and it was believed that these feelings blocked the organizing drive among the poor.

Another characteristic issue related to employment was the lack of authority of the target area director to select his own staff. Generally the board had full authority to hire or fire; at least its advice and consent was required, so that the executive had little control over the employees he supervised. In Santa Clara, the subprofessionals who had to be selected from a central roster and were paid by the EOC directly organized a protective association to seek improvements in their working conditions, and even went on strike for a few days early in 1967. The Oakland advisory committees were little involved in these issues since they had only consultative powers with respect to the employment of service center and delegate agency subprofessionals. When, however, they assumed responsibility for the community organization function in 1967, they found themselves facing similar conflicts.

Organizational Character

The TAOs like other organizations were constantly undergoing change in one form or another. Any description of their character refers to tendencies during a particular time span, in most cases 1965-66. Generalizations also tend to obscure the wide variations in and the lack of consistency among the operating systems of the TAOs. They differed in their composition and in their decision-making patterns. The 18 different TAOs were almost equally divided between pluralist and elitist decision-making systems, factional and consensual boards, and weak and assertive boards. The more assertive boards were most cohesive and characterized by pluralist decision-making systems. They also received strong leadership from either the chairman or the professional staff, or both. The more militant the boards were, the more likely they were to have members with a previous history of ethnic minority organization and membership in various organizations. Usually there was much more active participation when there was more at stake, for example, where the boards had or were seeking more power.

Although prolonged factionalism was found in eight out of the 18 TAOs, in only three of them were the disputes so disruptive that the TAOs were unable to function for a period of several months. In view of the very limited resources made available to historically deprived population groups whose anger had long been suppressed, it is surprising that there was not even more intense feuding over the spoils. The most frequent sources of these cleavages were ethnic and ideological differences, often complicated by struggles for personal power among TAO members, between TAO members and staff, among staff members. It was not always clear to what extent the recurrent factionalism reflected a more expressive style associated with some low-income or ethnic groups or the frustration from unrealizable and contradictory expectations aroused by the antipoverty program.

There was considerable variability in the response to such external issues as redevelopment, which was militantly opposed in the Mission, supported by Hunters Point and stalemated in the Western Addition. In Oakland, there was a wide discrepancy among advisory committees in their reaction to various project proposals; East Oakland, for example, was consistently among the most conservative and efficiency-minded, to the point of rejecting the proposal for a police review board when it was first introduced and being alone in favoring agency-sponsored over indigenous proposals. In Santa Clara there were opposing reactions to county-wide program proposals that reflected strong ideological and political differences between the ASC Boards.

The extent of member involvement in deliberations should not be exaggerated; in this regard the TAOs were like most voluntary associations, in which only a few members assume active roles. Attendance at most of the TAOs rarely exceeded 15 to 20 members, and only in the Western Addition, Mission, and Areas 3 and 5 in Santa Clara were there large public audiences. Most matters, including program reviews, were typically assigned to subcommittees of five or six members whose recommendations were then presented to the board, most of whose members were usually not too well informed about the issues. In making decisions on programs the chief criteria in most TAOs were political and ethnic interests and the possibilities for employment of the poor.

In spite of this somewhat perfunctory process, the level of understanding and debate was not substantially different from that in more established organizations with longer histories and greater experience. Indeed, the rapidity with which many low-income and working-class board members grasped the technical details of budgets and social service programming was quite impressive. In contrast to the narrowness of the protest role of similar organizations when confronted with urban renewal, the TAO members showed that when programs appeared to be in their interest, they could participate in more "constructive" and versatile functions such as planning, budgeting, and evaluation.

Also typical was a preoccupation with parliamentary procedure, almost to the point of ritualism; indigenous members, who were anxious to conform to the norms of formal organization, were deeply concerned with doing and saying the "right" thing. This emphasized the largely middle-class, task-oriented, agenda-centered nature of virtually all TAOs. They did not appear nor act like "poor peoples' organizations," whatever those may be. Their meetings were predominantly "business" meetings in the time-honored civic tradition, typically concerned with correspondence from the EOC, committee reports, and personnel and program matters.

What was unique about the TAOs, however, was their status as an arm of the federally sponsored and funded social service programs administered by the CAP. This role as local decision-making centers for the war on poverty tended to pre-empt all other organizational potentials. Because most of the members were neither consumers of OEO programs nor responsible to a low-income constituency, the TAOs did not fulfill the expected feedback function of their service role. Instead, as will be seen, they relied for these purposes, as well as for interpretation and encouragement to use the services, on the community organization function that they sponsored rather than on their own membership.

With but several exceptions the TAOs, although closer to certain strata of the low-income population, were still another layer of organization interposed between the poor and the CAP. Within a two- to three-year period, most TAOs took on the character of neighborhood councils, increasingly more formalized, autonomous, and parochial, rather than of broadly representative organizations responsible to a city-wide body.

Summary

As a new organizational hybrid, the TAOs invariably sought to acquire more authority and autonomy than originally granted to them by the CAP. The particular character and role assumed by the TAOs was greatly influenced by their original orientation toward community or program development, with the latter tending to become more dominant.

The decision to decentralize each CAP in varying degrees produced two rival centers of power. All TAOs regardless of their particular orientation and goals, were involved in a continual struggle with their EOC. Although the TAOs and their allies in each community ended up in "control" of the EOC, the neighborhood representatives did not vote consistently in a bloc, nor were they co-opted to any marked degree.

Apart from organizational maintenance, which took up considerable time, the leading issues debated by the TAOs concerned program development and review, staff selection, and their external relationships. Employment, in addition to being an incentive for participation, was one of the principal decision criteria in the evaluation of proposals and a source of conflict between TAO members.

As organizations, the TAOs were particularly subject to factionalism, mainly ethnic and ideological, elitist patterns of decision making, internal struggles for power, lack of representativeness, and assertiveness. The TAOs tended to become more middle class and distant from the EOC, and despite variations in their composition and extent of resident participation, there were few differences in the types of programs they supported. Their administrative and program functions pre-empted their other roles, and while not generally conceived of or controlled by the poor, they were at least for the poor.

9

WHY ORGANIZE THE POOR? THE DILEMMA OF SERVICES VERSUS ORGANIZATION

In the end, the community action program will succeed or fail, not on its record in delivering more or better social services, but on its record in involving the poor—in persuading them that they can control their own environment.[1]

In addition to the establishment of TAOs with their concerns for resident participation in decision making regarding program development, extensive efforts were made to contact neighborhood residents who were *not* members of the TAO. Many of the target area neighborhoods were canvassed by teams of professionals and their indigenous aides, often on a fairly systematic basis, for the purposes of

1. Informing residents about the CAP and the service center and encouraging and assisting them in the use of these and other community resources, as well as obtaining opinions regarding neighborhood needs, problems, program preferences, and priorities. In this *social service outreach,* the poor were perceived as client-consumers, many of whom needed social brokers, advocates, and expediters to help them obtain services to which they were entitled. Also imbedded in this function, which was largely information and referral, was a concern for case-finding.
2. Securing the participation of low-income residents in sub-area organizations and encouraging them to vote in the elections for representatives of the poor to the TAO. The *organizational maintenance* needs of the TAO required this form of community organization, in which the poor were regarded as individual potential members of a low-income constituency.
3. Involving the poor in new or existing organizations, usually with a

[1] Charles E. Silberman, "The Mixed-Up War on Poverty," *Fortune,* Vol. LXXII, No. 2 (August, 1965), p. 226.

self-help or neighborhood improvement goal. As part of a process of *urban community development,* small groups of residents were organized around common interests usually on a geographic basis such as blocks, neighborhoods, or districts, with a dual concern for increasing their skills in participation and bringing about changes in local neighborhood conditions.

4. Obtaining the participation of the poor in organized efforts to change the policies and practices of community institutions to conform to the wishes of the target area. This type of *social action* took three forms: prodding a community agency to do its job more effectively; pushing for a particular piece of legislation; or forming a temporary coalition of organizations united around a single policy issue. In contrast to the more "horizontal" character of community development, which was largely neighborhood based, social action was more "vertical" in its scope by cutting across neighborhood lines and affecting an entire community.[2]

These progressively more complex forms of resident participation were all described as "organizing the poor" and were the responsibility of a large number of indigenous aides, most of whom were members of the dominant ethnic group in the neighborhood, and whose job titles were: community aides, information and referral specialists, community development specialists, or neighborhood organizers. In most target areas, the information and referral function (social service outreach) and community organization (community development and social action) were not always carried out by two different groups of staff members, although when they were there was usually a working relationship between the groups.

The rationale for these attempts to communicate more effectively with the poor or organize them as a new constituency, client, or interest group was usually expressed in terms of the intrinsic values of participation as a form of sociotherapy; as a means of bringing about more effective delivery and utilization of social services; or as a source of power to bring about institutional change.[3] These justifications embodied the multiple and sometimes conflicting goals of the CAP, conceived as a social movement or a social agency depending upon its focus on changing individuals, neighborhoods, or community policies.

[2] The concepts of horizontal and vertical community action as they relate to community development and social action are derived from Roland L. Warren, *The Community in America* (Chicago: Rand-McNally & Co., 1963), pp. 161-66 and 324-25.

[3] For an analysis of the ways in which these forms of participation were promoted by six neighborhood centers see Robert Perlman and David Jones, *Neighborhood Service Centers* (Department of Health, Education and Welfare, The Welfare Administration, 1967), pp. 6 and 49-53. The experience of six projects funded by the Office of Juvenile Delinquency in attempting to organize the poor is described in Charles F. Grosser, *Helping Youth: A Study of Six Community Organization Programs* (Department of Health, Education and Welfare, Social and Rehabilitation Service, 1968).

Structural Patterns

In their attempts to promote these four types of community organization outside the TAO, the three CAPs varied considerably in their patterns of sponsorship, organization, philosophy, and practice. In Oakland, the responsibility for "organizing people in the community to enable them to have some control over the realities of their lives" was originally assigned to a delegate agency, the Oakland Council of Social Planning, presumably because of its experience with organizing district councils in various parts of the city prior to the antipoverty program.[4] Although the neighborhood organization component was originally supposed to include the responsibility for organizing the Target Area Advisory Committees, the Department of Human Resources later decided to organize the latter by themselves. Thus, two separate and parallel structures for resident participation evolved in Oakland with considerable distrust and suspicion between them. One system administered by the Oakland Department of Human Resources consisted of the advisory committees and the multiservice centers. The other systems, operated autonomously by the Council of Social Planning, employed a professional and two indigenous aides in each of the four target areas. This pattern persisted for 20 months before the neighborhood organization function was reassigned to the advisory committees by the OEDC.

In San Francisco two different trends were found within the Area Development Program, which absorbed one-third of the EOC funds during 1965-66. Whereas the information and referral functions of the areas were somewhat similar, the Western Addition program contrasted sharply with the others in being devoted principally to filling out the organizational structure within the area. Whereas most of the community organization efforts in Hunters Point, the Mission, and even Chinatown went into the development of indigenous groups of neighborhood residents *outside* the official structure of the EOC, in the Western Addition all of the resources went into the eventual organization of 28 neighborhood councils whose chairmen comprised the Area Planning Board. In this way community organization in the Western Addition was used primarily to develop and maintain the basic internal organizational structure for the TAO.

[4] The decision of the OEDC to subcontract the neighborhood organization component was the outcome of a pre-OEDC bargaining process in which the Council of Social Planning was unsuccessful in challenging the transformation of the Oakland Interagency Project into the Community Action Agency. The decision, in large part, represented a concession by the newly formed OEDC to the Council of Social Planning.

In Santa Clara County, central staff community organizers were originally involved in helping establish the ASC Boards, but once they were in operation, each area had its own specialists for information and referral, community development, group and individual services, and job and work training. In addition, the central EOC provided each area with several indigenous aides who were assigned by the area director to these specialists.

Philosophy and Priorities

Despite the notable differences in the structure and sponsorship of organization among the poor, essentially the same diffuse philosophy was articulated in all three communities, although their priorities and actual practices were dissimilar. Because of their hortatory character, these publicly stated goals may not have been meant to be taken seriously or even implemented. What was expressed was a mystique of participation that invoked such venerated symbols of community development as "grassroots," "self-determination" and "self-help" all of which were encouraged by a neo-Populist ideology promoted by OEO that served to legitimate the organizational program. Regardless of their origins and orientation, all of the CAPs probably endorsed the following statement of the Gilroy ASC philosophy in Santa Clara County:

> Man's satisfaction in belonging to a community can only be achieved as he is able to be involved in a process of self-determination through which he can achieve security and significance with dignity. CAP thus changed the antiquated concept of the relationship between donor-donee since its emphasis is on the "maximum feasible participation of the poor." This concept sees the poor person not merely as a recipient of services and programs over which he does not have any control, but as an integral participant in the effort of his community to eradicate the roots of poverty which degrade and cripple the human personality. For the first time the poor man achieves a sense of dignity and self-respect since he realizes he has a responsibility and opportunity to shape his destiny as he gets involved in a process of self-help, working in cooperation with neighbors, agencies, organizations and his community as a whole to resolve the problems which have made him dependent on society.[5]

Oakland's neighborhood organization was also described as seeking to

> Enable residents and groups of the target areas to further realize their maximum potential by participating in the making of decisions related to their own life . . . and enhance the effectiveness of

[5] "Statement of Philosophy of Gilroy Area Service Center," p. 1 (undated).

> the community institutions in resolving problems through the use of the community development process.[6]

Similarly, the goals of the Area Development Program in San Francisco also stressed community development, the objective of which was

> . . . a process of involvement in participation which will enable the residents to gain a meaningful place in the community and its affairs . . . (Chinatown)
>
> . . . to effectively increase the ability of local residents to use self-help methods in solving neighborhood problems, in determining the kinds of programs primary to solving their problems . . . (Hunters Point)
>
> . . . to stimulate the residents into growth producing activities and relationships in order that low-income residents will benefit from their increased participation in community life . . . (Mission).[7]

In San Francisco, the official stated philosophy had sociotherapeutic connotations, but its real intent was much more political. However, in actual practice, the Area Development Program served mainly social service and organization maintenance purposes.

The similarity of the expressive rhetoric of community development that the three CAPs employed, however, obscures considerable variations in their priorities and practices, although the outcomes were not remarkably different.

In contrast to the top priority assigned to community organization in San Francisco, Oakland's neighborhood organization program was regarded as but one among 20 other services provided by delegate agencies. It was also considered a program that had rather low status, owing, in part, to its being administratively separate from the advisory committees and the multiservice center. In Santa Clara, organization of the poor per se was not supported by the EOC and was encouraged only when it became necessary to comply with OEO deadlines for more representative participation from low-income persons. In Santa Clara, to a greater extent than in other communities, OEO pressures to speed up the reorganization of the ASC boards was mainly responsible for the greater emphasis on involving the poor in elections, but relatively little organizational effort was undertaken outside the TAO.[8]

[6] "Report on Component 12 Neighborhood Organization to Oakland Economic Development Council," Council of Social Planning, Oakland Area, Report No. 88 (December 1966), Appendix, p. 1.

[7] These statements are from the original proposals on Area Development submitted by Chinatown, Hunters Point, and the Mission.

[8] The result of this situation was that "The EOC has failed to organize the poor because it has had no program to do so." S. A. Skillicorn, "Sharing in the Action," EOC President's report, 1967, p. 2.

The extent of the difference in the priority assigned to all forms of community organization in San Francisco and Oakland is revealed in the rough comparisons in Table 3.

TABLE 3 [9]

Comparison of Resources Allocated to Community Organization by San Francisco and Oakland CAPs

Expenditures for Community Organization 1965-7 (30 months)

San Francisco	$3,727,339	(entire Area Development Program)
Oakland	414,210	(Neighborhood Organization program only)

Percentage CAP Funds Allocated to Community Organization

San Francisco	27%
Oakland	6%

Number of Staff (all types)

San Francisco Area Development	222
Oakland Neighborhood Organization	15

Ratio of Staff to Number of Poor Families in Target Area

San Francisco	1/160
Oakland	1/6000

Practice and Outcomes

Before the four approaches to organizing the poor are compared, the over-all pattern in each community will be briefly sketched.

In Oakland the dominant mode was a broad conception of community development in which a staff of four professionals and eight aides organized over twenty new neighborhood-based associations, as well as assisting numerous existing block clubs and tenant and parent groups in their efforts to improve physical conditions in the neighborhoods. There were substantial differences between the four target areas in the composition and structure of these groups, as well as in the issues selected and strategies employed by the staff. While the neighborhood organization staff disseminated information about the service center and referred residents to it and other community resources, there was considerable social distance and usually overt antagonism between the neighborhood organization

[9] It should be noted that these expenditures are not altogether comparable, although they do suffice for the purpose of indicating the gross differences in expenditures between San Francisco and Oakland. For example, in San Francisco, Area Development funds also included the costs of information and referral services and the operation of area and district offices. In Oakland, some of these costs were charged to the central administration and the separate service center budgets.

program and the advisory committees. The latter did not rely on the former for recruitment of members or other organizational tasks. Most social action was limited to mild, small-scale neighborhood efforts to compel better performance by several city agencies and the schools. Staff leadership was also given to a regional campaign directed at the employment and relocation policies of the Bay Area Rapid Transit District. The other major drive to change a community policy was the abortive proposal for a police review board.

A closer linkage between the four uses of community organization was found in San Francisco. Information and referral services were decentralized on a district basis for "walk-ins" and assigned on an outreach basis to either the community organization nonprofessionals or a separate staff of aides. Aside from rendering substantial direct services to individuals and families, this apparatus was also used on a fairly frequent basis to secure some feedback regarding needs and priorities as expressed by groups of residents. To a lesser degree only in Chinatown, hundreds of community aides were deeply involved in organizational maintenance functions of the TAO, such as conducting elections, and in trying, not always successfully, to sustain sub-area organization. The primary strategy to organize the poor in the Mission, Hunters Point, and Chinatown was through a community development process, stressing self-help, neighborhood improvement, and some social brokerage, with heavy reliance on block clubs and public housing tenant associations as the chief organizational structures. Social action was not often attempted; the most notable instance of it was the support of a large coalition in the Mission, which successfully fought redevelopment, as well as some rather effective attacks on public housing policy by Hunters Point tenant groups.

Most of the attempts to organize the poor in Santa Clara County were related to the maintenance needs of the ASC Boards as they were reconstituted to comply with OEO directives to include representatives of the groups and areas to be served. A limited social service outreach was promoted by small numbers of staff members working out of the area service centers and in some areas, extensive surveys of needs and priorities were undertaken. Sub-area organization, originally developed for election purposes, was usually not sustained owing to lack of staff, and as a result, a negligible amount of community development was promoted outside of the area service board itself. Most of the boards together with the EOC were, however, quite successful in one major piece of social action in the field of public housing.

In summary, then, although all communities stressed the social service outreach, San Francisco and Santa Clara expended considerably more resources in needs surveys and organizational maintenance than did Oakland. Community development programs in the form of self-help and neighborhood improvement groups were promoted much more extensively in San Francisco and Oakland than in Santa Clara, but in each community there were usually no more than one or two target areas where some form of social action was attempted.

1. SOCIAL SERVICE OUTREACH

One of the major purposes of the antipoverty program was to bring services closer to the people who needed them by means of neighborhood service centers offering some decentralized health, welfare, employment, educational, and legal services linked with outreach, referral, and follow-up. Eschewing the usual publicity devices, the target area stressed communication through personal contact by indigenous nonprofessional aides, who initially worked on a house-to-house basis informing residents about the service center and helping connect them with other community resources. The same contact often served two other purposes, as well, by providing a means of securing information from residents regarding their perception of needs, problems, program preferences, and priorities and possibly of recruiting the person into a new or existing neighborhood group sponsored by the TAO. The resident's need for services, whether in the form of information or follow-up, was a means of entry into the home and a basis for the establishment of a trusting relationship that could lead to further involvement in the future. Thus the aide was a combination messenger, publicist, salesman, recruiter, organizer, social worker, and expediter. In contrast to the community development or social action modes, which were *group* oriented, this type of community work was *individual* centered and viewed the resident as a client-consumer, or potential member, or both.

Two types of organizational structures were developed for the information and referral program with initial reliance on some form of outreach and subsequent emphasis on drop-ins to the service centers themselves. In most target areas, a large number of residents were attracted to the service center, which usually represented the most visible, tangible, and possibly constructive aspect of the CAP. For example, in Chinatown more than 80 per cent of the over one hundred "cases" each week were seen in the office as a result of a rather thorough canvass of the area during the first few months of the program.

The problem most frequently presented to the information and referral workers was usually that of unemployment; this was the one for which there were often the least resources. Referral to jobs or employment offices, training programs, and English classes were some of the major ways of dealing with the demands. Although hundreds of jobs were located through the energetic efforts of the aides who utilized the services of the Employment Department and its Youth and Adult Opportunity Centers, the Urban League, and other special job development and training programs, they could not possibly cope with the need. In contrast to the concrete services given in response to referrals for neighborhood legal services, which represented one of the innovative contributions of the CAP, response to requests for jobs revealed all too clearly the inadequacies of the CAP's orientation toward unemployment as an individual rather than a structural problem.[10]

Other types of problems dealt with by these previously untrained persons were the following:

> A landlord tried to evict a family on the basis of a lease that was changed after the tenants had signed it. The aide informed the family of their legal rights and at the same time pacified the landlord.
>
> An aide helped an 81 year old woman in a housing project find other quarters, since the project was being demolished and the project manager was not even aware that she needed assistance.
>
> A welfare recipient eager to become independent did not know that she could receive extra funds to go to school and additional money to pay a baby sitter from the Department of Social Services.
>
> A family was threatened by PG&E [Pacific Gas & Electric] to have their service discontinued but the aide interceded and helped the husband obtain a job, persuading PG&E to wait another month.
>
> An aide while going from house to house learned of a family just arrived from Texas with no funds or furniture. He enlisted the help of neighbors and local churches.
>
> A mother in need of medical care and unable to speak English was persuaded by an aide to go to the hospital. The aide obtained a baby sitter and then personally took the mother to the hospital and interpreted for her.[11]

These examples illustrate how nonprofessional staff members carried out their functions through interviewing individuals and families, making home visits, contacting other agencies, escorting and transporting clients,

[10] The CAP emphasis was mainly on education, training, personal counseling, etc. Typically, employment programs were largely "crash," such as the Concentrated Employment Program in 1967 or Summer Youth Employment, which was known informally as an "antiriot program." For a brief critique of the training programs sponsored by the war on poverty see S. M. Miller and Martin Rein, "Poverty, Inequality and Policy" in Howard Becker, ed., *Social Problems: A Modern Approach* (New York: John Wiley & Sons, Inc., 1966), pp. 506-10. Also, Sar A. Levitan, *Antipoverty Work and Training Efforts: Goals and Reality* (Ann Arbor, Michigan: Institute of Industrial Relations, University of Michigan, August, 1967).

[11] These examples are taken from the "Handbook for Community Aides," Mission Area Community Action Program, and prepared by Elaine Mikels. They are, however, characteristic of the types of cases found in the other target areas.

interpreting, expediting, following up on services, and playing an advocate role when needed. It was repeatedly found that many agency staff members did not know the benefits to which clients were entitled, and in some cases they more or less knowingly deprived clients of their rights. Other times, clients did not understand the social workers or vice versa, because of language barriers.

Out of this experience flowed a variety of direct benefits to thousands of individuals who were put in touch with needed services. The information and referral program also seems to have had some influence on public welfare departments, making them more sensitive to the needs of non-English-speaking clients. They began to use aides as interpreters and even employed some of them directly, as in San Francisco. A somewhat greater responsiveness on the part of some of these agencies to public assistance recipients was also credited to the effective performance of the advocate function by many of the aides, who reminded professional staff about the rights of their clientele.

Numerous unmet needs and service gaps were also pointed up by the aides in their day-to-day work or through the more systematic surveys that were undertaken, particularly in San Francisco and in selected areas in Santa Clara.[12] Yet, while involving residents as respondents in a survey might have been a useful way of approaching them and informing them about services, most TAOs were not in a position to do very much about their findings regarding needs and priorities. The frequent use of surveys in Hunters Point had a boomerang effect by increasing frustration and disillusionment with the antipoverty program and the unfulfilled expectations that it aroused. In this way, unintended by-products of the outreach program contributed to the difficulty of organizing the poor. Furthermore, the discontent arising out of the malfunctioning of the service systems, which might have been channelled into community organization, was utilized only at Hunters Point, the Mission, and in three areas of Santa Clara. In the other target areas, social service issues were rarely used as a basis to organize the poor. Instead, as will be seen, the low-income person was perceived primarily as a resident rather than as a client or recipient.

[12] Because the Oakland Neighborhood Organization staff did not operate out of a service center sponsored by the TAO, they devoted more time to direct organizational work than to information and referral. In the other communities it was rather curious that the needs and priorities "discovered" in the community through meetings, questionnaires, and interviews usually turned out to be precisely in the same order as those of the TAO staff. For example, "community organization" was found to be the primary need in the Mission and in Hunters Point. In the Western Addition there were many accusations of tampering with the responses of the "grits and gripe session" in which priorities were also expressed. Perhaps the most intensive collection of such data was in area 3 of Santa Clara, where 8,000 questionnaires were returned after a canvass of 14,000 residents.

Many information and referral workers uncovered inequities but tended to deal with them on a case-by-case basis, seeking redress for an individual or family but rarely trying to organize a group of victims for collective action.[13]

2. ORGANIZATIONAL MAINTENANCE

Organizational efforts were also undertaken in the neighborhoods on a rather unselective basis to establish and sustain the TAO. As a means rather than an end in itself, the involvement of residents in elections and occasionally in attempts to maintain a sub-area organization occurred to the greatest extent in the Western Addition and to a lesser extent in Santa Clara, Mission, Hunters Point, Chinatown, and least of all, Oakland. Neighborhood organizers were credited with "rescuing" the elections in the Western Addition, which had fallen into the doldrums after the first few months. Similarly, the Santa Clara areas with the highest percentage of residents voting were those that had invested substantial amounts of effort in community organization prior to the election. In Area 8, for example, community aides were able to produce a 50 per cent turnout after contacting thousands of voters. Area 3 also had relatively high proportions of voters in the sub-area elections. In Santa Clara County, the EOC relied completely on the ability of the community aides to carry out the rather complicated and seemingly endless election procedures in reconstituting the ASC boards. The considerable turnover among the elected representatives in the TAO in Santa Clara made it necessary to schedule elections almost continuously, and because in most instances there were no on-going sub-area organizations, it proved increasingly difficult to stir interest in voting.[14] As a result, the commitment of staff

[13] This experience contrasted with that of Mobilization for Youth, where social brokerage was used extensively. See George Brager and Harry Specht, "Mobilizing the Poor for Social Action," *Social Welfare Forum* (New York: Columbia University Press, 1965), pp. 197-210. Also Harry Specht, *Urban Community Development: A Social Work Process* (Walnut Creek, California: Contra Costa Council of Community Services, Publication No. 111, 1966), pp. 35-36.

[14] The difficulty of holding elections was acknowledged by the EOC chairman, Dr. Skillicorn, in his farewell message. He noted that the Santa Clara EOC was unable to mobilize the 75 poor persons, a minimum of 25 from each area, once a year to choose their representatives. S. A. Skillicorn, "Sharing in the Action," p. 2. There was considerable disparity between the publicized number of voters and the information gained from our interviews regarding the turnout. In some districts in the Mission it was asserted that only the staff members voted, and the area acknowledged that only 400 votes were cast in the 1966 election in the entire Mission. Evidently, the voter turnouts were sufficiently low for OEO to refuse to fund any further elections. A roundup of the elections in the early part of 1966 showed the following percentages of low-income persons voting: Philadelphia 2.7, Los Angeles .7, Boston 2.4, Chester, Pennsylvania 6, Cleveland 4.2, Kansas City, Missouri 5, Huntsville, Alabama 15.6. "Where were the poor on Election Day?" *U.S. News and World Report* (March 21, 1966), p. 94.

to these maintenance functions took an increasing proportion of their time, and in the Western Addition, temporary part-time aides were even hired during some of the key elections.

Because of limited staff and the absence of unifying issues, sub-area organizations proved most difficult to sustain in Santa Clara and in the Mission, and this difficulty accentuated the low accountability of the system. Only one target area acted on the widespread recognition that if the poor were organized in some sort of bloc their representatives would be more than a useful fiction. Central City in San Francisco was the single area to abandon mass, geographic-based elections after almost a year's experience and substitute a system whereby neighborhood organizations with working-class and low-income memberships selected their delegates to the TAO. Oakland, which did not really have community-wide elections of low-income persons until December, 1966, was among the last of the CAPs to adopt this method of selecting the representatives of the poor.

It seems clear that regardless of the ideological commitment to the development of an indigenous structure, the maintenance of organizational membership proved to be a pre-emptive task with little payoff. Because of the low voter turnout and the failure to sustain sub-area organization, it is safe to say that a "second government," in the sense of a parallel electoral process, did not develop.

3. COMMUNITY DEVELOPMENT

Various forms of community development were promoted in different degrees by all three communities as part of their attempt to secure "maximum feasible participation." Whether new groups were organized or existing ones strengthened through the provision of staff services; whether all the residents of a block, neighborhood, or district were eligible for membership, or only those constituting a special interest group; whether the focus was on better meeting the needs of the individuals or families themselves, or improving the condition of the neighborhood, the dominant theme was that of collective participation in some form of planned change and the development of indigenous leadership. The assumption was that poor people knew or could be helped to identify what their problems were and that if they were organized, they could develop the skills to wield the political power necessary to solve many of their problems. Through community organization, then, efforts were initiated to bring together people who had some common interest and to form them into a self-help or pressure group to push for more and usually better social services.

The goals, structures, composition, character, strategies, and influence of the groups involved in some form of community development were quite similar in Oakland, Hunters Point, the Mission, and Chinatown. Most groups were small, with a nucleus of three to five persons and a membership that ranged from 10 to 50, although many more attended one or two meetings and dropped out. For example, it was claimed that over nine thousand persons attended one or more group meetings in Oakland, but this obviously includes considerable duplication. Membership, even liberally construed, was slightly over six hundred in more than twenty organizations. It was claimed that approximately one-half of these members were low income, although these statistics were questioned by the Department of Human Resources.[15] In the Mission, 11 groups were organized, each with a membership of 40 to 60, of whom 10 were regarded as active persons; at Hunters Point, 13 block clubs were organized in three districts. Whereas Hunters Point tried without success to sustain an inter-block council, there was no attempt to bring together these various groups in Oakland. The largest organization was the Ping Yuen Improvement Association, which claimed 250 members and was the first public housing tenant association in Chinatown.

These community development groups were organized primarily around residence, and just as the recruitment strategies employed in the organization of the TAO shaped its character, role, and influence, so the use of the block, neighborhood, or district as the basic unit of organization determined the composition, type of issue, structure, character, and strategy of the new associations. Potential members were invited less because they were poor, a member of an ethnic minority, interested in a particular issue or service, or committed to a specific ideology than because they lived in a sector of the target area unit that was being organized. As a result, most groups had a heterogeneous membership the majority of whom were not impoverished or alienated, nor were the issues selected always those that were most salient to the poor. In the Mission these neighborhood and public housing tenant associations, all but several of which disintegrated within a year, sought such improvements as a well-baby clinic, a girl's club, school lunches, clean-up campaigns, improved garbage collection, and rodent extermination. Oakland neighborhood groups were involved in securing improved lighting, traffic signs, and one-way streets; sponsoring anti-litter campaigns; and blocking permits for poolhalls, taverns, and a half-way house for mental patients. Block clubs at Hunters Point were concerned with improving the physical

15 *Evaluation Analysis of the Council of Social Planning's Neighborhood Organization Program* (Research Division, Department of Human Resources, December, 1966). Questions regarding the validity of the DHR evaluation could also be raised since comparable statistical data were not always collected by these two organizations.

aspects of the neighborhood, such as modernizing the restroom facilities in an elementary school and guarding another school on weekends to prevent vandalism. Hunters Point, together with the Mission and several Oakland neighborhoods, was among the few target areas to help organize indigenous groups that were later funded as delegate agencies providing child care and educational, housing, and employment services. In general, however, there was a noticeable absence of functional, self-help associations formed either through initial organizing strategy or through later "spinoff."

Some of the consequences of organizing residents on a geographic basis, rather than by selective recruiting of the poor or organizing people on an interest or issue basis, were perceptively noted by one neighborhood organizer in Oakland:

> When the organizers come in, they canvass everyone—low and middle income alike. Everyone is invited to small block meetings where they hash out a whole range of problems. It is all very democratic, and the poor get outvoted without anyone realizing exactly how it happened. Everyone is encouraged to ventilate their grievances: "The neighborhood children tear up my yard." "I need a job." "The schools are no good." "The police never come when you need them and they are all over you when you don't." "My landlord promised to fix my stove when I moved in two years ago but he still hasn't done it." "The street is full of broken glass and the city won't clean it up." "There is no recreation for the kids." Everyone talks about the problems as they see them. Neighbors meet each other, often for the first time, and get a sense of their power and possibilities. There is a strong pull for getting an issue or a project that everyone can agree on, and if someone in the group doesn't pull for this, the organizer does. That is his job. And that is where a major goal of the program goes down the drain.
>
> Only a few people need jobs, not everyone has personal complaints about the school or trouble with his landlord. In the search for an issue on which everyone can agree and take action they end up with the lowest common denominator. Street cleaning or the need for a stop light are not the most pressing problems poor people face but they are the problems that face everyone in the neighborhood: poor and non-poor alike. That is why the group turns to them as issues. It is at this point that the poor start dropping out.
>
> . . . The upshot is that the goals of helping poor people get organized to help solve their problems have been in direct conflict with the goal of organizing neighborhoods so they can solve theirs.[16]

Most of these neighborhood organizations were quite conventional in their structure, observing formal parliamentary procedure and utilizing agendas and a fact-finding consensual model of decision making similar

[16] "Report on Component 12 Neighborhood Organization to Oakland Economic Development Council," Council of Social Planning, Oakland Area, Report No. 88 (December, 1966), pp. 12-13.

to those used by middle-class improvement associations or councils. Generally, they provided opportunities for participation to the more upwardly mobile, although this was less true in the Mission and at Hunters Point, where some new indigenous involvement occurred in the block clubs when many of their most active members obtained jobs with the EOC and replacements were sought. Another characteristic of these groups was that they, too, had difficulty maintaining an ethnic "mix," and just as the more middle-class members tended to drive out the poor, one ethnic minority usually took over the group.[17]

Many individual participants benefited from these attempts to involve them in a voluntary association, but the costs to the TAO in the amount of staff time required to maintain the organization were considerable. It was found that there was considerable membership turnover; attendance waxed and waned depending on the issue, and many of the groups did not persist for more than a few months, particularly when staff support was curtailed.

In community development, considerable emphasis is placed on a democratic rational process whereby problems and needs are articulated, goals and solutions considered, consensus developed, and plans formulated and implemented. In one of the few evaluations of this type of community organization, the Oakland Department of Human Resources concluded that this process did not occur in the expected manner. Instead, it found group goals manipulated by staff, and the pursuit of special interests about which there was no consensus. Perhaps more significantly, although the Oakland groups identified problems and talked about them, they were rarely able to formulate and implement any plans.[18] Although based on a rather limited study of the Oakland experience, this generalization was also applicable to most of the groups in San Francisco as well where there was a similar lack of continuity, and a failure to set possible goals and train indigenous leadership.

Three sets of factors may help explain the relatively meager results of the community development efforts outside the TAO, despite the substantial investment of funds and personnel in San Francisco and to a lesser extent in Oakland.

[17] This difficulty has been described as follows: ". . . it is probably too much to hope for that middle class and lower class people can work effectively over long periods of time in a citizen organization. Perhaps this is too pessimistic. Evidence to the contrary would be refreshing. But so far there is little evidence or logic to support the view. This does not mean this should not be tried or that it could not work for short run specific purposes." David Hunter, *The Slums* (New York: The Free Press, 1965), p. 195.

[18] *Evaluation Analysis of the Council of Social Planning's Neighborhood Organization Program* (Research Division, Department of Human Resources, December, 1966), pp. 50-57.

1. The level of commitment, skill, and morale of the *staff* was not conducive to a successful program of community development. All but a few of the staff members were indigenous nonprofessionals, and most of them did not receive adequate training and supervision for their new jobs. Considerable insecurity was attached to their staff positions, and they had a natural concern not to endanger them; so many "played it safe" and were perceived by residents and co-workers as having been co-opted. Because they were the lucky ones to be selected from a large number of equally qualified applicants, envy, distrust, and resentment were aroused in the population they hoped to organize. They also had to bear the brunt of being identified with the antipoverty program and with all the hopes and promises it could not deliver. In San Francisco, this burden was compounded by the image of a conflict-ridden organization that was widely promoted in the mass media.

2. There were two sets of *situational and organizational constraints:* (a) the lack of tangible, short-run inducements to participate and (b) the continual imposition of OEO guidelines and deadlines. As one organizer put it: "It's difficult to reach people if you have nothing to offer them, neither money, nor the chance to earn it, nor direct services. . . ." The limited array of social services in the target areas and the information and referral assistance available to the poor appeared either irrelevant or inadequate to satisfy the primary needs for jobs or income on the part of those whom the organizers wanted to involve in a community development process. The need to comply with shifting OEO policies on resident participation and the role of CAP staff, the uncertainties of annual funding, and the urgency to demonstrate tangible results that would justify continuance of the program all contributed to limit the possibilities of building new organizations on a solid basis.

3. Finally, *the poor themselves,* the community to be organized, consisted of people who, in the words of the Mission staff,

> . . . were primarily interested in services and jobs rather than organization. They were not revolutionary, militant, cohesive (easily organized). They did not participate readily because they were preoccupied with daily self and family needs and generally lacked information and knowledge on actions which can legitimately be taken.[19]

[19] Mission Area Community Action Program, "Rationale for Budget Application February 1967 to January 1968," p. 13. On the political character of the poor and its significance for organization, see Allan Haber, "The American Underclass," in *Poverty and Human Resources Abstracts,* Vol. II, No. 3 (May-June, 1967), 5-19. The lack of dissent among minorities is discussed by Earl Raab in "What War and Which Poverty?" in *The Public Interest,* No. 3 (Spring, 1966), 54.

This is similar to an observation made about Spanish Harlem:

> The poor do not want organization for its own sake, nor should anyone else. They want better housing, better jobs, better schools, etc.—they want results. If organization gets them these things, they will buy it. If government gives them these things, as it should, the poor may not need to organize. Organization is only a means to an end, not an end in itself.[20]

Thus the crisis-life of the poor, which accounts for the apathy or alienation frequently ascribed to them, as well as the low salience of the issues around which the community development process was oriented, may account for their lack of incentive to join and maintain a neighborhood organization.

4. SOCIAL ACTION

The goal of social action was often described as institutional change, whereby the poor as a newly organized interest group in the community were expected to bring pressure on established agencies to modify some major policy or practice. A desired by-product was the development of increasingly sophisticated and effective indigenous leadership that would gain knowledge and skill from their experience of participating in such efforts for change. In contrast to the more horizontal character of community development then, social action was directed at vertical community forces, and it was concerned with both the mobilization of power and the development of leadership.

The following were the major types of issue-oriented social action that were characteristic of each community:

a. *Attempts to persuade or pressure public bureaucracies to perform their duties more effectively or equitably in the neighborhood.* These efforts included the campaigns waged by neighborhood groups in East Oakland to get the city to cooperate in providing better and more frequent street-sweeping, litter signs, neighborhood clean-ups, traffic safety measures, new street lights, and more adequate library facilities. These groups had legitimate grievances and were assisted by staff to direct their complaints to the attention of the appropriate public bodies and to ask for remedial action. In most instances, this was granted without any substantial controversy. The work of the area staff at Hunters Point to avert the evictions of individual families was another example of pressures directed at a single agency, the public housing authority. In general, how-

20 Patricia Cayo Sexton, *Spanish Harlem* (New York: Harper Colophon, 1965), p. 187.

ever, for reasons that are not at all clear, techniques of social brokerage whereby residents were organized around a common grievance were utilized infrequently in all the CAPs.

b. A second type of social action is represented in those efforts by target area organizations to secure *legislative action,* as in the successful campaign to establish public housing authorities in San Jose, Gilroy, and Santa Clara County. All but two of the ASCs in Santa Clara collaborated in securing passage of ordinances establishing public housing programs for the first time. Area 3 in Santa Clara County was most successful in giving leadership to this project as well as in obtaining capital improvements from the city of San Jose.

c. A third type of campaign involved efforts by an *ad hoc* coalition *to change the policy of a political jurisdiction* covering a much wider scope than a local neighborhood, such as JOBART and MCOR. Both of these examples, however, need to be qualified somewhat. MCOR affected only the Mission Area of San Francisco, but because it was such a large area MCOR had implications sufficiently broad to be included in this category. Also, although MCOR was an independent organization, it received major support and assistance from the TAO staff. In Oakland JOBART, which had been foundering for almost a year as a loose coalition of human relations groups, civil rights organizations, Negro ministers, NAACP, and other such groups from San Francisco, Richmond, and Oakland, was staffed by one of the neighborhood organizers from the Council of Social Planning. JOBART was regarded by the Department of Human Resources as the most successful of both the issue-oriented as well as the geographically based groups organized by the CSP, even though its record of accomplishment was not impressive.[21] Although there were many public meetings and negotiating sessions and numerous demonstrations and picket lines whose objective was to force BART to provide jobs for minorities, halt construction of the "Richmond Wall," and compensate adequately residents who had to move, few of these goals were achieved. Negotiating sessions were broken off after four meetings when JOBART concluded that representatives of the District were not acting in good faith. The goal of jobs for minorities was not achieved; and the Richmond City Council voted to accept BART's plans calling for a wall to be built around the tracks separating the south and north sides of Richmond. While JOBART was successful in getting the state legislature to pay for moving expenses, only 34 out of the 400 displaced persons could benefit from this legislation, coming as late as it did.

[21] Appendix 3, "Evaluation Analysis of An Organization Staffed Under the Auspices of the Council of Social Planning's Neighborhood Organization Program in Target Area C" (Research Division, Department of Human Resources, December, 1966).

Both MCOR and JOBART constituted part of the "spillover" effects of the CAP, as did numerous other groups that developed outside the official antipoverty structure and did not share the conventional, melioristic quality of most of the organizations sponsored directly by the TAO. In Oakland there were a number of small social protest groups whose development was stimulated by the war on poverty and the discontent it stirred. Among those participants who did not drop out in disgust or cynicism from the TAO were some who became sufficiently aware and angry to join other more militant groups in attacking the schools or the public housing authority. Unfettered by the constraints of the OEDC and its staff, these organizations were able to function in a more aggressive manner. The *least* assertive groups were those developed strictly within the TAO structure itself, as in the Western Addition. Those organized *outside* the TAO, such as those in the Mission and Hunters Point, were more active in seeking community improvement and more likely to become involved in conflict. In this connection, it was found that TAO support of some existing structure in the community was more productive than the organization of new groups such as welfare rights associations.

Another example of social action that sought to alter the balance of power was the OEDC proposal to establish a police review board. This attempt to bring about a change in a community policy dragged on for over twenty months, as the OEDC failed to persuade the Oakland City Council that some sort of review process was necessary. The demand for a police review board alarmed and challenged the council sufficiently so that the conflict brought out into the open the previously ambiguous character of its control over the OEDC. One consequence was the council's assertion of its prerogative by denying the right of the OEDC to receive funds from the Ford Foundation for any purpose related to a police review board. Followed by other attacks on the autonomy of the OEDC, the police review board issue eventually led to the decision of the CAP to separate itself from the sponsorship of the city of Oakland.

The experience of MCOR, together with that of the OEDC, was among the relatively few instances where EOC- or TAO-sponsored action resulted in a head-on clash between the CAP and local government.

Fighting the Power Structure

The recurrent strain between the EOC and city hall in both San Francisco and Oakland had somewhat less to do with the character of any social action initiated by the CAP than with the basic issue of who should control the policy-making body. In both communities, controversies were exacerbated by a particular social action issue—the police review board in Oakland and MCOR in San Francisco—but there was a long-standing and fundamental conflict between the mayors and the EOC regarding their interests and conception of the CAP's appropriate composition, role, source, and exercise of authority.

In San Francisco, the administrative turmoil deriving from the conflict between central and area staff, as well as factional fighting in some of the area boards over the commitment to community organization ahead of program, served as a continual source of discord. The Mayor placed the blame for the controversy in the city on the Area Development Program; it was this policy, he asserted, that influenced the abandonment of redevelopment plans for the Mission and a Model Cities application for Hunters Point, and also revived objections to redevelopment in the Western Addition. Mayor Shelley frequently expressed his displeasure with the program, but although he was convinced it was headed in the wrong direction, he was rather circumspect in his attempts to influence it.

Oakland's Mayor Reading also criticized the neighborhood organization program on the grounds that it sowed discontent, involved too few poor, and was overly influenced by the staff. He claimed that Oakland was over-organized and that neighborhood organization took money from more significant programs such as education and training, which would lead to jobs. In his view, neighborhood organization should have been given the lowest priority because the poor did not want organization, they wanted jobs and neighborhood improvements. The Mayor was also concerned about the existence of "two governments" and pressed for the OEDC to be directly responsible to the city council rather than to OEO, on the grounds that the city had insufficient authority over the OEDC and its work.[22]

In retrospect, the reactions of the mayors appear somewhat out of proportion to the facts of the situation and probably unwarranted. Not only did they have much more influence than they admitted publicly, they had much less to fear in the form of a challenge to their power. The San Francisco mayor appointed 49 per cent of the membership of the EOC and had control over the vital 10 per cent of the city's share. In Oakland, the staff was part of the city apparatus directly responsible to the city manager, and all requests for funds were approved by the city council. Rarely did the TAO or any of the groups organized in the neighborhood attack city hall itself or constitute a new political force or threat, as ex-

[22] These opinions were expressed by Mayor Reading in his testimony before the Senate's Sub-Committee on Employment, Manpower and Poverty, May 10, 1967, San Francisco, California, and in response to questions directed to him by Senators Joseph P. Clark and Robert Kennedy.

pected by many. Despite the fears that federal support would be used to attack local governmental institutions, the number of such instances is surprisingly small considering the resources ($3.5 million) that were poured into the community organization function in San Francisco and Oakland. Somewhat coercive tactics were used at Hunters Point against the Public Housing Authority and by MCOR, but almost not at all in Oakland. Examples of conflict, however, were overshadowed by the instances of conventional pressure directed against a public bureaucracy whereby a group of citizens took democratic collective action and functioned as a lobbying interest for the poor in the manner in which the residents of cities have traditionally acted. These measures were hardly radical. Rather they were, as Cloward has noted, distinctly middle class in their emphasis on self-help, local initiative, and democratic cooperative action. They were very much in keeping, for example, with the community council tradition.[23] What was different was that these milder forms of citizen action had never been developed in most low-income areas and were stimulated and sustained by the war against poverty.

Thus, the feared political insurgency of the poor did not really develop in any substantial way in these three communities, and there were very few attempts to confront agencies or government directly in a militant manner.[24] Indeed, it could be argued that government itself was much more the aggressor in San Francisco and Oakland, although this was much less so in Santa Clara County. The response of the CAP to the congressional budget cuts in late 1966 was also remarkably restrained. Beyond the usual telegrams and resolutions and several sporadic attempts by Headstart, parent, and other similar groups to protest, there were few organized or mobilized efforts to oppose the proposed reductions in funds.

[23] Richard A. Cloward, "The War on Poverty: Are the Poor Left Out?" *The Nation*, Vol. 201, No. 3 (August 2, 1965), 55-60. Other characteristics of low income self-help organizations are described in John B. Turner (ed.) *Neighborhood Organization for Community Action* (New York: National Association of Social Workers, 1968), pp. 14-21, 125-26, 182-85, 192-93.

[24] The lack of social protest and the failure of all but a few CAPs to use a strategy of developing power for the poor sometimes through purposefully created conflict was noted in the *Report of the Committee on Labor and Public Welfare*, U.S. Senate on S. 2388 (Economic Opportunity Amendments of 1967), 90th Congress, First Session, pp. 36-37. The dominant role of governmental officials and their appointees on the CAP Boards was earlier noted in the report of the Advisory Commission on the Intergovernmental Relations, *Intergovernmental Relations in the Poverty Program* (Washington, D.C.: Government Printing Office, April, 1966), p. 49. Useful summaries of the national experience with resident participation are Sanford L. Kravitz, "The Community Action Program in Perspective," in Warner Bloomberg, Jr. and Henry J. Schmandt, eds., *Power, Poverty and Urban Policy*. (Beverly Hills, California: Sage Publications, 1968), pp. 259-84, and Howard W. Hallman, "The Community Action Program: An Interpretive Analysis," *ibid.*, pp. 285-312.

In spite of the frequent bluster about "fighting the power structure," relatively little of this occurred. Why was this so? In addition to the operation of the factors cited earlier affecting staff, sponsor, and the poor, which inhibited the community development process, there were these special, limiting conditions on social action:

1. Internal factionalism, in which much of the available militancy went into squabbling within the TAO or against the EOC so that little energy and fewer resources were left for an attack on more substantial elements in the power structure. This was particularly true in San Francisco and Santa Clara, and was neatly expressed in an interview with George Napper, the former director of Hunters Point:

> I wonder if EOC wasn't planned to get people fighting among themselves so they wouldn't engage in certain (troublesome) activities.[25]

2. The character of the sponsoring organization. In Oakland, the Council of Social Planning was committed to a policy of community development on a neighborhood basis in which a council-type structure was considered to be a model. This strategy led to the organization of neighborhoods that were preoccupied with self-help and improvement and operated against more vertical and assertive forms of social action. In addition, sponsors such as the Council of Social Planning or a CAP could not be expected to promote the use of agitational methods of organization and confrontation tactics, which some have claimed are the only means by which the poor can be mobilized to confront the power structure.[26] Such strategies, if successful, would have brought the CAP into serious conflict with the institutions upon whom it was dependent for support. In the Western Addition, and to a lesser degree in Santa Clara, there was ideological backing for a more assertive organization, at least on the part of some staff members. However, structural requirements, such as the conducting of elections and staffing neighborhood councils, in addition to the internal dissension, effectively limited the goals and issues around which residents were organized.

3. The staff included persons with a wide range of political ideologies, ethnic attachments, and commitments to social action. Because of the lack of a coherent and consistent policy in any of the three communities, staff members tended to go their own way and improvise according to their needs and interests. Perhaps more than any other factor, the ideology and

[25] Quoted in the *San Francisco Examiner,* October 26, 1966.

[26] This argument has been advanced notably by Saul Alinsky in numerous interviews and publications, such as "The War on Poverty: Political Pornography," *Journal of Social Issues,* Vol. 21, No. 1 (January, 1965), 41-47.

capabilities of the staff influenced the character of any social action undertaken. The more radical ones tried to organize groups around issues that might involve conflict, while others, just as deliberately, sought to promote innocuous projects. Relatively large numbers of the poor were reached by the community organization staff, but the staffs' major approach was informational, in an attempt to help persons make use of the social service programs, and they did not conceive their purpose as organizing the poor for a radical assault on power.

4. The last factor pertains to the nature of the poor themselves, who were much less interested in ideology, political issues, and power than in more immediate and tangible needs.

Summary

Of the four approaches to organizing the poor outside the TAO, some form of community development was the usual method, with social action occurring much less often. More neighborhood residents were, however, contacted through the social service outreach, which was used mainly for information and referral purposes. Together with the organizational maintenance requirements of the TAO, these two modes of community organization preempted most of the staff resources.

This experience of attempting to organize the poor in the three communities demonstrated that it was possible, with the investment of a substantial number of staff, to organize and sustain for relatively short periods of time small neighborhood associations that could involve a selected group of residents in a variety of self-help and neighborhood improvement activities. The block clubs at Hunters Point, the neighborhood improvement associations in Oakland, the neighborhood councils in the Western Addition, the public housing tenants' associations in the Mission and Chinatown, and the sub-area organizations in Santa Clara usually involved residents who were predisposed to participate in community affairs. More often than not, the more sophisticated and upwardly mobile members dominated and those with less income and organizational experience tended to drop out. There were thus three sets of displacements in these groups organized outside the TAO: social service concerns prevailed over community organization and social action; the middle class prevailed over low-income groups; and ethnicity took precedence over poverty and single ethnic groups dominated multiple ethnic groups.

The issues selected by these groups were generally of immediate local concern, represented the lowest common denominator of interest, and rarely involved the development of any long-range plans. Usually engaged in seeking remedial action in a consensual manner rather than through protest or direct action, most of these meliorative organizations were quite middle class in their character, observing parliamentary procedure and the other characteristic traits of voluntary associations. They demonstrated some ability to bring about minor adjustments and modifications in environmental conditions, but very few groups made the transition from a concern with social services to more political involvement.

The deficiencies in block organizations and neighborhood councils that have been noted over the years were also found in these groups; namely, the rise and fall of attendance, the limited scope of activity, the extensive factionalism, lack of effective leadership, and the need for continual input of critical issues and extensive staff support to sustain themselves. They tended to have a limited impact on the conditions of poverty as well as a negligible amount of social action.

Three subtypes of social action were found, and the most effective forms of protest were undertaken outside the CAP, often as a part of the spillover from the frustration aroused by the war on poverty. Although elected officials feared and fought the specter of an organized attack against city hall, the persistent, internal factionalism among these groups and the lack of commitment, plan, and methodology mitigated against this; as a result there were very few assaults on the establishment and its policies.

10

RESIDENT PARTICIPATION AND ITS INFLUENCE: WHAT DIFFERENCE DID IT MAKE?

Few undertakings in our time have generated as much hope, produced as many immediate and beneficial results, or excited as much controversy, as the anti-poverty program . . .[1]

The task of identifying the results of the participation of the poor in three communities is beset by more than usually formidable obstacles to the assessment of the outcomes of planned social change. The ambiguity of the goals of resident participation; the difficulty of separating out the influence of other aspects of the CAP; the effects of other complex and often unknown variables; the relatively short duration of the program; as well as the elusiveness of reliable substantive evidence inevitably make any conclusions highly tentative. Nevertheless, subject to these limitations, it may still be convenient to bring together some generalizations about the apparent consequences of resident participation in San Francisco, Oakland, and Santa Clara County on four target systems: 1) social service agencies; 2) minority groups; 3) the poor; 4) local government.

1. Social Service Agencies

Four sets of interrelated strategies were utilized by the CAP with the objective of changing the attitudes, policies, and practices of governmental and voluntary agencies to make them more responsive to the needs of the poor. All but one of these relied primarily on various modes of resident participation.[2]

[1] President Lyndon B. Johnson, Message on Urban and Rural Poverty, March 15, 1967, p. 3.

[2] Underlying these strategies was the assumption that the social service bureaucracies needed pressures from their clientele in order to make them more responsive to the poor. However, there may be other reasons why the bureaucracies may not function effectively. For example, they may have insufficient funds, or their technology may be inadequate.

These strategies were:

1. "seduction" or persuasion through financial incentives ("bribery"), demonstration projects, or both as an inducement to offer or modify a particular service;
2. "infiltration" by indigenous nonprofessionals employed by delegate agencies or by the CAP itself;
3. "monitoring" by low-income persons serving on delegate agency advisory or CAP policy-making bodies;
4. "attack" by organized pressure groups from the target area, an approach previously described in Chapter 9.

If one starts with the most ambitious goals of the CAP and seeks to determine the cumulative influence of these measures on redirecting the focus and content of any part of the social service system, one finds relatively little change in the basic orientation of health, education, and welfare agencies. It may be unfair to take seriously the goals and claims of OEO and the CAP regarding the "quiet revolution" of innovations and transformations. What actually took place among the established community agencies, at least in Oakland and San Francisco, was much more in the nature of a "decentralization of the status quo." One of the very few instances of what might be described as a major shift in organizational mission as well as methodology occurred in the Legal Aid Society in Oakland and to a much lesser extent in the state department of employment, but in both cases, the changes were due less to the participation of the poor than to the first strategy, "bribery." The extension of some conventional social services, previously unavailable to a deprived clientele; the emergence of new, indigenous forms of sponsorship for other traditional social programs; and some involvement of residents in evaluative roles were among the more tangible results of the leverage exerted by the CAP. This does not minimize the value of legal, health, employment, remedial, or compensatory educational programs, but the departures from tradition were much more in the decentralized mode of delivery, sponsorship, and planning process than in the nature of the services themselves.

"SEDUCTION"

Not surprisingly, the most substantial impact on an agency's goals and program occurred when there was a rapid expansion financed by "disproportionate" OEO funds, as in Oakland, where the Legal Aid Society expanded its staff from 2 to 20 attorneys over a two-year period, as a result of a ten-fold increase in its budget. A redirection of legal aid services was implicit in any amount of OEO funding, owing to the guidelines for neighborhood legal services, but expansion of agency income at such an accelerated rate was bound to alter its organizational character. Also, the funds available to the state department of employment, which permitted extensive decentralization and the opening of adult and youth opportunity centers in the target areas, may account for the increased proportion of low-income persons in their clientele and possibly in some alteration in staff perspective and modes of work.[3]

The converse of this may also explain why, despite the large sums allocated to the San Francisco and Oakland schools, there appear to be relatively few notable modifications in their practices, although this was much less true for Oakland than for San Francisco. The amount of OEO funds granted to the schools was very small in proportion to their total budget and even in comparison with funds available to them under the Elementary and Secondary Education Act of 1965; hence the CAP influence was not too noticeable.[4] More than fifteen established agencies were involved in the San Francisco EOC, but with the exception of the Urban League, OEO funds financed a very small, specialized service that was often not a major portion of their program. With different staff, budgeting, financing, and reporting procedures, these poverty projects were usually isolated from the mainstream of the agency's ongoing operation; as a result, there was little spillover.[5] It therefore appeared unlikely that these agencies would continue to extend some of their prevailing social services or inaugurate new or redirected ones without some form of continuing subsidy. In view of the fact that the CAP had somewhat less than 1 per cent of the total community expenditures for health, welfare, and education available for leverage, its meager effects on agency policies were to be expected. Finally, the low impact on the dominant features of the established agencies was also a consequence of the basic failure of the CAP to involve as delegate agencies such key public bureaucracies as the Public Social Service and Health Departments in San Francisco, the Wel-

[3] It was asserted in an interview with the regional manager of the state department of employment that 80 per cent of their clientele now came from the target areas. It was not possible to verify this statement.

[4] In Oakland, the schools received approximately $3 million of their total budget of $40 million from all federal and philanthropic sources including the Economic Opportunity Act, Elementary and Secondary Education Act, and the Ford Foundation. In San Francisco, the proportion of OEO funds amounted to less than 1 per cent of the $89 million school budget.

[5] A notable exception was the San Francisco Family Service Agency, which, in contrast to the more segmental involvement of its counterpart in Oakland, began reaching out to low-income groups in the Western Addition and to assume advocate roles for them on numerous social issues. These actions were, however, due more to the pre-EOC professional goals of the executive who sought to change the role and character of his agency than to the specific influence of the EOC. The latter provided the executive, who already had some board support, with sanctions and opportunities.

fare Commission, the Police Department, and the Public Housing Authority in Oakland, and some school districts in Santa Clara.

If, however, one lowers expectations to a more realistic level and looks for changes of lesser magnitude than redirection, there were some differences in agency policies and practices that were probably related to their participation in the antipoverty program. (However, as will be seen, the necessity for compliance with OEO guidelines and the pressures generated by some types of social action were much more influential than resident participation.) Among some of the more substantial changes that were reported were the following: the establishment of a new department of special urban services in the Oakland schools; the appointment of school advisory committees and the facilitation of joint housing arrangements with two indigenously sponsored schools for drop-outs; the break with norms opposed to "grantsmanship" in Alameda County by the health department and its use of indigenous personnel in program development; the employment of new types of indigenous and professional staff by the department of employment, their elimination of "rap sheets" and revamping of the definition of "permanent employment" from 3 to 30 days; alterations in its rate schedule and a moratorium on evictions by the San Francisco Public Housing Authority; the addition of some compensatory education programs by the San Francisco schools and the sponsorship of the bail bond project by the bar association in that city.

There were, in addition, reports of changes in the attitudes of some agency professional staff and board members, as well as on the part of low-income indigenous staff and participants. On the positive side, several executives thought that the agency had better public relations in the minority community; that there was a greater appreciation by its middle-class professional staff of the needs and desires of low-income people and a "better understanding" of the establishment by many of the nonprofessionals, together with some modification of the antiprofessionalism of the members of the TAO. Typically, the professional staff were more convinced that changes had occurred in their agency than were "outsiders." On the other hand, there were widespread feelings in San Francisco and to a lesser extent in Santa Clara on the part of the target area board members, as well as professionals, that many of the established agencies had been antagonized by their treatment by some of the CAP staff, as well as the conflict in the CAP, which circumstances produced even greater distance and lack of understanding than there were before. Evaluating the reality of imputed changes in attitudes as well as practice was particularly difficult, not only because of these contradictory impressions, but also because it was not possible to trace the consequences of any allegedly new or different perspectives in humanizing the service systems.

In attempting to ascertain the relative influence of the various modes of resident participation on the service systems, it seems evident, as noted earlier, that some of the most substantial changes in agency behavior were less a response to the participation of the poor than to the necessity for compliance with OEO guidelines. In a few instances changes were due to some form of social action. As in other aspects of the CAP, a process of self-selection took place in which those agencies that were already interested in extending their services to low-income persons in the target area applied for funds and of necessity had to adapt their programs and staffing patterns to OEO specifications. For most established agencies, then, the most salient prerequisite was their *own* decision to apply for OEO funds, since this usually meant that they were willing to have their proposal reviewed by target area representatives, work with a low-income clientele, assign professional staff to a neighborhood, possibly employ indigenous personnel, and at least consult with target area representatives on matters of program and staff.

Generally, most of the initative to participate in the CAP came from the agencies themselves, and major reliance was placed on this process of agency self-motivation. Attempts to induce established agencies to take over some existing service started by the target area or an indigenous organization, ostensibly as a "demonstration," were infrequent and ineffective. This inducement seems to have been part of the plan in Santa Clara, where the direct operation of child care and educational programs was assumed by the Area Service Centers with the hope that eventually other agencies such as the schools would be willing to take on this service as part of their regular program. This objective was rarely achieved because of the resistance of the schools to adding a new service to an already overburdened budget, and the reluctance of some of the Area Service Centers to give up sponsorship of a tangible program on the grounds that other groups did not really have the requisite skills to work with the poor. The most that could be expected from the use of demonstrations as a prod was some contribution in kind and possibly a transfer of technique, as when the San Francisco schools provided several teachers for the language training centers sponsored by the areas and considered adoption of some of their teaching methods. On the other hand, it was not clear whether the new indigenous delegate agencies such as those in the Mission and Hunters Point were supposed to serve a demonstration function or whether they were to continue as permanent organizations, subsidized by OEO or local community funds.

"INFILTRATION"

Of all the types of resident participation, the *employment* of nonprofessionals by the delegate agencies was the one on which high hopes had been pinned on its being a source of major improvement in the character of services offered to the poor. As a bridge to the poor, the nonprofessionals were expected to educate the professionals and to improve communication between them and their clientele. It is true that changes in the attitudes of professionals were ascribed by some of the executives to interaction with the indigenous staff, but no alterations in agency policy or practices were ascribed or traceable to their presence, apart from the Alameda County Health Department, where it was believed that the employment of aides had influenced the agency's decision to train home health aides and refer them for employment. At best, the nonprofessionals may have affected the mode of delivery of some services, making them more available.[6] Those low-income persons employed by the TAO or delegate agencies who functioned as social brokers or expediters were often able, in these advocacy roles, to secure some modification of policy on a case by case basis in the public welfare department or public housing authority. These interventions provoked varying reactions, from the agency's resentment toward the EOC staff to a greater sensitivity to the needs of bilingual clients. In both San Francisco and Oakland, the welfare departments eventually employed several indigenous case aides.

The relative lack of impact of indigenous personnel on their employing agencies might be explained by the following factors, apart from their co-optation: the small number of nonprofessionals employed by any agency, high turnover, and the fact that most of them were, as in Oakland, employed as part-time teaching aides in programs such as Head Start. They may have also presented a threat to professionals, particularly teachers, and the aides' own disabilities as untrained, poorly paid persons in dead-end jobs with no evident future also minimized their influence.[7]

"MONITORING" BY LOW-INCOME PERSONS

Another channel of influence for low-income persons on attitudes, policies, and practices was their presence on the advisory committees of

[6] In a study of nine cities it was found that while personal relationships between professionals and nonprofessionals were good, there was "no evidence of significant change in the policies and values of the institutions or of the professionals employing them." Oscar Ornati, "Program Evaluation and the Definition of Poverty," Paper presented before the Industrial Relations Research Association, December 27, 1966, San Francisco.

[7] Most of the pressures to bring about change in the Oakland schools came from the outside, such as the Ad Hoc Committee on Quality Education, rather than from the indigenous aides. For further data on the attitudes of the nonprofessionals employed in the Oakland schools, see Harold Nawy in collaboration with Martin Thimal, *The East Bay Community Action Program, Part II, Strategy or Stratagem* (Berkeley, Calif.: University of California, School of Criminology, 1967), pp. 42-49. For a contrasting set of findings on the effectiveness of new careerists in the Richmond schools see Robert Blauner and Anatole Shaffer, *New Careers and the Person,* Contra Costa Council Community Services, Publication No. 116 (Walnut Creek, Calif.: July, 1967).

delegate agencies,[8] as well as their membership in target area program review committees. From either vantage point, the opinions of the neighborhood could be brought to bear on the agency's administrative process. This form of consumer consultation was quite unprecedented in the social services, and as a requirement for OEO support, it provided a sanction for access by clientele to the agency staff and board members responsible for developing and operating program. There was considerable variation in the forms and structure of this *monitoring* function, ranging from occasional consultation on the selection of indigenous personnel, inclusion of low-income target area representatives on a policy-making board or membership on an advisory committee along with professional staff, to a wholly indigenous advisory committee attached to an agency such as the school. Where the target area representatives became part of the decision-making structure of the agency, even on an advisory basis as in the San Francisco Family Service Agency, they had more influence at least on attitudes than when they served as members of a wholly indigenous "watchdog" subcommittee responsible to the board of a target area organization, as in the Mission. In the latter case, there was a tendency for the indigenous staff or board members assigned to this function to lose interest and report irregularly or not at all to the target area. In the former case, the participation of low-income persons usually increased over a period of time, and they were perceived by the professionals as making a rather generalized contribution to the deliberations.

The fact that professional staff had to meet and confront target area representatives on a regular, formalized basis meant that program plans had to be discussed with the latter and their reactions taken into account, serving as a check on and reducing the range and content of unilateral agency planning. For the delegate agencies this meant sharing the details of administration with persons who were relatively unsophisticated and inexperienced in these matters. Those professionals who were more committed to the principle of resident participation spoke more favorably of the rapid learning that took place and the useful contribution that was eventually made. Attitudes on the part of the target area representatives were also reported as changing from initial suspicion and antagonism to a "better understanding" of the agency's viewpoint. As one low-income member of an advisory committee commented, "At least, they listen now." Yet, evidence of actual changes in policy and practice stemming from the work of monitoring committees was not found in any of the three communities.

[8] See "Neighborhood Councils and Program Advisory Groups," Regional Community Action Agency Bulletin, WR-4-67 (February, 14, 1967), as the only official OEO statement regarding this function.

The major significance of the institutionalization of monitoring was that the range of citizen participation in agency decision making was broadened by inclusion of individuals and groups who had been, in effect, excluded from these processes in the past. Through formalized and structured involvement rather than *ad hoc* consultation, regular channels of communication were established between several agencies and target area representatives, particularly in Oakland, to a much lesser extent in San Francisco, and virtually not at all in Santa Clara.

In all of the communities, delegate agencies also had to participate in a review of their programs and budgets by committees including representatives of the intended consumer—the poor or their stand-ins—in addition to the traditional community influentials with whom they were familiar. In San Francisco, this process tended to alienate the agencies much more so than in Oakland, although some agencies were believed to be more likely, out of a feeling of duress, to consult with EOC before making any major changes than they had been. Although the number of established agency programs that were funded declined over a two-year period in Oakland and increased in San Francisco, there was much more agency respect for the OEDC than for the San Francisco EOC, a fact that was probably related to the aversion of most social agencies to conflict.

What are the long-range implications of these developments? Will these forms of resident participation continue without an OEO? Although formal organizations try to limit the number of decision makers; and agencies may not be too interested in consulting with neighborhood groups if they are not required to do so as a condition of funding, forces have been set in motion that may serve to continue the practice of including low-income representatives of the clientele in the councils of agencies as well as in consultation with representative organizations in the areas to be served. For one, a precedent has been set that operates against maintenance of traditional "welfare colonialism," which ignored the consumer in its decision making. As a result, a substantial number of persons have become familiar with the concept of maximum feasible participation and have acquired enough sophistication to be able to embarrass or persuade agencies to involve persons affected by their program, as well as to extend it to other areas of community life. There is probably no turning back, even though there may not be any continuing mandate or sanction from OEO for the participation of the poor. The idea is now abroad and has become linked with the growing demands for Black Power or "Brown Power" (for Mexican-Americans); it can be sustained by an urban ethnic Populism that has succeeded the civil rights movement. To replace OEO ideology and compliance with its directives, then, there is now an informed constituency of former nonprofessionals and participants, supportive caretakers, and ethnic minority leaders who can be expected to invoke precedent and exert pressure to sustain planning *with* and not *for* the poor. There is also much broader public acceptance of the concept of the client-citizen, as evidenced by the following statement from an enlightened business leader, the first vice-president of the Federal Reserve Bank of Philadelphia.

> . . . responsible citizen action must include all groups, *including the economically and culturally deprived.* There should be no question in our minds that our disadvantaged citizens can and will provide new insights and perspectives, and will create a new community enlightenment. We see this happening. We observe a growing and justly deserved respect for the poor and dispossessed of our society, and a growing confidence in their ability to contribute to the making of a better society, not just for them, but for all of us.[9]

Because the decentralization of social services for the poor is one of the objectives of much federal legislation aimed at humanizing the urban ghetto, it is quite likely that the participation of low-income persons will become increasingly a part of established public policy.[10] Given the precedent of the war on poverty and the social conditions in most racially segregated low-income neighborhoods, provisions for more indigenous participation would appear to be a political necessity.

B. Effects on Minority Groups

From its inception, the ethnic character of the CAP was one of its most pervasive features. The interests of ethnic and racial minorities were dominant not only in the initial selection of the executive leadership, but also in the designation of the target areas, in the struggle over representation of the poor, and in the subsequent development and distribution of programs and service benefits.

[9] Robert N. Hilkert, speech at 41st Annual Meeting, Philadelphia YMCA, May 12, 1967, quoted in the *Congressional Record,* H6867, June 7, 1967.

[10] The involvement of neighborhood residents in the Model Cities program is described in *Program Guide: Model Neighborhoods in Demonstration Cities* (Washington, D.C.: Department of Housing and Urban Development), 1967, pp. 13-14, 26. For a similar expression of the need for federal support of resident participation see Warner Bloomberg, Jr., "Community Organization," in Howard Becker, ed., *Social Problems: A Modern Approach* (New York: John Wiley & Sons, Inc., 1966), pp. 422-23. Among the governmental constraints on resident participation was the growing tendency of OEO to promote "package programs" such as Head Start, legal services, health centers, etc., which effectively reduced the area and incentive for participation since the local community was offered an option of accepting or rejecting a program designed by Washington. Another limitation was the increase in the local share of from 10 per cent to 20 per cent, which took place during 1967.

Although political and geographical factors shaped the division of the Santa Clara County into nine approximately equivalent areas, in San Francisco and Oakland ethnic considerations were the primary determinants of the boundaries of the neighborhoods selected as target areas, as well as of the selection of the chairman and executive of the Community Action Agency. That 80 per cent of the minority population was included in the target areas, despite the fact that most of the poor were white, made evident the informal understanding between some officials and ethnic spokesmen in these two cities that this was to be a "Negro program." The lack of an equivalent acknowledgment for the Mexican-Americans in Santa Clara, who comprised 16 per cent of the poor, was largely responsible for the original attack on the EOC in Santa Clara County.[11]

The ethnic dimension of this first phase of the antipoverty program laid the groundwork for the next stage of development, in which minority spokesmen in San Francisco and Santa Clara seized upon the concept of maximum feasible participation as sanction for their drive to increase representation of the poor on the governing board and to give more autonomy to the neighborhoods. By assuming that ethnicity, residence in the target area, and poverty were synonymous, representatives of organized minority groups, few of whom were themselves poor, were able to challenge the original cross-sectional, "balanced" community coalition. Eventually, they came to constitute the majority on the policy-making boards in all but a few of the TAOs. Because of the ambiguity of the principle of maximum feasible participation and the lack of organization of the poor, minority groups could purport to speak for the poor with greater plausibility than could any other community interest. Although the Mayor of San Francisco and the executive leadership of the Santa Clara EOC contested this claim, neither was able to prevent the "takeover" by minority interests and the subordination of the antipoverty program to ethnic power politics, both Negro and Mexican-American.

A NEW POWER CENTER

In this way, control over the resources available through the CAP passed into the hands of middle-class and working-class Negroes in San Francisco and Oakland and their Mexican-American counterparts in Santa Clara. The result was that jobs, power, and status went almost exclusively

[11] Some of the consequences of the ways in which the target area boundaries were drawn in San Francisco were that approximately one-third of the poor did not reside within them, and competition between minority groups was increased since ethnicity became the most important criterion. Similarly, on a national basis, Negroes comprised more than one-half of the participants in all federal antipoverty programs even though more than two-thirds of the nation's poor were white. *San Francisco Chronicle,* February 16, 1967, p. 17.

to the more upwardly mobile members of these respective groups in all three communities, rather than to the hard-core poor. Beyond conferring material benefits, principally in the form of preferred employment of minority persons in both professional and nonprofessional positions, the CAP enhanced the political role and influence of ethnic groups by serving as a new community forum and decision-making arena, where indigenous leadership could emerge and "practice." In the target areas, and particularly on the EOC level, where there were many decisions involving hundreds of thousands of dollars, the CAP was a highly visible public setting. Even its most routine deliberations were regarded as newsworthy. Because of the high stakes involved, there was no lack of incentive for organized minority groups to take advantage of these unprecedented opportunities. Out of their participation, ethnic groups gained public attention, control over some new social service resources and the patronage connected with them, as well as an increased measure of political sophistication.

As a vehicle for political socialization, the CAP provided access to interaction with governmental and community influentials representing the established centers of power, most of whom were confronting minority persons as peers for the first time. The controversy that was engendered by this experience, however, tended to repel many of these influential people, who dropped out or played an insignificant part. Because of this, the CAPs gradually lost much of their original character as community coalitions and became instead separate enclaves of ethnic interests and power.

Apart from structuring interaction between majority and minority representatives in the community, the CAP contributed to the political education of Negro and Mexican-American groups, particularly through generating controversial issues as well as the means for their resolution. Because of their novel but ambiguous mandate, their status as new decision-making centers in the community outside the existing institutional structure, and their concern with controversial issues in which there were tangible and high stakes, conflict was endemic in the CAPs. Many members wearied of the recurrent squabbling, but the necessity of having to deal almost continually with conflict meant that those who persisted—and survived—acquired invaluable training in organizational politics. Even in the Western Addition, where the discord was perhaps greatest, it could be argued that the disruption and waste of resources were outweighed by the lessons and skills learned by the participants. Similarly, on the same scale of values, the gain in Mexican-American self-identity and pride as a result of "beating the Anglos" in Santa Clara County and their experience in forming a coalition for the first time might compensate somewhat for the scapegoating of the executive and the alienation of most of the establishment. On these grounds, conflict regarding the control of the CAP could be regarded as constructive because it involved previously inactive segments of the community.[12]

In this perspective, then, the use of the CAP by ethnic groups to acquire some power and the resultant struggle may have served as a training ground for future political action, particularly in cities where the racial minorities will within a decade or two become a majority. Resident participation in the CAP may have provided the first major foothold for Negro and Mexican-American groups to gain control of an urban community decision-making center and the use of some social service and economic resources. So far it is an unexploited and underdeveloped political resource, and it may even have rather small leverage because of the close ties of the CAP to the social service system.[13]

LEADERSHIP CHANGES

In addition to these opportunities to control a new resource allocation system, the leadership structure of the ethnic groups was also affected by the process of resident participation. Within each minority community there was an internal struggle for leadership between social classes, moderates and militants, older and younger generations, and integrationists or assimilationists against ethnic separatists.[14]

In San Francisco, where the EOC was the natural successor to the civil rights movement, Negro activists were largely responsible for achieving ethnic control over the program. The intergenerational *modus vivendi* of the traditional political and professional spokesmen for Negro rights and the leading activists who had become EOC staff members was strained as

[12] It has been suggested that ordered conflict in the market place of community decision making might reduce disorder and destructive strife. Earl Raab, "Organizing Recipients," Memo to State Department of Social Welfare, February 15, 1966. It has also been argued that the dysfunctional consequences of conflict tend to be limited or eliminated to the extent that a community is characterized by many controversies, high participation, and increasing organizational experience among the citizenry. James S. Coleman, *Community Conflict* (New York: The Free Press, 1957), pp. 19, 21-22.

[13] In the future battle for control of the city in the decades ahead, the CAP may be viewed in retrospect as the first beachhead where the minorities established their position. Richard Cloward and Frances Piven have projected the future battle for control of the city in which the suburbs would use regional planning as their major weapon against the likely dominance of the central city by ethnic minorities. See their article, "Black Control of Cities," *New Republic,* Vol. 157, No. 14 (September 30, 1967), 19-21. In this connection the opposition of minority spokesmen to regional government in the San Francisco Bay area has already been expressed.

[14] Because of the nature of the minority communities and the reliability of the data collected on these issues, the generalizations in this section should be regarded as quite tentative.

the alignment between the two groups shifted in the recurrent factional and personal disputes. In the process, many of the middle-class leaders were discredited and lost a great deal of whatever influence they may have had in the ghetto. The public image of a Negro-dominated poverty program seemingly confirmed the belief that the minority neighborhoods could not be trusted to administer an enterprise as complex as the EOC. The inability of the Area Development Program, particularly in the Western Addition, to organize the poor after an expenditure of almost $3 million also contributed to the disillusionment.

The EOC provided opportunities for some of the more assertive, indigenous "nitty-gritty" types to participate in areas such as Hunters Point and Mission. Many of them, however, secured employment in the Area Development Program and, it was widely believed, became much more interested in holding on to their jobs than in keeping in touch with their neighbors. The fact that such a large number of Negroes were employed in the program may also explain the relative lack of community action on minority rights. Their concern with holding on to their own jobs and the increasing preoccupation with program, as well as the internal politics of the EOC, meant that while individuals gained, their groups did not.

In San Francisco, as the concept of Black Power was gradually popularized, the influence of moderates became weaker, and a "black backlash" was noticed in which younger, more militant voices were increasingly heard. Integration lost much of its attraction; most of the effort at Hunters Point, for example, was devoted to rehabilitating the ghetto to make it more livable for the next 10 to 15 years. Within the EOC, however, "welfare" ends increasingly superseded the initial concern with ideology and the achievement of "status" goals.[15] Much of the energy that might have been directed against discrimination in the community or toward opening up more jobs was instead utilized in a series of intramural targets within the EOC. Thus the major trend in the pattern of leadership was increasing fragmentation, in which older middle-class spokesmen could no longer presume to speak for the Negro. Instead there were a host of competing claimants, none of whom seemed to have any substantial following.[16]

[15] This discussion relies on several concepts discussed in James Q. Wilson, *Negro Politics: The Search for Leadership* (New York: The Free Press, 1960), pp. 176, 185, 214-15. These include the notions of welfare and status ends, militants and moderates, as well as the distinction between Negro leaders and leaders of Negroes.

[16] Some evidence of the shift in Negro leadership can be found in the following: "Negroes Told of Ghetto Hate," *San Francisco Chronicle*, August 10, 1967, p. 2; "Black Backlash," *San Francisco Sunday Examiner and Chronicle*, September 10, 1967, Section A, p. 7; "New Activists Move for Black Power," *San Francisco Chronicle*, July 3, 1967, p. 3; "Negro Group Confronts Mayor on Jobs," *San Francisco Chronicle*, July 6, 1967, p. 1; a thoughtful analysis of some changes in the Negro ghetto nationally is found in Andrew Kopkind, "King and Black Power," *New York Review*

In Oakland, there appeared to be the making of a new minority "establishment" in the OEDC, with Negroes comprising almost three-quarters of the members. Despite the continual reminders and rumors that Oakland might become another Watts, a combination of highly efficient police control measures, various training and youth employment programs, and the opportunities for ventilation of grievances at TAO and OEDC meetings seems to have drained off considerable discontent.

In contrast to the images of other CAPs, the image of the OEDC in fighting city hall and as a source of some benefits for low-income persons, may have supported the belief that at least there was one place in the community where the voice of the minority groups could be heard. The OEDC was not completely identified with the establishment, and its leaders did not deceive themselves that services would solve the problem of poverty.

At the same time, the minority community in Oakland during 1966 witnessed a series of failures: the failure of a school boycott, of attempts to organize a coalition of grassroots groups, to bring Saul Alinsky to Oakland, and to establish a police review board. While the OEDC tended to drain a considerable amount of leadership and participation from other existing minority organizations, it also stimulated the development of some indigenous new groups, many of which were attracted by the possibility of obtaining funds and which moved quickly from the role of critic to that of delegate agency. In comparison with leadership in San Francisco, indigenous leadership in Oakland emerged very slowly, but there was much less internal factionalism in Oakland than in San Francisco.

As far as can be ascertained, there were no major shifts in the Negro leadership structure comparable to those in San Francisco. If anything, there was a narrowing of the distance between the middle-class Negro professionals on the OEDC who represented organizations such as NAACP and CORE, and the indigenous working-class and low-income Negroes who represented the TAO. They formed a strong alliance on the OEDC, being primarily concerned with program and job development, and there was much less controversy as this bloc prevailed. Some of the moderates claimed that there was more communication between them and the more deprived and militant elements than there was in other communities, but in both San Francisco and Oakland there were signs of an increasing polarization between those Negroes identified with the anti-

---

of Books, Vol. 9, No. 3 (August 24, 1967), 3-4, 6; and Tom Haydon, "The Occupation of Newark," *ibid.,* 14-23. A somewhat similar discussion in the mass media is found in articles by Claude Brown and T. George Harris, "Is the Race Problem Insoluble?" *Look* (June 27, 1967), p. 28. A view of the Oakland ghetto is found in the *Oakland Tribune,* October 1, 1967, pp. 17-21.

poverty program and its middle-class goals of education, training, and employment, and a ghetto underclass, primarily of militant young adults who were completely alienated from the community and its "Negro leaders" and ripe for violence and rebellion.[17]

MEXICAN-AMERICANS

The war on poverty came along at a critical point in the development of the Mexican-American community, assisting it in becoming more self-conscious, assertive, and political as it moved through some of the earlier stages of development that characterized the Negro movement of self-emancipation.[18] In Santa Clara and Oakland, the CAP helped unify Mexican-American organization leaders, who were drawn together by their opposition to the EOC and their demand for a greater share of representation and jobs. A loose structure for communication and interchange was developed in Santa Clara, and more assertive tactics were employed as Mexican-American spokesmen belatedly discovered the effectiveness of picketing and walkouts. All this contributed to a greater sense of identity and newfound "Brown Power" on the part of some. Smarting at the amount of public concern over the Negro, Mexican-Americans pointed out how much worse off they were in education, housing, and unemployment, and began to insist, particularly in Oakland, on separate but equal representation on the policy-making boards. In contrast to the Negro coalition in San Francisco, which sought representation for the poor, the Mexican-Americans in Santa Clara and Oakland were more obvious in their demands for more representation and jobs for Mexican-Americans.

Out of their participation in the battle for representation in Santa Clara came some dramatic gains, as the EOC became largely identified with the Mexican-Americans. Jobs, representation as individual and organization delegates, and experience in community decision making were some of the benefits accruing to individuals. Also in Santa Clara, additional efforts at community organization and more militancy on the part of a CSO chapter were stimulated by the Mexican-American takeover. The original coalition was fragile, however, and the Round Table disintegrated after

[17] A three-fold division in the community between "traditionalists," "militants," and "survivalists" was found in Watts and is described in Nathan E. Cohen, "The Los Angeles Riot Study," *Social Work*, Vol. 12, No. 4 (October, 1967), 14-21. A more comprehensive analysis of conditions in the Negro ghetto is found in U.S. Riot Commission, *Report of the National Advisory Commission on Civil Disorders* (New York: Bantam Books, Inc., 1968).

[18] An excellent account of the position of the Mexican-Americans in California is found in Helen Rowan, "A Minority Nobody Knows," *The Atlantic*, Vol. 219, No. 6 (June, 1967), 47-52. See also Celia S. Heller, *Mexican-American Youth: Forgotten Youth at the Crossroads* (New York: Random House, Inc., 1966).

the reorganization of the EOC, although attempts were made to revive it.

In the EOC the votes of the Mexican-Americans became important for the first time in a community decision-making arena, and the organizations were enhanced by the community image projected by their leaders as well as by the program funds received by the CSO. At the same time, there were many doubts as to the degree to which these spokesmen were close to the low-income Mexican-American community. Most of them were middle-class and belonged to more than one Mexican-American association, so that the organized Mexican-American community may not have included more than several hundred persons. Increasingly some of the younger, more indigenous and activist elements began to challenge these *de facto* leaders, but neither group seemed to have had much of a following.

The role of the Mexican-American in the Negro-dominated OEDC in Oakland was but a faint echo of the pattern in Santa Clara. There was only a brief temporary unity in protesting the original formation of the OEDC in January, 1965, on the part of several Mexican-American organizational leaders, which quickly faded. The two Mexican-American representatives then concentrated on trying to obtain funds for a Spanish-speaking community center and ran into considerable opposition from some of the Negro members on the OEDC, who regarded the project as a form of minority self-segregation. For almost two years the Mexican-American group was under-represented on the OEDC, with only 2 out of 40 places, in part because of the basic structure and the inability of the Mexican-Americans to be selected as representatives from Fruitvale, where they constituted somewhat less than half of the membership. Only when the OEDC was reorganized, largely as a result of target area pressures, did the Mexican-Americans benefit from this and obtain a separate, fifth advisory committee for themselves along with some increased representation.

With traditions that did not encourage or sanction participation in social action, Mexican-American and Chinese leaders saw their groups severely handicapped in the war on poverty, in which rewards went to those who were most assertive. Yet neither the Mexican-American nor the Chinese representatives were sympathetic to the more militant tactics employed by Negroes in the civil rights movement, although the Mexican-Americans in Santa Clara learned to appreciate and utilize them when needed.

Part of the Negro–Mexican-American strain and the disdain with which minority groups other than Negro viewed conflict tactics was related to the difference in their social goals and their feelings of cultural superiority and distinctiveness. In contrast to the Negro, who emphasized integration, Mexican-American and Chinese groups supported a form of cultural pluralism that would permit and even encourage ethnic identity, if not separatism. The movement toward Black Power as an attempt to strengthen the social organization and capabilities of the Negro community grew in 1966, but integration goals were much more prominent in the early stages of the war on poverty.

Because of their commitment to cultural pluralism and the largely immigrant basis of the poverty found among the Mexican-Americans and the Chinese, these groups gave a priority to language training, which clashed with the Negro emphasis on employment. Although the struggle for power within the Negro community in San Francisco angered the other minorities, in all of the groups the position of minority "leader" still tended to be defined by the non-ethnic majority and its mass media and was usually assigned to someone who was visible and articulate and not necessarily to anyone who had a following.

Because the antipoverty program in general was more effective in changing individuals than in changing systems, its impact on minority persons was possibly much greater than its influence on ethnic organizations or on the status and power of the minority group. As employees and as members of the CAP, many minority members acquired increased political awareness, knowledge, and skill in participating in community affairs. Various forms of involvement gave those who persisted a greater sense of personal competence, influence, and community recognition. At the same time many others, who became cynical and hostile toward the community and its "phony war" on poverty, dropped out.

These positive changes in role perception were particularly significant in the indigenous nonprofessionals, many of whom belonged to the TAO and moved rather freely between staff and member roles. In carrying out their duties they acquired considerable knowledge about the way in which different community systems operate; over four hundred and fifty persons in the three communities learned how to be "caretakers" in their neighborhoods. Despite the problems of turnover, morale, and lack of training, the experience gained by these aides in organizing groups, conducting elections, serving as social brokers and advocates and, in Santa Clara, in organizing a protective association, was significant. In this way, the war on poverty again served as a training ground for the development of a cadre of indigenous community workers, many of whom might be expected to become much more influential informal, and possibly formal, leaders in the future.[19]

[19] For a similar finding in another Bay Area community, see Anatol Shaffer, Evelyn Knight, and David Williams, *Final Report, Richmond Community Development Demonstration Project* (August, 1967). Also Robert Blauner and Anatol Shaffer, *New Careers and the Person.* Contra Costa Council of Community Services, Publ. 116, Walnut Creek, California, July, 1967.

C. The Poor

Those who were employed in the CAP gained experience and skills and many of the CAP participants improved their understanding, but there was widespread recognition among both groups in all communities that the hard-core and unaffiliated poor had really not been reached, nor did they benefit in any substantial way from the programs and services of the war on poverty. This opinion was, of course, in sharp contrast to the official reports of the CAPs and their "quiet revolution." For example, in San Francisco it was claimed that "nearly everyone of the hundred and eighty thousand poor is engaged in at least one community action program," and in Oakland the Department of Human Resources reported that half of the target area population, amounting to 48,000 persons, was served in 1966.[20]

With respect to the attitudes and the economic condition of the poor, those closest to the program staff, particularly the indigenous members and participants in the TAO, were in agreement that the program helped a very small number of those already climbing out of poverty by means of jobs, information, and services. Admittedly, the task of evaluating the over-all impact of the CAP was beyond the scope and intent of this study,[21] but at least it should be noted that in Oakland and particularly in San Francisco, the dominant attitudes consistently found were that the poor had lost confidence in the program because of unfulfilled promises and the negative public image of the EOC. In addition, in the Mission, Western Addition, and Hunters Point areas, aides reported considerable resentment directed toward them because they had been able to obtain jobs. The

[20] San Francisco Economic Opportunity Council, *Progress,* 1966, p. 19, *OEDC Reporter.* Apart from generally loose and inconsistent statistical reporting, which rarely resulted in non-duplicative counts, it was very difficult to distinguish between the effects of the CAP and its service programs from those of resident participation.

[21] Further evidence regarding the ability of the CAP to reach the hard-core poor in San Francisco and Oakland is found in *Examination of the War on Poverty,* Staff and Consultants' Reports, prepared for the Subcommittee on Employment, Manpower and Poverty of the Committee on Labor and Public Welfare, U.S. Senate, Vol. VII (Washington, D.C.: Government Printing Office, September, 1967), 2179-2241. This document also contains a concise analysis and program evaluation of the CAPs in San Francisco and Oakland. Similar evidence from another community is found in "Study Finds Poor are Hard to Reach," *The New York Times,* September 3, 1967, p. 37, which reports that an Atlanta study revealed that 79 per cent of those questioned in target areas stated that no one had ever suggested that they visit one of the agency centers for antipoverty program. It also was noted that the CAP in Atlanta had involved those residents who were accustomed to taking part in various civic and church activities.

lack of interest of the poor in participating was stressed in all the TAOs, along with the observation that the hard-core poor were much more interested in the here-and-now and emergency needs and not in long-range programs that would not directly and immediately affect their condition.

There was, however, recognition that resident participation had stimulated awareness of the existence of poverty and had popularized the idea; that it had contributed to some new hopes, provided opportunities for minority groups to obtain control over additional resources, and made it possible for a top stratum of persons to obtain jobs and to participate in decision making in the community. Some of the costs of the greater awareness that was stimulated were, of course, the frustrated expectations that turned to apathy, anger, or a more profound recognition of the formidable obstacles to improvement of the conditions of the poor.[22]

D. Local Government

The effects on city politics of resident participation were, as noted in the previous chapter, minimal. Although a new center of minority influence was established in each community, the CAP did not appear to disrupt the prevailing structure and balance of power in any significant way. City agencies, with the exceptions of the San Francisco Redevelopment Agency and Public Housing Authority, were rarely attacked, although many were antagonized by the actions of the TAO and the EOC staff and occasionally, board members.

Few of the activists used the CAP as a springboard for political office, apart from three of the unsuccessful candidates for the Oakland City Council in 1967, who were associated with the antipoverty program. Some of the TAOs stimulated interest in voter registration and in election issues, but with little discernible impact on any particular election.

In general, then, the impact on local government was an unfulfilled potential in San Francisco and Oakland, although in San Jose the city council was much more responsive to the needs of the Mayfair area. The mayors of San Francisco and Oakland regarded the CAP as a challenge to their power and may have feared the increased political consciousness of the poor, but this threat did not materialize to any significant degree. The political systems in all three communities were sturdy and resilient

[22] Yet it should be noted that in the 32 cities that rioted during the summer of 1967 none of the buildings housing poverty programs was burned or destroyed and the only damage was negligible. "OEO and the Riot—A Summary," *OEO News Summary of the War on Poverty*, Vol. 2-26 (September 11, 1967), 1-2.

enough to absorb this new structure without the distribution of power being seriously altered.

Summary

While there are many methodological difficulties in assessing the impact of resident participation, some generalizations can be made about its effects on the social agencies, minority groups, the poor, and local government.

Three channels of influence were available to low-income persons to modify the attitudes, policies, and practices of social service agencies: indigenously operated demonstration projects; employment in a delegate agency; and monitoring and social action. Of these, pressure group tactics were most effective, although some minor changes stemmed from the other modes. Equally powerful in stimulating redirection or a greater responsiveness to the needs of the poor were the necessity to comply with OEO guidelines and the effects of a disproportionate infusion of OEO funds. A significant precedent was established by the antipoverty program in legitimizing the involvement of neighborhood residents in agency program planning, and there appears to be sufficient support in the low-income community and in government to assure the continuance in some form of this type of participation.

Members of minority groups were the major beneficiaries of the war on poverty. Ethnic interests were dominant in the initial selection of executive leadership, in the designation of the target areas, and in the allocation of program benefits. Jobs, power, and status accrued to the members of the principal ethnic group in each neighborhood, and the CAP also contributed to their political socialization. A cadre of indigenous leadership was developed that may play an important role within their own ethnic group and possibly in the future political struggles for the control of the city.

The ethnic leadership structure was shaken somewhat by internal struggles as newer, younger, and more militant spokesmen increasingly challenged the *de facto* middle class leaders. Growing polarization was evident within the Negro community between those identified with the goals and methods of the antipoverty program and an angry, alienated, and rebellious underclass.

There was general agreement that the hard-core and unaffiliated poor were not reached by most of the TAO and CAP programs. There were modest gains in heightening public awareness of poverty and in providing limited opportunities for jobs, services, and participation, which may not have offset the social costs of the frustrated expectations that were stirred up.

In its impact on local government, the CAP, as a new center of minority influence, did not achieve its political potential, nor did it materially alter the balance of power.

11

CONCLUSIONS: THE FUTURE OF THE PARTICIPATION OF THE POOR

Contrary to the hopes of a few and the fears of many, CAP is not a social revolution.[1]

Along with CAPs in almost a thousand other communities throughout the United States, five Bay Area CAPs sought to develop programs to combat poverty with the maximum feasible participation of the groups and areas to be served. Because of the basic ambiguity of the concept of maximum feasible participation, it was perceived in divergent ways by various groups with high stakes in the war on poverty. Four different modes of resident participation were promoted, each containing contrasting interpretations of purpose and the role of the poor in policy making, program development, community organization, and employment.

The outcomes of each of these types of participation can be summarized as follows:

Summary of Outcomes of the Four Modes of Resident Participation

CAP POLICY MAKING

1. A new decision-making center was created outside the existing institutional structure with influence over some limited social service resources. Essentially, it had the character of an emergent interest or pressure group controlled by some of the more upwardly mobile and assertive members of ethnic minorities, whose role had shifted from participation in a community coalition to control of the CAP. Although it was ostensibly still

[1] Howard W. Hallman, *Examination of the War on Poverty,* Staff and Consultants' Reports, prepared for the Subcommittee on Employment, Manpower and Poverty of the Committee on Labor and Public Welfare, U.S. Senate, Vol. IV (Washington, D.C.: Government Printing Office, September, 1967), p. 900.

allied with the economic notables and traditional community influentials of the established agencies, the latter were underrepresented, and the CAP was predominately a federally supported ethnic power base.

A new organizational vehicle, not an "umbrella" nor a "second government" nor a "third force," was established. Instead, one more planning, policy-making and budgeting center for federal funds emerged in the form of a quasi-governmental, nonprofit corporation with a sanction to operate decentralized, compensatory social services and provide a small number of jobs as well as opportunities for community and individual development. There was no substantial shift in the distribution of power, but a new structure with an unfulfilled political potential had appeared.

PROGRAM DEVELOPMENT

2. The recruitment and organizational strategies sponsored by the CAP in organizing the target areas screened out the hard-core poor and resulted in a "creaming" process whereby previously affiliated residents with strong ethnic identification prevailed in a pseudodemocratic system with very low accountability to an amorphous electorate.

These previously neglected segments of the working class and low-income persons were much closer to the social service clientele than were the traditional community decision makers, and they participated in a variety of processes of planning, developing, reviewing, and operating conventional, supplementary social service programs. Although considerable expertise was gained by a small number of activists, these program development concerns preempted other social change activities and involved relatively few persons who were officially "poor." There was also little direct relationship evident between a high degree of resident participation when encouraged by staff and ethnic pressures and the existence of better or even different programs.

Decentralization produced two rival centers of power. Target area organizations over a period of a year or more moved from the advisory functions originally delegated to them and won much broader authority. Each tended, however, to become another neighborhood association, increasingly autonomous and somewhat removed from the EOC, rather than a broadly representative body responsible to a citywide organization. Many were consumed by internal factional disputes, with middle-class persons tending to push out low-income members and program and organizational maintenance concerns dominating.

SOCIAL ACTION

3. Most of the efforts to organize the poor to lift themselves out of poverty fell far short of their goal, owing in large part to the lack of suit-

able inducements as well as to factors inherent in the staff, strategies, sponsor, and the nature of the poor. The organizing apparatus was used more often for social service and organizational maintenance functions than for community development or social action, although several instances of the latter were effective in modifying agency policies. Neighborhood improvement and self-help were stressed, with social service issues prevailing over political concerns. Some progress was made in establishing the legitimacy of the poor as an interest group, but their expected insurgency did not materialize.

EMPLOYMENT

4. Jobs in the CAP were a major inducement for participation, a criterion for decision making, and a source of conflict as well as growing ethnic power. Patronage considerations dominated, and hundreds of members of indigenous minority groups, relatively few of whom were co-opted, acquired community caretaking skills that may contribute to the political socialization of minority groups.

At the outset of this study it was noted that underlying the different interpretations of maximum feasible participation were two orientations toward poverty, which resulted in a strain between competing goals and methods. The conflicting and ambiguous character of the CAP goals generated tensions because of opposing expectations regarding the extent to which the CAP was: (1) a way of breaking the cycle of poverty through social services and job preparation; (2) an effective tool to centralize planning and coordination of local services; (3) a compensatory device to give a greater political voice to the poor; (4) a protagonist for "creative disorder" whereby an apathetic clientele would be moved to stimulate changes in the social service bureaucracy.

Different, often incompatible strategies were required to achieve these various goals, in which the CAP was perceived as a social movement (a cause) or a social service agency (a function), or both, thus constituting a curious blend of professionalism, bureaucracy, social action, and reform. These strains were reflected in the continuing conflict around the *control* and *purpose* of the CAP, in which it became increasingly obvious that the CAP could not represent the interests of the poor *and* the establishment, nor successfully promote the development of social service programs *and* at the same time organize the poor effectively.

CAP Control: Accountability to Whom?

By the end of 1967, it became evident that the conflict over control of the CAP between the ethnic minorities and local government and between the TAO and the EOC had ended. These controversies had evidently so frightened big-city mayors and Congressmen that the prospect of an independent CAP, particularly one in which the poor comprised 51 per cent of the governing board, could no longer be tolerated. When Congress realized what had been wrought or at least what might be wrought in the name of maximum feasible participation, it moved to vest in local government the authority for deciding on the form of a CAP. It also required that the board, whether under governmental or corporate auspices, would consist of no more than one-third poor people, with the remaining places equally divided between governmental officials and representatives of other community groups.[2] As a result, the nonprofit corporation, the form chosen by almost 80 per cent of the CAPs in the United States, had exhausted its political durability within three years, thus drastically curtailing the experiment in resident participation.

The 1967 Amendments to the EOA, by confining the CAP within the traditional political framework, prematurely ended the debate about the viability of a nongovernmental, federally financed agency. However, it may still be useful to examine some of the issues regarding sponsorship and control and assess their significance. The findings in San Francisco, Oakland, and Santa Clara, which are supported by similar conclusions elsewhere, show that the extent of independence and the actual political challenge of the CAP was much less than believed. This study has suggested that both the alleged benefits and the costs of the nongovernmental CAP, even when it was "controlled" by the representatives of the poor, were somewhat exaggerated. In the first place, the necessity for local matching funds and the power of the mayors to appoint or ratify the selection of CAP board members meant that the established political structure had substantial influence over the program. Secondly, the extent of insurgency promoted, the actual power gained, and the established institutions changed were much less than claimed by both critics and defenders. The noisy sounds of contention, while they may have alarmed many, obscured a general inability to organize a meaningful constituency in the neighborhoods around issues that would help sustain the collective efforts of low-income groups. In general, the ability of the ethnic coalitions in all three communities to gain power was not matched by their capacity to exercise it effectively for political purposes.

Ultimately, the significant element was much less what the CAPs actually did than how they were perceived, what they represented, or what

[2] The Economic Opportunity Amendments of 1967 set a deadline of June 30, 1968 for compliance with the provision limiting the representation of the poor to one-third, and February 1, 1969 as the deadline for local governmental decisions regarding their sponsorship of the CAP.

they could become. Given an urban political structure where even a strong mayor has difficulty asserting his authority over city departments, it can be understood how a new, self-perpetuating quasi-public bureaucracy with direct channels to a federal agency and neighborhood organizations could constitute a potential threat. Thus, it was the degree of political power at stake rather than the type of CAP—independent or under governmental control—that shaped the character and outcome of its relationship with government. For example, despite their differences in autonomy and sponsorship, there was much more similarity between the CAPs in Oakland and San Francisco in their fight with their respective mayors, than between the CAPs in San Francisco and Santa Clara, both of which were independent, nonprofit corporations. The major conflicts in Santa Clara, like those in Oakland until it began to acquire more power and to assert itself, were mainly intramural. Also of greater importance than the particular sponsorship of the CAP were such factors as the ideology and capabilities of the leadership, particularly the professional staff; the extent of poverty in the community and particularly in the target area; and the degree of ethnic organization. The extent to which these variables were maximized seemed to be more closely related than any other factor to the degree and effectiveness of resident participation and in explaining the differences both within and between the CAPs.

Another consequence of the multiplicity and conflict in CAP goals was that all of the CAPs, regardless of their particular auspice and the way in which the conflict over control was resolved, faced dilemmas regarding their accountability and their relationship to a constituency. Whether they were located outside the governmental structure, as in San Francisco and Santa Clara, or partly within it, as in Oakland, the CAPs as federally sanctioned and funded agencies were really *in the middle:* between OEO and the local community, as well as between the poor and the social service bureaucracies. Their distinctive locus and relationship to OEO posed this question: To whom were they accountable—to OEO, to local government, to the electorate, to the entire community, to the target area, or to the poor? While some CAPs, particularly San Francisco, declared that their primary accountability was to the "invisible poor" (were they ever found?), their case rested on some dubious assumptions regarding their relationship to this constituency. On the one hand, the relationship between OEO and the CAP might appear to be similar to the relationship between the Department of Agriculture and the County Agricultural Committees. That is, just as farmers vote for their representatives, who have the power to fix acreage and crop quotas, so the poor elect their representatives to the TAO, who make decisions regarding social service programs affecting them. This analogy may not be altogether apt because the poor, as a vast, amorphous mass of people with diverse needs, did not all have the same stake in OEO-financed programs, whose benefits turned out to be relevant to less than one-fourth of the low-income population. Furthermore, the elections from which the CAPs derived their authority to speak for the poor could easily be faulted on the criteria for voting and the exceedingly small number of ballots cast, but more tellingly on the basic lack of accountability of the representatives to a defined electorate.

As a quasi-public nonprofit corporation, then, the CAPs were in a no-man's-land of legitimacy. They needed a constituency for political reasons but were constrained in the development of one by the diverse character of their target populations, their limited resources and organizational capabilities, and their social service preoccupations. Yet, if the CAPs had been able to develop a constituency, their legitimacy would have been enhanced but they would have presented an even more formidable threat to the establishment and drawn more fire. In other words, the CAP was damned if it did and damned if it didn't develop an active constituency.

It became increasingly clear that an independent CAP controlled by the poor was not a viable organization and that it could not serve two masters, the poor and the established agencies and government. Consistency eventually required that the CAP declare to whom it was accountable and whom it represented. Evidently there was no resolution to the dilemma of dual loyalty apart from governmental sponsorship of the CAP.

Yet, although the somewhat questionable representativeness of the CAP may have impaired its claim to legitimacy to speak for the poor, the importance attached to representativeness may also have been exaggerated. First, those participating in the CAP were much closer to the low-income groups who would presumably benefit from the services than others who had previously been in decision-making roles; TAO members were similar to clientele by virtue of ethnicity, residence, and usually income. Second, it could be argued that it may not have been that important for the hard-core poor or the actual beneficiaries to be directly involved. Since the scope and content of program benefits were largely determined by OEO, the extent of local discretion was quite narrow. Given the resources and the orientation of the CAPs, it is difficult to see in what ways wider participation would have affected the use and the outcome of the programs. From another standpoint, the fact that the CAP was not able to deal with the more substantial requirements of most of the poor for more income or better paying jobs was probably more significant than its lack of formal accountability to them.

CAP Purpose: Services versus Organization

In the course of three years, the degrees of freedom available to a CAP became less as the number of "prepackaged" programs increased along with the local share of costs, as the amount of "versatile" funding decreased. More and more, the CAP became a conduit for OEO funds, concerned with "grant management," program development, coordination, budgeting, financing, and direct services. It was primarily concerned with the design and redistribution of compensatory social services for certain strata of the poor. The strong pull of a services orientation is best illustrated by the experience of San Francisco where, despite control of the EOC by representatives of the poor, and highly autonomous TAOs with a determination to use their limited funds to organize the poor to exert pressure on institutions, the drift toward social service programming was inescapable. One would also have thought that if the CAP were an independent organization it would have been freer to stress community organization, but the Santa Clara program, which had even fewer ties to government than did San Francisco's, did not even consider organizing the poor until the end of its third year.

The utilization of the CAP to promote service delivery rather than to organize the poor was a nationwide trend. A review of 35 CAPs completed by the summer of 1967 found that the service role was the predominant one and that the CAP programs differed only from more conventional ones in their greater degree of citizen involvement.[3] Maximum feasible participation also meant an attempt to promote all four modes of resident participation, but the CAP did not succeed in involving the hard-core poor nor in effectively promoting a process of community development, or stimulating social action to change the social service bureaucracies. Manifestly, it was, of course, impossible for all of these goals to be attained, and various reasons for this have been noted: the absence of a consistent commitment and strategy; the paucity of qualified staff and of demonstrable benefits to serve as incentives for participation; the necessity of having to meet OEO guidelines and deadlines; and the competing demands of organizational maintenance.

Underlying these factors was the strain between services and organization, which can be viewed as a consequence of the attempt to contain two opposing strategies of change within one organization: (1) a "planning"

[3] *Examination of the War on Poverty,* Staff and Consultants' Reports, prepared for the Subcommittee on Employment, Manpower and Poverty of the Committee on Labor and Public Welfare, U.S. Senate, Vol. IV (Washington, D.C.: Government Printing Office, September, 1967).

mode, which sought to use funds and persuasion to develop and coordinate social service programs involving established agencies; and (2) an "action" mode in which the clientele of these agencies were to be organized to pressure for change. The latter strategy, while infrequently attempted, would have involved the CAPs in assisting clientele to pressure the very social service bureaucracies on whom the CAPs were dependent. Since the effective administration of programs of social service, community development, or social action require different ideologies, structure, resources, and staff skills, it would be unlikely to find them within the same organization. In being unable to reconcile these two strategies of social change, the CAPs were in a long line of other unsuccessful attempts to weld such functions together.[4]

At the same time, the CAPs showed that, contrary to the experience of urban renewal, people in low-income neighborhoods could certainly do more than protest.[5] Residents of the target areas, including a very small proportion of low-income persons, demonstrated their ability to serve in policy-making, advisory, program planning, review, administrative, and budgeting roles. As the outcome of federal intervention, a significant precedent was set for community decision making in that the definition of who should be included in that community was broadened. In the often confused and contentious efforts to develop and conduct programs with the participation of the residents of the target areas, numerous economic and political benefits accrued principally to various members of minority groups. Although the CAP asserted the right and demonstrated the capacity of previously excluded groups to be involved in decision making, there was usually much more emphasis on the forms than on the substance of participation. Whether perceived as an opportunity to be exploited or an OEO requirement to be complied with, resident participation easily became an end in itself, and often took on the character of a "numbers game" preoccupied with elections and percentages of membership. People forgot that involvement is a means and could be no more effective than the social goals to which it was related.

As a result, much of what took place in the name of maximum feasible participation during the first three years had little to do with the reduction

[4] For an analysis of previous efforts to deal with the requirements for social planning and citizen participation, see Peter Marris and Martin Rein, *Dilemmas of Social Reform* (New York: Atherton Press, 1967). Another assessment of this experience is found in Arnold Gurin and Joan Ecklein, "Community Organization For What? Political Power or Service Delivery," *Social Welfare Forum, 1968* (New York: Columbia University Press, 1968).

[5] A classic statement of this position is found in James Q. Wilson, "Planning and Politics: Citizen Participation in Urban Renewal," *Journal of the American Institute of Planners*, Vol. XXIX, No. 4 (November, 1963), 242-49.

of poverty or changing institutions, but could best be justified on socio-therapeutic grounds. Some individuals benefited through employment and their involvement in decision making, but the groups that were organized both within and outside the CAP framework did not and probably could not develop sufficient political power to affect those social policies and practices in employment, education and housing that perpetuate poverty. Nor were these organizations functionally linked to realistic programs that might have provided more income and better housing for slum residents. Instead, one of the dominant assumptions was that the causes of poverty lie mainly within the individual and not in the economic, social, and political structure that supports unemployment, underemployment, and racial segregation. In any realistic hierarchy of needs, however, services are secondary and supportive to the provision of adequate income and housing. To rely on service programs, "participation," or both as the means for eliminating or reducing poverty is both ineffective and misleading. Because of its minuscule resources and unfulfilled expectations, the CAP, in the long run, may have contributed to an even greater sense of relative deprivation in the low-income neighborhoods. As a result, caution should be used in promoting the participation of the poor in future programs that do not have any direct impact on the major deficits in their life. To avoid further despair and the growth of more hostility, cynicism, or apathy, the next steps in the involvement of ghetto residents should, ideally, be functionally linked to a massive federally supported program of rebuilding the ghetto, which would provide employment and housing along with a community development process.

The experience of the CAPs suggests that there is great need to organize the poor around community development and social action objectives, but that such efforts require a degree of commitment, skill, and autonomy that can no longer be expected, if it ever could, from the CAP. It is quite unlikely that any community body that depends on annual Congressional approval of public funds and must meet programming and funding deadlines and, in addition, is charged with planning, coordinating, budgeting, and administrative functions could be expected to commit itself to the development of independent organizations of poor people.

Despite its record of social service program development and lack of political militancy, the CAP in the future will undoubtedly have an even more limited role in the promotion of these milder forms of social action and self-help among low-income groups, and other sponsors may have to be found. As the precursor of an alliance between Washington and the urban ethnic poor, the CAP will have to compete with and probably be superseded by such programs as Model Cities and other more comprehensive efforts to rebuild the slums. Its future bound up with the precarious fate of OEO, the CAP appears destined to succumb more and more to local governmental sponsorship and control and become increasingly "deradicalized" and institutionalized as it evolves into another social service bureaucracy with which the poor must contend. At the very least, a diminution can be expected in its mandate, incentive, resources, and capabilities to involve the poor in other than organizational maintenance and consumer consultation.

A lower priority will probably be given to organization of the poor outside of the CAP's own decision-making framework, and the range of participation within the CAP may be somewhat contracted due to a lessening of local discretion. Nevertheless, it will still have the potential of supporting the participation of low-income persons as advisors to and reviewers of delegate agency programs; financing indigenous, housing development and community organization agencies; and promoting a greater use of nonprofessionals. If, as expected, the CAP becomes more and more of a limited social service planning center, the eventual separating out of the third mode of resident participation—community development and social action—may ultimately prove helpful to the CAP in achieving more clarity and specificity in goals and greater congruence between its purpose and capabilities.

NEXT STEPS IN RESIDENT PARTICIPATION

This means that if further efforts are to be made to organize autonomous groups of low-income persons, sponsors other than the CAP must be secured outside the framework of local government. The rationale for continuing to do so rests on ideological, socio-therapeutic, and political grounds. First, there is a commitment to fulfill the potential of a democratic pluralistic society that sanctions and benefits from the creation of new structures for the organized expression of diverse interest groups in America. Secondly, the CAP has dramatized the ways in which participation by some low-income persons can heighten their stake in society and by reducing their sense of powerlessness, raise their morale and improve their social functioning. Finally, while middle-class social reformers have traditionally spoken for the needs of the poor, it is questionable whether in view of the relationship between race and poverty such groups have a strong enough commitment to those massive measures required for the redistribution of power, status, goods, and services. Even with this conviction, a reformist alliance that did not include organized constituencies of the urban poor would lack effectiveness if not legitimacy.

Both the socio-therapeutic and political arguments for community organization can be viewed in the light of three urban trends, which constitute the context and an additional set of compelling factors: (1) the continued growth of the minority population, together with that of an underclass in the central cities, with no appreciable narrowing of the gap between the low-income population and the rest of the city; (2) continued suburbanization and resistance to integration, along with the increasing political influence of ethnic minorities, who will constitute the majority of the voters within the next 10 years in at least 10 to 15 large and intermediate-sized cities; (3) direct federal-city relationships involving more comprehensive forms of planning and providing for resident participation.

Under these circumstances, the social and political health of urban communities would be enhanced if technical assistance and other resources could be provided to a diversity of low-income groups by a wide range of sponsors as part of an extensive and long-range process of community development. The probable payoffs in increased social awareness, organizational know-how and political sophistication among those who are destined to play a major role in the future of the city would certainly justify the effort. In this perspective, community development can be regarded either as an end in itself or as a means of preparing residents for more substantial forms of participation in rebuilding the ghetto and as a potential source of power to press for a greater federal investment in the transformation of low-income neighborhoods.

Because the poor are not a homogeneous group with shared class consciousness and a common set of needs and demands, there is no single set of organizational goals and structures or sponsor that is suitable for all. Among the forms of community development that offer the most flexibility and potential are several which were relatively neglected by the CAP. They all involve the organization of or support of indigenous functional organizations or corporations, including mutual benefit associations and cooperatives in which low-income persons comprise the policy-making board and staff, as well as users, beneficiaries, or customers. Arising out of neighborhood and individual needs, such organizations have purposes that vary in scope and size from sewing or child-care cooperatives to food buying clubs, home repair services, and credit unions to neighborhood corporations.

It is the autonomous neighborhood corporation in particular that constitutes the most feasible model whereby low-income residents could acquire a base of power that could affect the quantity and quality of resources available to them.[6] As a tax-exempt legal entity, democratically structured with the authority to receive funds and acquire property, the

[6] The literature on neighborhood corporations is quite limited. For a study of one of the first and evidently promising ones, see Institute for Policy Studies, *Review of the Neighborhood Foundation Project* (Columbus, Ohio, October 1965). A discussion of neighborhood corporations in Columbus, Ohio and on the Lower East Side of New York City is found in Harry Schwartz, "An Approach to the Problems of the American Urban Slum," *International Review of Community Development,* Nos. 15-

neighborhood corporation could operate a wide range of enterprises for the benefit of the community as consumers and employees. It can be a single- or multiple-purpose organization; as a broadly based corporate body it would be eligible for federal funds to rehabilitate slum housing or develop moderate income housing as well as administer educational, job training, health, and recreational programs. Self-governing and duly accountable to the residents as stockholder-members, the neighborhood corporation can avoid some of the electoral dilemmas of the TAO and might lead to a revitalization of democratic processes in low-income areas. While still subject to the hazards of goal displacement and co-optation, the neighborhood corporation is free of some of the other political and organizational constraints on the CAP, and offers a promising structure with the possibility of improving the local environment to benefit residents and at the same time also providing a basis for political action in their interest.

The immediate tangible benefits of such functional corporations constitute a strong incentive to join, and participation in the management of the affairs of the corporation can yield dividends in increased self-confidence, organizational experience, and the acquisition of needed services and goods. They can also constitute one of the most constructive outlets for the striving toward nationalistic or ethnic identity found in the Negro ghetto, and represent a way of channelling and further developing minority interests originally articulated by the CAP.

Along with the creation of new functional associations, there is also a need to strengthen existing low-income indigenous organizations—social, religious, and civic—by providing them with staff, technical assistance, funds, and other resources so that they can operate their own programs and serve as another arena where participation and leadership skills can be developed. Although such groups are not ostensibly political, they can be related to issues as they arise. For example, a community maintenance service could lead a battle against slum lords; a credit union could take on local merchants; and a co-op could protest against low-quality foods at higher than regular prices. Neighborhood corporations, which would include such functional associations, could also play an important role in any citywide coalition of reformist political groups.[7]

---

16 (1966), 245-57. As a political solution to some of the sources of racial conflict, neighborhood corporations are strongly endorsed in Aaron Wildavsky, "The Empty-head Blues: Black Rebellion and White Reaction," *The Public Interest,* No. 11 (Spring, 1968), pp. 3-16. An opposing view toward decentralization of functions, particularly education, is presented by Irving Kristol, "Decentralization for What?", *ibid.,* pp. 17-25.

[7] Some of the social action possibilities of neighborhood corporations are also noted in "Participation of the Poor: Section 202(A) (3) Organization Under the Economic Opportunity Act of 1964," *The Yale Law Journal,* Vol. 75, No. 4 (March, 1966), 625-29. See also W. H. Ferry, "The Case for a New Federalism," *Saturday Review,* June 15, 1968, pp. 14-17.

Among those who could provide the funds necessary to organize and sustain autonomous community development in the low-income community are religious, ethnic, and civic organizations, foundations, universities, the United Fund, unions, and some governmental agencies. Because community development in its early stages is relatively noncontroversial, investment in this process would be regarded as "safe" by those sponsors especially concerned with low risk, who could not tolerate community conflict. It is even conceivable that a community-wide federation or holding company might be organized to receive and allocate funds to indigenous groups for these purposes. Other sponsors, such as some religious or ethnic groups, might be willing to support more politically oriented voluntary associations based on residence, race, client status, or *ad hoc* issues.

For both types of sponsors, there are some lessons that have been learned from the CAP experience that may be of value in the promotion of urban community development in the low-income neighborhoods. Efforts to organize poor people around shared needs should be based upon the knowledge of the life styles found among poor people, and should use a selective recruiting strategy, convening them not so much as poor persons but rather as members of other social groupings such as ethnic minorities, agency clients, or participants in a mutual-benefit or functional association. The issue, interest, or function around which they organize should be selected by them and preferably be of a tangible nature, so that some practical benefits may be achieved in a relatively short period of time. Trained staff, whether professional or indigenous nonprofessional, should be available as organizers and technical assistants, committed to a long-range strategy of helping develop and sustain an autonomous organization. The sponsors should be willing to assign qualified staff members to serve at the pleasure of low-income groups or to provide them with funds to obtain their own staff. It is critical for the community development process that it function as independently as possible, and the sponsor should be prepared to grant such autonomy and to expect some conflict and factionalism as the inevitable accompaniment of the development of organization among low-income groups. Because continuity and a stable source of support are essential, a minimum investment of operating funds for a three-year period seems essential, after which time most of the groups should be self-supporting.

Finally, it is essential to have a realistic conception of the possibilities and ultimate goals of these types of community development. At the very least, they can be justified by the possible psycho-social benefits to individuals who may modify their self-image and perception of the world as they gain experience and some tangible benefits from their participation.

It is true that various forms of community organization may be useful—indeed, often the only way to initiate a process of reducing alienation and increasing social competence—but unless they can become politicized, they may perpetuate a misleading mystique in the possibilities of neighborhood-based self-help. There is no assurance, however, that groups evolving out of this process would utilize their experience and limited power for "constructive" political purposes or that they would have a substantial impact on the living conditions of the poor. At the same time there are no insurmountable obstacles to these desired outcomes. The community development process is no substitute for that massive commitment of national resources required to eliminate poverty by rebuilding the ghetto and restoring full citizenship to minorities, although it may be able to mobilize support for these social policies. Nor is this type of low-income organization necessarily an effective antidote or countervailing force to growing use of violence in the ghetto. There is, however, the possibility of educating a leadership cadre and establishing a base for urban ethnic political power to accelerate needed action to eliminate the inequities that sustain poverty and segregation. Whether this can occur before we are overwhelmed, whether a strategy of community development or one of violence will prevail, will depend in part on the extent to which we have wisely considered the lot of the poor—and ours.

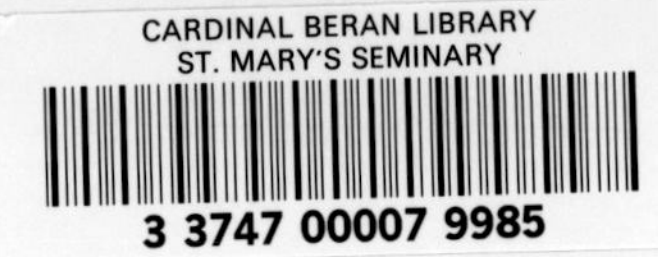

Date Due			